LIVING COUNTRY BLUES

LIVING COUNTRY BLUES

by *Harry Oster*

MINERVA PRESS
New York

To Sarah,
Rosie,
Eddie,
and Jack

ACKNOWLEDGMENTS

THE WRITING OF THIS book was greatly facilitated by four research grants and a year's sabbatical leave given by Louisiana State University, by the services of its secretaries in typing the manuscript, and by a fellowship of the John Simon Guggenheim Foundation during 1961-1962.

Among the many individuals generous with help and advice have been two English experts on blues and Negro records, Francis Smith and Paul Oliver, who spent many hours tracking down recorded sources and parallels for songs in my collection; Karl Knudsen, partner in the European record company, I. S. Dansk Grammofonpladeforlag, who allowed the use of his extensive record collection; Pete Welding, who read and corrected part of the manuscript; Alan Wilson, blues specialist, and Thomas Rees, jazz musician, who both worked on transcriptions of melodies. I am especially grateful to the folk whose songs are here included, most notably, Robert Pete Williams, Hogman Maxey, Guitar Welch, Butch Cage, Willie B. Thomas, Leon Strickland, Roosevelt Charles, Otis Webster, Herman E. Johnson, and Smoky Babe.

I wish also to thank Richard B. Allen, Associate Curator of Archive of New Orleans Jazz for his generous assistance in collecting in New Orleans and for helping me on several trips to Angola, and Warden Victor Walker and Educational Director J. D. Middlebrooks and other officials of the Louisiana State Penitentiary at Angola for their active co-operation.

In addition I am grateful to the various music publishers who have generously permitted me to publish folk variants of their material—Leeds, Duchess, Pickwick, Northern, Venice, Music Corporation of America, and Arc. Mr. John McKellen of MCA Music has been especially helpful.

Finally, I owe a general debt of long standing to Harold W. Thompson, who introduced me to the rich fascination of folklore studies during my four years of graduate work at Cornell University.

—HARRY OSTER

University of Iowa
Iowa Cty, Iowa

CONTENTS

CONTENTS

PHOTOGRAPHS

RECORD LABEL ABBREVIATIONS

Ald	Aladdin	Mlt	Melotone
Ban	Banner	Mod	Modern
Bb	Bluebird	LFS	Louisiana Folklore
Br	Brunswick		Society
BrB	English Brunswick	OK	Okeh
Bwy	Broadway	Or	Oriole
Cen	Century	Pa	Parlophone
Cir	Circle	PaE	English Parlophone
Co	Columbia	Para	Paramount
Cq	Conqueror	Per	Perfect
Cr	Crown	PrB	Prestige Bluesville
De	Decca	Rom	Romeo
DeE	English Decca	RPM	Revolutions Per
Exclo	Excello		Minute
Ft	Feature	SIW	Sittin' In With
Fkwy	Folkways	Sp	Specialty
FL	Folk-Lyric	Stin	Stinson
JDvs	Joe Davis	Supr	Superior
Gnt	Gennett	Supt	Supertone
GS	Gold Star	Trd	Tradition
Hrld	Herald	Vg	Vogue
Im	Imperial	Vic	Victor
ISD	Storyville, I. S. Dansk	Vo	Vocalion
	Grammofon-	VoE	English Vocalion
	pladeforlag	VRS	Vanguard Recording
Lon	London		Society

1. *Walkin' with the Blues*

Spoken: Yes, it's me, an' I'm walkin' with the blues again,
Every which way I go I'm talkin' with the blues,
Man, you know, it's bad when you gotta sleep with the blues,
When I go to eat, I eat with the blues;
So it musta be the blues in the way that I start.
Every time I go to set down to take my rest,
The blues is settin' down by the side o' me.
I guess I musta been born with the blues,
Man, it ain't nothin' but the blues, no whichaway I go,
Blues to sleep, an' blues to sing;
Blues to sleep, an' blues to sing;
Just right down I must be the man of the blues.
This is the blues themself, walkin' with me,
This is the blues themself, walkin' with me, talkin' with me,
No, go ahead an' make me blue.
Yeah, yeah, blue as I can be,
Yeah, blues ain't nothin' but me,
Blues is carryin' me down gradually by degrees;
Each day an' night as I pass by,
It's the blues an' me,
It's the blues got me;
Well, go on then, blues, won't you let me take my rest?
Because I'm a worried man,
An' I'm a blue man, an' I stay blue all the time.
Blues, why don't you leave me be?
I don't know why you wants to worry me an' trouble me this-
   away, blues,
Blues just won't leave me alone for nothin' I try,
So that leaves me with the man of the blues.

*Roosevelt Charles, vocal; Otis Webster, guitar; Angola, Nov. 19,
1961.*

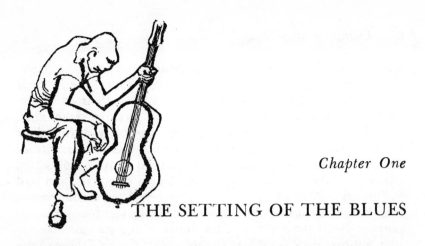

Chapter One

THE SETTING OF THE BLUES

DESPITE THE IMPORTANCE OF THE BLUES and the fascination they have held both for members of a folk audience and for sophisticated intellectual listeners, no book has as yet been devoted to an examination of a substantial number of blues collected in folk communities. Most of the blues discussed in print have been those in commercial recordings, principally because there were few other materials available for study. To satisfy this need, the following collection offers some two hundred and thirty examples selected from the four hundred I have found while recording all kinds of Negro folk music in Louisiana between 1955 and 1961. Although the material (except for a few songs obtained on a trip to north Mississippi) was recorded in one state, the songs are typical of a much larger area. The performers are broadly typical of Louisiana, Mississippi, Georgia, Texas, Alabama, Arkansas, and Tennessee. Some of them, Hogman Maxey and Roosevelt Charles, for example, have been as far afield as Arizona and California. Much of the material was obtained in the Louisiana State Penitentiary at Angola. Enclosing some three thousand caged and womanless Negroes, this huge prison is a fertile breeding ground for blues, and it contains a revealing cross-section of blues singers from various ages, backgrounds, and regions.

Although a prison, especially one with a large Negro population, is in theory an ideal place to record folk music which has disappeared or faded badly elsewhere, in reality the mass media of entertainment exert almost the same influence on the inmates as on the performers outside. In each camp there are radios which pick up the standard popular music from stations in Louisiana and Mississippi and there are also fifty-eight television

1

sets, spread all over the prison. In addition the prisoners attend movies once a week. Since most of the prisoners are in their early twenties, they are accustomed to getting their entertainment from radio, television, and motion pictures rather than from folk sources. During the average stay of two years their musical tastes change little. There is, however, a minority of older prisoners, who are still a rich potential source of folksongs, especially blues, and in much lesser degree spirituals, and still less group worksongs. While the younger prisoners continue to sing blues, just as in the world outside prison there are important distinctions between the blues of the younger generation, approximately eighteen to thirty years old, and those of the older prisoners. The former generally try to perform a song just as they have heard it, whereas the older group, like Roosevelt Charles, Hogman Maxey, Guitar Welch, and Robert Pete Williams are sufficiently at home in the form to improvise freely, drawing on a mental reservoir of thousands of blues phrases, some of them original, most from live tradition and from the innumerable records which have appeared since 1920. Since there is no necessary continuity between stanzas, the old style blues singer often goes through a song by free association. If a listener asks Hogman or Robert Pete the name of the song he is going to sing, he is likely to scratch his head and reply, "Wait till I've sung it."

Most of the prison recordings were made over a two year period beginning in January, 1959, in the old part of the prison, which consists of white-washed dormitories, grouped in camps, each housing about four hundred prisoners. In Camp H the principal "studios" were the laundry room, presided over by a one-legged convict, justly apprehensive that the convicts crowding in to hear the music might steal pieces of laundry, and the tool room, which is decorated with primitive murals of dancing figures and clippings of pictures from newspapers. In the background a leaky pipe hissed steam insistently.

A grimmer and more secluded setting for recording was the abandoned upper story of the building which houses the "chronics," the aged and persistently ill convicts. As we recorded in the huge dusty room, the happy songs of birds floated in from the trees outside while from below came the appallingly venomous rumbles and shouts of endless quarrels among the senile and sick prisoners. (I once asked Andy

Mosely, the cheerful thirty-year old convict who took care of them, what the current quarrel was about; he told me they were arguing about something which happened eight years ago.) In Camp A, where the Lomaxes found Leadbelly in 1934, the most frequent recording site was the "Apache Station," so called because several of the prisoners active in the station (which broadcasts through a loudspeaker on the roof) had been members of Mardi Gras tribes in New Orleans, exponents of wild dancing and singing of Haitian origin, wearing gaudy costumes patterned after American Indian ceremonial dress. Generally in Camp H and A (except when we were in the building for chronics), attracted by music pouring out the window, convicts of all ages crowded in to listen; the frequent variations of their expressions from moody sadness to raucous laughter demonstrated that to them the blues form was still vital and alive.

The most talented and creative users of the tradition were Robert Pete Williams and Roosevelt Charles. An illiterate country Negro who is probably as close to pure folk tradition as anyone of his generation, Robert Pete Williams was born March 14, 1914, in Zachary, Louisiana, where the members of his family were share-croppers. He worked as a farmhand, picking cotton and cutting cane until 1928 when he moved to Scotland-ville, a Negro community on the outskirts of Baton Rouge. In Scotlandville he worked in a lumber yard for several years, after which he got a job washing and cleaning barrels.

In 1954 he was sentenced to life imprisonment at Angola for killing a man in a barroom brawl.

He learned to play the guitar in 1934 on a crude instrument he had fashioned out of five copper strings and a cigar box. After a while he managed to buy himself a cheap guitar, "an old box, strings about an inch from the neck."

Once he had started playing music engulfed Williams. He says colorfully:

> Music begin to follow me then. I been tryin' to stop playin', thinkin' 'bout lookin' out for preparin' my soul for Jesus. I was a Christian man before I got here. I can play church songs too, jest as well so I kin blues. . . . What Jesus gave me, He didn't take it away from me. I walked away from Him. He sent me to be a preacher, and I didn't take it. . . . So by me not takin' up preachin' an' leadin' the peoples, he throwed it on my little

kid, he's right at eight years old. Yes suh, he's preachin' now himself. Well, I didn't take it. Jest look like to me I can't put music down. Time I get hold of one guitar an' maybe sell it to somebody, well music jest come back an' worry me so, I jest have to go back an' buy me another guitar.

All the music I play, I jest hear it in the air. You can hear the sound of it, comin' out, soundin' good. Well, all of my blues that I put out, that was made-up blues. I make up my own blues you see. Why, I may be walkin' along or ridin' in a car, an' blues come to me, an' I jest get it all in my head. Well, I come back an' I get my guitar an' then I play it.

These remarks suggest that Robert Pete Williams feels the traditionally sharp dichotomy between the singers of sinful songs and the singers of spirituals. Usually once a Negro has gotten religion, he puts aside his guitar and refuses to sing any more blues, songs which are so frequently concerned with sex and drink. It is also significant to note that the description of the process of composing a song suggests that the musician passively receives music which comes to him through a powerful inspirational force from outside himself. Certainly many of his best songs are the results of improvisation, of responding freely and spontaneously to the thoughts which flow into consciousness. The most powerful expression of his feelings is the "Prisoner's Talking Blues," which he spoke and sang in a voice choked with emotion.

 2. *Prisoner's Talking Blues*

Spoken: Lord, I feel so bad sometime', seems like I'm weakenin'
    every day.
You know I begin to get grey since I got here, well a whole lot
    o' worryin' causin' that.
But I can feel myself weakenin', I don't keep well no more.
    I keeps sickly.
I takes a lot of medicine, but it looks like it don't do no good.
All I have to do is pray; that's the only thing'll help me here,
One foot in the grave look like,
An' the other un out.
Sometime' looks like my best day gotta be my last day.
Sometime' I feel like I never see my little ole kids anymore.
But if I don't never see 'em no more, leave 'em in the hands
    of God.

You know my sister she like a mother to me.
She do all in the world that she can;
She went all the way along with me in this trouble till the end.
In a way, I was glad my pore mother had (de) ceased because
    she suffered with heart trouble,
An' trouble behind me, sho' woulda went hard with her.
But if she were livin', I could call on her sometime'.
But my old father dead too,
That'd make me be motherless an' fatherless.
It's six of us sisters (*sic*). Three boys.
Family done got small now, looks like they're dyin' out fast.
I don't know, but God been good to us in a way,
'Cause ole death have stayed away a long time.

Sung: Lord, my worry sho' carryin' me down,
Lord, my worry sho' is carryin' me down;
Sometimes I feel like, baby, committin' suicide.
I got the nerve if I just had anythin' to do it with.
I'm goin' down slow, somethin' wrong with me,
Yes, I'm goin' down slow, somethin' wrong with me;
I've got to make a change while that I'm still young,
If I don't I won't never get old.

Vocal and guitar, Angola, March 21, 1959. (The recording
may be heard on *Angola Prisoners' Blues,* LFS A-3, 1958.)

The early background of Roosevelt Charles is in many ways
typical of the folk Negro who keeps getting into trouble with
the law until his life is a succession of terms in prison alternating with occasional periods on the outside. When I last
saw Charles in 1960 he was serving his fourth sentence at
Angola. In a talking blues he traced his early years:

 3. *Trouble Followin' Me*

Spoken: You know it's been bad luck an' trouble been followin'
    me,
Ever since I was six months old.
When I was six months old my mother laid down an' died.
She left me in this world all alone, boys,
An' it was hard to say that I was motherless an' fatherless too.
Father he laid down an' died a month before my birth.
You know that was bad, sad news, sad in min'.
I, . . . (in) the beginning, at the age o' nine, I runned off to
    big L. A.
I was strange, I didn't know nobody,

I found a place to stay, people was nice an' kind to me there.
So a lady she taken me in, she raised me as her own dear child,
Treat me as a mother would, mother's love I don't know,
That was sweet too.
One day I was walkin' out on the career,
Lookin' at the birds, how they were treadin' the mighty air,
I looked at automobile', how they was runnin' the track;
It looked sweet to me, decide I better run the highway,
Seen a freight train comin', I decided to better get on board,
I couldn't be left behin';
I grabbed the freight train, an' looked down,
Wanted to put it down, but it was movin' along the rails too
    fast,
Thought if I put it down, bad luck would overtake me over
    there.
I didn't know I was already in bad luck as it was.
Now you talkin' about bad luck, that's been followin' me all
    of my life.
Bad luck an' trouble. When bad luck leave me, my trouble
    just begin.
Came on back down in ole Arkansas,
That's where my real trouble just begin;
Sister was a young lady, she had been married,
An' left me all out by myself, didn't want to stay there;
That was sad to me, but sweet to some people too.
I decided I begin to ramble,
I grabbed me a armful o' freight train;
I fell down in ole Louisiana, stopped in a small town they call
    Bastrop,
That where big trouble just begin.
I commits a murder, that how I fell down in ole Angola.
Boy, that was sad news, sad in min' when I fell down here.
I went before the judge, the judge said,
"Well, son, say you mighty young,
But say when you come back, you'll know better next time."
I looked at the judge, an' he didn't crack a smile.
I said, "Judge, is you jivin', just sayin' somethin' to be sayin'
    somethin'?"
He said, "If you think I'm jivin', wait they get you on the river."

Sung: It was early one mornin' just about the break of day,
Well, I could hear that big bell tonin',
Heard somebody say, "You know you got to go." . . .

*Roosevelt Charles, vocal; Otis Webster, guitar; Angola, Nov.
19, 1960.*

Such blues of introspective examination of course have their counterparts in the free world since bad luck and trouble, loneliness, insecurity intensified by having no parents to turn to, the wanderlust of the rolling stone, the impulse toward violence are frequent themes in blues. A lonely and tired field hand seated on his shabby sagging porch sometimes expresses similar thoughts, his guitar wailing and commenting ironically after each line.

A more typical setting for blues in the country occurs when a few friends gather in a little shack to drink their "googaloo" and cut loose in a jam session. Even though the texts of many of the songs are sad, the style of performance is gay and spirited. As the performers begin to pick up steam, to become possessed by the spirit, the excitement of the music draws a crowd into the tiny building; the walls seem to bulge. A field hand seizes a partner and they gyrate wildly. Members of the crowd exuberantly laugh and shout encouragement. Some of the guests chip in to buy more wine, whiskey or beer. Before long the whole rickety shack begins to rock and the floor to heave under their stomping feet. Often the swingy infectious music and dance sweep on until a new day calls for shuffling off to the back-breaking toil of farm work, or drearier jobs as janitors and laborers in nearby towns.

Such an atmosphere surrounds the home of Butch Cage, old-time dance and blues fiddler, where I have recorded jam sessions about twenty times. The liveliness and gaiety with which the blues (and other types of folksongs) are performed is in striking contrast to the harshness of the life Butch has led, a life which in its essentials is typical of most country Negroes.

Butch (James) Cage was born on March 16, 1894, in Franklin County near Meadville, Mississippi, where his parents were sharecroppers. They grew cotton, corn, sugar cane, and rice among "hills and hollows red as paint, a poor place like Nazaree." "When we cleared new ground," says Butch, "water'd wash out the top soil in three years. Don't know how we got along plenty of times. Yessuh."

After the crops were gathered, Butch and other sharecroppers would cut lumber and make cross-ties, 6″ by 8″ by 8′; although suitable timber was hard to find, the standard price for these was 10 cents.

When Butch was ten years old, his father died; his widow had to take care of the thirteen children. Somehow she managed to keep the family together. They moved about every year or two to another unproductive farm. Their living quarters were crude—board shacks without inside sealing and without a loft. Butch says, "We could look out the holes in the roof at the stars." Often in the fall Butch knocked around Louisiana and Mississippi, scrounging for any work he could find on cane farms, sugar houses, and railroads. During these years Butch went to school a total of three weeks.

Though almost everything else was lacking, there was plenty of music. "All of my folks was some sort of musician. I had sisters play accordeen, an' another brother play the fife. My mother was a good songster, an' she was the best dancer in Franklin County." Butch also heard two old Negro fiddlers, Frank Felters and Ole Man Carol Williams; he sat at their feet listening and watching until he too could scrape away on their favorites—"Dixie," "Arkansas Traveller," "Hell Broke Loose in Georgia," "Old Wagoner," "Hen Cackle," "Ole Mule," and many breakdowns, square dances, and buck dances. He took part in the moaning and shouting at the local church. He danced to blues and he also heard popular hits like "Oh You Beautiful Doll" and "If You Like Me Like I Like You." He fell under the fascination of phonograph records when he heard a cylinder phonograph played in 1907. He also played the fife in "an old field band," which consisted of fifes, kettle, snare, and bass drums. The fifes were generally hand-made out of cane reeds.

Although Butch was picking up some money playing at white and colored dances on weekends, he felt that he was not getting anywhere. In 1927, the year of the worst flood disaster on the Mississippi, he made only four bales of cotton. That year he left to join his brother who was farming a patch of land in Louisiana on shares.

Butch helped him, and also he worked as a day laborer on cane and strawberry farms. From 1941 to 1945 he did menial jobs on the railroads, taking out and replacing ties and rails, levelling track, tamping rails, etc. Then he got a steady job as a laborer for the city of Baton Rouge—cleaning ditches, picking up trash, putting in pipes.

In 1960 Butch retired to live on social security and his city pension. With his wife Rosa he lives in a little shack in Zachary, Louisiana.

Despite the rough life he has lived, Butch is an attractively serene and jovial man, full of exuberance and high spirits. Seeing him perform is almost as important as hearing him. His face crinkling in a warmly infectious grin, he holds the fiddle on his chest in the old-time country style; with his hand about three inches from the end of the bow, he saws away with wicked syncopation, waving the fiddle as he plays and stamping both feet with crashing intensity for the basic beat.

The trail of the blues has also led to the State Mental Hospital at Jackson, where a near-psychotic young patient sang an unusual blues about dope addiction—to New Orleans where the blues tradition of the younger generation is exemplified by blind Snooks Eaglin, that of the older generation by Lemon Nash, an old-time medicine show bally man (an entertainer whose job it is to attract a crowd) originally from Arkansas, and by Billie Pierce, a red hot mama from Florida—to towns in southern Louisiana near the Gulf of Mexico, in one of which Leon Strickland worked—and to southwest Louisiana to Abbeville where lived Godar Chalvin, a Negro who had grown up in a Cajun community and whose style represents an interesting blend of Negro and French tradition. Whenever possible I have made at least several visits to each locality in order to gain rapport with the performers and to record their repertoires in depth. The blues which follow are the most significant fruits of the search.

Chapter Two

A BRIEF HISTORY OF BLUES
AND A DEFINITION OF THE FORM

THE BLUES PROBABLY HAD THEIR ROOTS in songs of lament in the days of slavery. Aged Negroes in New Orleans, some born in the eighteen-sixties have attested, "The blues was here when I come."[1] Little is known of sad secular songs which slaves no doubt performed, for no one wrote them down, except for a few fragments, and because many slave owners discouraged mournful singing since it might impair efficiency. Frances Kemble, who lived on a Georgia plantation from 1838 to 1839 wrote:

> I have heard that many of the masters and overseers prohibit melancholy tunes or words, and encourage nothing but cheerful music and senseless words, deprecating the effect of sadder strains upon the slaves, whose peculiar musical sensibility might be expected to make them especially excitable by any songs of a plaintive character and having reference to their particular hardships.[2]

No doubt musical expressions of despair often resounded in the slave cabins out of earshot of the owners and overseers.

It is generally agreed that the principal ancestor of contemporary country blues is the field holler or cry, which John W. Work of Fisk University has described as a "fragmentary bit of a yodel, half sung, half yelled":

> Approaching his house or that of his sweetheart in the evening, or sometimes out of sheer loneliness, he would emit his

1. Marshall Stearns, *The Story of Jazz* (New York: 1956), p. 79
2. Frances Kemble, *Journal of a Residence on a Georgia Plantation in 1838-1839* (New York: 1863), pp. 162-163

11

holler. Listeners would say, "Here comes Sam," or "Will Jackson's coming," or "I just heard Archie down the road." . . .

In these 'hollers' the idiomatic material found in the blues is readily seen; the excessive portamento, the slow time, the preference for the flatted third, the melancholy type of tune . . . many . . . could serve as lines of blues.[3]

Odum and Johnson in *Negro Workaday Songs* have used a phonophotographic approach in an attempt to isolate and define the holler's basic elements. While admitting their inability to describe fully the complex components of the sound, they identify sudden changes of pitch and a greater amount of vibrato than is typical of most white singers. They also single out a "snap" of the vocal chords,[4] a use of the falsetto voice probably of West African origin.

The examples of hollers among the recordings of the Library of Congress reveal central elements of the blues. "Arwhoolie" makes use of falsetto, sliding from note to note (portamento), and blue tonality; "in fact, it is a blues without the rhythm and the European harmony."[5]

The early blues drew on worksongs as well as hollers. Robert Pete Williams' "Levee Camp Blues" is a significant example of how elements of hollers and worksongs often combine to form blues. Its form and musical characteristics give a revealing glimpse of the probable evolution of blues in the nineteenth century.

 4. Levee Camp Blues

1. Oh, that ole gal o' mine, stays out all night long;
Oh, that ole gal o' mine, she stays out all night long;
Oh, I can't do nothin' with you, woman, no matter what the pore boy do.

2. Oh, Captain, Captain, oh, you better count yo' men;
Oh, Captain, you better count yo' men;
Oh, some gone to the bushes (escaped), oh Lord, an' some gone in.

---

3. John W. Work, *American Negro Songs* (New York: 1960), pp. 34-35
4. Howard W. Odum and Guy B. Johnson, *Negro Workaday Songs* (Chapel Hill: 1926), pp. 257-263
5. Stearns, *The Story of Jazz*, p. 76

3. Oh, I can eat more chicken, boy, oh boys, than the cook
can fry; (2)
Oh, I can pop more leather than the contractor can buy.

4. Oh, that ole gal walk like Mattie Campbell, oh boy, but she
walk too slow,
Oh, she walk like Mattie, but the pore gal walk too slow.

5. Oh, it's pay day tomorrow, oh buddy, how you know? (2)
Oh, I know, boys, 'cause the Captain he tole me so.

6. Oh, that ole gal o' mine, she won't do nothin' she say,
Oh, that ole gal er mine, she won't do a thing she say.

Vocal and guitar, Angola, Jan. 26, 1959. (The recording may
be heard on *Angola Prisoners' Blues.* LFS A-3, 1958.)

Each verse begins with a long drawn out cry which suggests
the influence of the holler. The singer sometimes sustains a
syllable and runs it through a short melodic phrase, e.g., "No
mat-ta— — — — — what the po' boy do— — — — — —," "Oh— — —, that
ole gal— — —," (underlined words followed by a long dash indi-
cate the syllable is sustained through a melodic phrase). There
are frequent slurs, and usually at the ends of lines the last note
tapers off downward into nontonal grunts—survivals of African
style. The effect is to intensify the emotion and to sustain it
beyond the limits of the words. In accordance with the performer's expressive impulses, the length of lines, the pauses between, the number of lines in a stanza all vary freely. The
accompaniment consists of basically one chord in the Aeolian
mode with—to the western ear—only suggestions in the bass of
the dominant and the subdominant.

The singer meanders spontaneously from thought to thought,
from the infidelity of his woman, to escape, to boasting about
his appetite and skill as a worker, back to the woman, this time
finding fault with her for another reason, then to an ironic
comment on the relationship with the boss (apparently pay
day is not a regular event and occurs at the whim of the boss),
and finally to his depression over his lying gal. The ideas he
expresses and the tendency for their sequence to follow the
natural rambling pattern of the flow of thought are characteristic of both worksongs and blues.

Another form which originated early in the history of blues
is the *talking blues.* In a non-literate society there is much

less separation between speaking and singing than in one which is dependent on written language. In all probability then, in the nineteenth century, a slave field hand relaxing in his hut in the evening, plunking moodily on a banjo, or thumping a rhythm on a drum or barrel, would often let his voice wander, sometimes speaking semi-rhythmically, sometimes slipping into a few lines of song, moving freely and naturally from one to the other without a perceptible break, as Smoky Babe (Robert Brown) does in expressing his reactions to farm life without a woman.

 5. *Workin' Blues*

1. *Spoken:* Well, I always get up every mornin', 'tween five an' oh, six o'clock,
Boys, I'm tellin' you it's a mess, it's a mess,
You know it's a mess, oh, you know it's a mess.

2. Well, if you ain't got yo' wife aroun', you ain't ain't got no woman,
She ain't at home, I'll tell you true, yo' bed ain't made up,
Yo' floor ain't swept an' everythin', I'm tellin' you true,
It's rough, oh peoples, it's rough.
I gotta go out there an' feed my ole hogs,
An' fool aroun' ole cow an' everythin',
You know everythin' I mean, you know get everythin' lined up out there,
You know out in the field there, mean ole boss an' everythin' in the mornin' time,
You know how you feel that mornin', don't wanta get up,
But you gotta get up.

3. *Sung:* Well, I'm goin' to work now, baby, I'm goin' out there an' do what I can do.
Spoken: Boy, it's rough, it's rough, it's rough out there,
I'm tellin' you the truth, I'm tired, but you got to make a livin',
Got to work anywhere you go, anywhere you be,
You see what I mean, you gotta work.
If you ain't a-workin' for yourself, yo' home, yo' garden, an' everythin' like that, you know what I mean,
You ain't gonna miss nothin' if you go out doin' it;
I'm talkin' about now I got to go out here work for my boss a while,
To get some money for Saturday night, you know,
Have a good time then, hm.

4. *Sung:* Well now, this work is hard, this work is hard, an'
it's killin' me.
Spoken: Oh no, Robert Brown, is it killin' you?
Oh, it's just gettin' me down, ha ha,
I just can't hardly be myself, hardly believe myself.

5. *Sung:* Well, I'm gonna find my little woman, she lovin'
somebody else.
You know how you gonna find her?
Yeah, ha, she done left you all alone, see,
She done quit you, done gone to another home,
'Cause you ain't got nothin' but work up the cotton pickin'
blues,
Or either got a job in somethin' else, at home work or outside
work, or anythin' like that,
Just tell her, well, baby, please—

6. *Sung:* Baby, please, baby, please come back home,
Fix me a meal, or either, either leave poor Robert Brown alone,
Well, these ole cotton pickin' blues, all I got to say,
I'll let her go.

Vocal and guitar, Scotlandville, April 18, 1961.

The language and phrases in this example are not standardized;
there are no tightly constructed epigrammatic verses likes those
in "A Thousand Miles from Nowhere," a modern blues on a
similar theme:

I wake up early in the mornin', feelin' I'm 'bout to go out
of my min', (2)
I got to find me some kinda companion, if she dumb, deaf
crippled or blin'.

Smoky Babe's song, on the other hand, is much looser in
construction. Although the guitar accompaniment maintains
a precise beat, the poetic form of the text takes shape mainly
from the natural conversational flow of his reactions.

Before there was a large storehouse of traditional verses for
singers to draw on for their improvisations, many of the early
blues were essentially like Smoky Babe's "Workin' Blues."

By late in the nineteenth century, folk Negroes were singing
phrases essentially similar to those which appear in the country
blues of today. Although these are taken from songs collected
between 1905 and 1908, they were probably well known by folk
Negroes many years before:

Went to the sea, sea look so wide,
Thought about my babe, hung my head an' cried.
O my babe, won't you come home?

I got the blues, but too damn mean to cry,
Oh, I got the blues, but I'm too damn mean to cry.

Got nowhar' to lay my weary head,
Oh my babe, got nowhar' to lay my weary head.

I'm po' boy, long way from home,
Oh, I'm po' boy, long way from home.[6]

Typical of the early blues is a song W. C. Handy heard in
1892 while sleeping on the cobblestones in St. Louis; there he
heard "shabby guitarists picking out a tune called 'East St.
Louis.'" It had numerous one line verses which they would
sing all night, lines like:

I walked all the way from old East St. Louis, and I didn't
have but one po' measly dime.[7]

Around the same time, an approximation of the classical
blues form and the most common blues tune had already appeared widely in the familiar "Joe Turner" song, which deals
with the notorious Joe Turney, brother of a governor of Tennessee. Joe Turney had the job of taking Negro prisoners from
Memphis to the penitentiary in Nashville and to the "farms"
along the Mississippi. The real purpose of his visit was not
to punish criminals for the sake of law and order, but to round
up cheap labor, workers who would only have to be fed and
housed. The system was to get a stool-pigeon to start up a crap
game. When enough Negroes were rolling the dice, the law
would suddenly swoop down on them, arrest the number needed
for work, rush them through a token trial in a kangaroo court,
and hand them over to Joe Turney. Turney would handcuff
eighty prisoners to forty links of chain and lead them off. The
reaction in song was expressed in three-line stanzas which consisted of one line repeated twice, as in the variant Willie B.
Thomas sang for me in 1961:

---

6. Odum and Johnson, *Negro Workaday Songs*, p. 18
7. W. C. Handy, *The Father of the Blues: an Autobiography* (New York:
1941), p. 142.

> Joe Turner in this town,
> Tell me Joe Turner in this town,
> They tell me Joe Turner in this town.[8]

Some verses were more developed in form, approximating the standard blues framework of today:

> He come wid forty links of chain, O Lawdy,
> Come wid forty links of chain, O Lawdy,
> Got my man and gone.[9]

The same tune and the three-cornered form began to be used as a convenient mold for emotional reactions to other disturbing events.

W. C. Handy has presented a vivid picture of a folk Negro singing a blues and accompanying himself in the knifeblade style which was later to become one of the most important and effective approaches to the guitar. In 1903 in a railway station in Tutwiler, Mississippi:

> A lean loose-jointed Negro had commenced plunking a guitar beside me while I slept. His clothes were rags; his feet peeped out of his shoes. His face had on it some of the sadness of the ages. As he played, he pressed a knife on the strings of the guitar in a manner popularized by Hawaiian guitarists who used steel bars. The effect was unforgettable. His song, too, struck me instantly.
>
> > Goin' where the Southern cross the Dog.
>
> The singer repeated the line three times, accompanying himself with the weirdest music I had ever heard.[10]

Handy also quotes typical verses of field hands:

> Boll Weevil, where you been so long?
> Boll Weevil, where you been so long?
> You stole my cotton, now you want my corn.[11]

This is an early example of the kind of blues about the boll weevil which still survive in the Deep South.

---

8. Willie B. Thomas, "Joe Turner Blues," Scotlandville, Oct. 4, 1960, No. 126 in this collection
9. Handy, *Autobiography*, pp. 145-146.
10. Handy, *Autobiography*, p. 74
11. Handy, *Autobiography*, p. 75

Around the same time, the roustabouts who came into Clarksdale from the Mississippi eighteen miles away would sing:

Oh, the Kate's up the river, Stack O' Lee's in the ben',
Oh, the Kate's up the river, Stack O' Lee's in the ben',
And I ain't seen ma baby since I can't tell when.[12]

Phonograph records began to play a vital role in the creation and dissemination of blues during the nineteen-twenties. On August 10, 1920 Mamie Smith, "contralto with Rega Orchestra," cut Perry Bradford's "Crazy Blues" (OK 4169), a song with a chorus based on a twelve-bar structure, the first disc of a singer using a blues form.[13]

Despite the fact that the "Crazy Blues" was on the fringe of folk blues—described by Paul Oliver in *Blues Fell This Morning* as "half-vaudeville performances which marked a late stage in the development of blues from a simple folk music to a form of sophisticated entertainment"[14]—the early sales of about 7,500 discs a week suggested that Negroes were eager to hear their own music on records. At the same time, it helped create a wider demand for the music and influenced the style of folk performers who heard and liked it. Thus a basic pattern in blues development was begun in which the oral informant of a traditional society was often replaced by a disc which exposed his listeners to the style and repertoire of singers not in their immediate circle. The cycle of development then ran from folk singer to professional performer to record, and back to folk singer, the progress marked by constant changes. Both professional and non-professional performers built up a large reservoir of blues phrases and verses which they would draw on, sometimes by free association.

While in the earliest days of recording the emphasis was on young girls singing city blues, the record companies quickly discovered that there was a considerable market for country blues singers. At first they brought the performers North to the studios; later they took mobile units South, for they discovered that what country Negroes in the South liked best were singers from their own neck of the woods, performing country blues.

---

12. Handy, *Autobiography*, p. 75
13. Paul Oliver, *Blues Fell This Morning* (London: 1960), pp. 1-2
14. Oliver, *Blues*, p. 2

In July 1924 Paramount Records issued Papa Charlie Jackson singing the "Lawdy Lawdy Blues" and in April 1926 Paramount advertised their first record by Blind Lemon Jefferson, "Booster Blues" and "Dry Southern Blues": "Here's a real old-fashioned blues-singer—Blind Lemon Jefferson from Dallas. ... With his singing he plays the guitar in real southern style."[15] Lemon was indeed a genuine folk performer and he had an enormous impact on country Negroes, mostly through records. Herman E. Johnson, who has been much influenced by Lemon and at one time owned a dozen of his records, says of him, "Lemon was a genus (*sic*). Couldn't nobody play the guitar like Lemon."

The great popularity of his records had an important effect on hardening the blues form into a classical mold. Although he himself did not follow a twelve bar form in many of his blues, he did make use of a three line form, which consisted of a verbal line, followed by an antiphonal guitar line, then a repetition of the verbal line, followed by a response from the instrument, and a concluding verbal line, all often of lengths varying freely from stanza to stanza. The form which Lemon used freely, amateurs and professionals began to use rigidly until thousands of recorded and folk blues had essentially a standard structure, tune, and even guitar breaks. Also, when singers performed with several accompanying instruments, relatively standardized patterns of harmony and rhythm became necessary. Marshall Stearns has pointed out:

> When the blues became a group performance some preconceived plan was needed, for everyone had to agree on when to start and stop. Leadbelly furnishes an example of an intermediate stage. Performing alone on recordings, he sometimes disregards what have become the conventional chord 'changes' and the usual duration of each chord, strumming along until he remembers the words that come next. Perhaps he is searching his memory, but as long as he is alone it makes little difference. On the other hand, when Leadbelly plays with a group, he automatically adopts a common harmony and timing.[16]

With the addition of a musical instrument, it was natural for the singer to fall into a call-and-response pattern, which is

15. Samuel B. Charters, *The Country Blues* (New York: 1959), p. 63
16. Stearns, *The Story of Jazz*, p. 79

characteristic of most spirituals and worksongs—a device prob- ably inherited from an African past. The instrument served the function of a second voice answering the singer and com- menting on his remarks. As was typical of the folk Negro's approach to instruments, he often made the instrument, usually the guitar, imitate the human voice. The inclination toward a variable third and a seventh, a characteristic of Negro singing, he expressed on the guitar by often pushing the strings across the fingerboard with his left hand, thus causing notes to go sharp and then to drop in pitch, creating pitches which cannot be depicted accurately in European notation; frequently also he would bend notes by sliding a bottle neck, glass, knife blade, knife handle, thimble, or any hard slippery object on the strings. The use of such a *glissando* makes it easy to play notes in between the standard pitches. Originally (and in some cases still) the performer did not follow European harmony. "Gui- tarist John Lee Hooker . . . employs a drone which sounds very much like the skirl of a bagpipe, and he says his grand- father played that way."[17] Big Bill Broonzy insisted that

> for me to really sing the old blues that I learned in Mississippi I have to go back to my sound and not the right chords as the musicians have told me to make. They just don't work with the real blues . . . the real blues is played and sung the way you feel and no man or woman feels the same way every day.[18]

If some of the most successful professional performers have felt this way, it is not surprising that many back country performers like Robert Pete Williams (who when I was recording him had never been outside of a Negro folk environment in Louisiana) are still accompanying themselves with chords and progressions which are outside the traditions of European harmony.

By the middle twenties, when the recording business was only in its infancy, the combined annual sale of records of Negro performers to the colored market totalled between five and six million copies.

By the end of the twenties Vaudeville and tent-show singers, circus artists, and barnstormers, medicine-show entertainers

---

17. Stearns, *The Story of Jazz*, p. 77
18. William Broonzy, *Big Bill Blues* (London: 1955), pp. 88-89.

and wandering troubadours, street beggars and field-hands, folk minstrels with guitars and gin-mill pianists, vocalists with washboard, jug and jazz bands were to be heard on records all singing and playing some form of blues.[19]

Records were sold not only in record shops but also by mail order and in "saloon bars, barber shop parlours, drug stores, cigar stands and Negro business establishments of every description."[20] The more popular blues performers appeared on a great number of records. Big Bill Broonzy, Lonnie Johnson, Bumble Bee Slim, and Leroy Carr collectively put out over a thousand titles, a small fraction of the total issued. Inevitably this flood of material had considerable effect on Negro folk singers.

The market for race records shrunk during the depression of the thirties, but in 1945 the success of Cecil Gant's "I Wonder" induced record companies to plunge heavily again into blues. "Categorized as 'Rhythm and Blues' in 1950, a hit sold about 100,000 copies and commercial white bands often recorded their own diluted version."[21] In general, Rhythm-and-Blues are blues with a heavy rhythmic background, musically simpler and less imaginative than country blues in their natural setting or in some of the early phonograph records. The current vogue is "Rock and Roll," in many of its manifestations a much coarsened and simplified outgrowth of blues, which began its popularity in 1955 and continues to sell millions of records to colored and white youngsters. Its heavy crude style has influenced the younger blues singers in the South.

In the meantime, a significant number of musicians whose blues still keep a close link with their folk roots continue to record for a Negro folk audience. The giants of this area, which is essentially Rhythm-and-Blues, are John Lee Hooker and Muddy Waters (McKinley Morganfield) of Mississippi, Howling Wolf (Chester Burnett) of Arkansas, and Lightnin' Hopkins of Texas.

Among the folk blues singers of the Deep South of today, styles of performance survive which represent all the principal stages of the history from hollers to Rock and Roll.

---

19. Oliver, *Blues*, pp. 2-3
20. Oliver, *Blues*, p. 3
21. Stearns, *The Story of Jazz*, p. 80

If we define "blues" to include all the forms and types of songs these performers call by that name, the result is much broader than the conventional definitions. A blues may be any of these:

1. An expression of an emotion, or of emotions in the classic blues pattern, sung with an instrumental accompaniment. The melody consists of twelve bars, usually in 4/4 time, broken up into three units of four bars each. The first phrase is built on the tonic chord, the second on the subdominant, the third on the dominant seventh. To go with each musical phrase there is a line of text. The second verbal line repeats the first, sometimes identically, sometimes with a slight variation for rhetorical emphasis, and the third line, which rhymes with the first and second, resolves the thought expressed in them; if they express grief, it gives a reason, or it concludes the verse in startling or epigrammatic fashion. The verbal phrases take up less than four bars each, leaving a break in which the instrument answers the voice or embellishes the melody. The singer "worries" the third and often the seventh and/or the fifth of the scale, wavering between flat and natural. The same effect appears in the accompaniment, readily accomplished on a guitar by pushing the strings sideways and distorting the pitch, or by sliding a hard object along the strings so that pitches not in the European scales are sounded and notes are "bent." The effect is approximated on the piano by rapid alternation between major and minor intervals and by superimposing a minor third over a major chord while remaining in a major key. Although ideally the blues is an improvised form, frequently the singers perform a song essentially as they have before, or as they have heard it on a record. Further, it is important to note, the emotion expressed may be sad, happy, or a combination of both. As Iain Lang has written of blues on records: "One need not, in fact, have 'the blues' to sing or play the blues. There are scores of fast-tempo blues with riotously cheerful themes, although it is true that the characteristic blues time is slow."[22]

2. An instrumental performance which follows a similar pattern.

---

22. Iain Lang, *Jazz in Perspective: the Background of the Blues* (London: 1947), p. 109

3. Songs with a rough fluid approximation of the classic form, but with variations from verse to verse in the number of bars, the lengths of verbal phrases, and the instrumental breaks between lines, within a verse, and between verses. The chords may differ from those in European harmony, or the order of chord resolutions may be essentially the same as in the classic blues, but the proportions varied to suit the whims of the singer.

4. Talking blues, semi-rhythmic speaking or a mixture of speaking and singing, accompanied by rhythmic guitar. The speech has a fluid conversational flow though it is more rhythmic than ordinary conversation. At the same time it is less rhythmic than a Negro folk-sermon or than the talking blues of white performers in Southern mountain tradition, which usually have the poetic stresses coinciding exactly with the accented beats of the accompaniment. In the Negro talking blues, the lines are of approximately equal duration in time, but may vary considerably in the number of words. When the talking blues include singing, the performer slips from speech to song and back so naturally that the shift is scarcely perceptible. On records there is a significant number of examples of this tradition.[23]

5. Songs not in a three unit form, but which are similar to more standard blues in the sentiments they express, their language and verbal conventions, and the instrumental style of their accompaniments. In this category the most common forms are two line and four line. The former approximates an eight bar construction, and the two lines rhyme. The latter is usually around sixteen bars with the opening verbal line sung three times and a rhyming concluding line, a favorite form in revival spirituals.

It is also necessary to make a distinction between country blues and city blues. While there is often considerable over-

---

23. Some typical examples are William Moore, "Raggin' the Blues," Para 12761, Chicago, c. Jan., 1928; Romeo Nelson, "Head Rag Hop," Vo 14447, Chicago, Sept. 5, 1929; Blind Willie McTell, "Travellin' Blues," Co 14484-D, Oct. 30, 1929; Bukka White, "Special Stream Line," Vo 05526, March 1940; Champion Jack Dupree, "Me and My Mule," King 4876, c. 1929; Big Bill Broonzy, "Blues in 1890," VgF LDO30, Paris, Sept. 21, 1951; Big Bill Broonzy, "Mule Ridin', Talking Blues," Fkwy FG 3586, Chicago, 1957; and Lightnin' Hopkins, "Come Go Home with Me," Fkwy FS 3822, Houston, Jan. 16, 1959

lapping and even a symbiotic relationship between the two—each in a sense feeding on the other—one can set up a continuum with pure country blues at one extreme, pure city blues at the other.

COUNTRY BLUES	CITY BLUES
Spontaneous expression of thought and mood.	Planned, arranged texts and music.
Wide range of subjects.	Concentration on love.
Fluid use of form.	Precise classical form, predictable twelve-bar structure.
Non-European harmony, use of drones, tendency toward single chord accompaniment.	Standard chord progressions, clearly defined use of tonic, subdominant, and dominant chords.
Unaccompanied voice, or most commonly solo performer accompanying himself on a guitar; in groups, reliance on folk and sometimes home-made instruments, e.g., guitar, harmonica, country style fiddle, percussion in the form of a washboard.	A. For the accompaniment of the so-called "classic blues singers" of the twenties and early thirties, women like Ma Rainey, Bessie Smith, Clara Smith, etc. the use of a group of formal instruments, piano, trumpet, trombone, sometimes clarinet, saxophone, plus a rhythm section, playing in the idiom of the small jazz band of the twenties.
	B. With the supplanting of the "classic blues singers" by mostly male performers, whose singing and playing were rooted in country styles, the use of some informal instruments for accompaniment, guitar and mandolin, plus piano and a rhythm section of drums and bass. However, as in *A*, adherence to definite arrangements.

Classified by these criteria, among the performers included in this study, Robert Pete Williams is a pure country blues singer while Billie Pierce—a barrelhouse pianist, a member of New Orleans jazz bands since 1929, vocally a disciple of Bessie Smith—is typical of city blues singers.

Chapter Three

THEMES AND FUNCTIONS
OF COUNTRY BLUES

First the blues started in slavery times when they allowed them to sing. . . . The Negro's type of singin' was the blues 'cause he had the blues.

After that, later on the blues came outa the cotton fields and the canefields. When Negro people was workin' at that time, when Negro people tooken wives, they didn't marry, they most jus' taken 'em up; as long as they taken a wife on the place, as long as they exchange on the plantation it was all right. Saturday one had a dollar an' a half, an' the other one had two an' a half, an' probably one had three dollars, an' the one with the mos' money, he got the woman. An' so, that Saturday night when the drinkin' was all over, when he got home he foun' his wife gone, his woman gone, an' that Monday mornin' he had the blues. Then he began to sing such songs as this:

Oh, don't yo' bed look lonesome, when yo' woman is gone.

He sing these thing till the next Negro get it, an' go to sing it; an' perhaps he could sing it better an' he'd add more to these blues 'cause he had the same trouble. The thing runned on until a smart man heard it, an' then he went to singing' an' they put it on records, an' from that record soundin' out, the whole community got to singin' the blues.

That's where blues originated—from sorrow, broken-hearted, from a woman done quit her man. An' that's where most of the blues come from. An' on an' on. He felt sorry that the man told him afterwards he had to leave the plantation what he was on. After, the Negro got so he could leave an' move to different plantations, an' he took the blues. He got broke an' he didn't have no money; he be walkin' up an' down the road, an' he got to singin':

> Don't a man get hard luck sometime'
> He's broke an' he ain't got a dime.

That give him the blues. An' the blues come through many different kinds of trouble. He feel sad because he feel lost, or feel the need of someone, an' blues is a matter of sadness. An' that's where blues was originated from . . . just the idea of a man feelin' sad. . . . That's where it originated from—from sorrow an' sorrowful joy.

Willie B. Thomas, July 15, 1961

I had a good religious mother, a good religious father; they both was members of the Baptist Church. I has one brother an' one sister, an' they is members of the Baptist Church, an' apparently I was the on'iest jack (maverick) of the family. I don't belong to any church.

So my life was just that way, to keep out of trouble, drink my little whiskey, an' go an' do little ugly things like that, but just in a cue-tee (quiet) way. An' in 19 an' 27 I taken up the habit of playin' the guitar, an' I imagine it must have been the good Lord give me the talent to compose things. An' durin' those times, I was raisin' cotton, plowin' the mule. From that, milkin' in milk dairies, from that, driftin' on to larger cities, workin' on barge lines where there was ship docks, workin' at scrap metal companies, where we was handlin' iron eight hours each day, from that, on construction jobs, an' then we worked pourin' concrete an' whatsoever other things was necessary. We did this until it ranned out. We run another industry then, the Solvay Process; we worked there in those chemical things like that; then we would leave home again, pick up quite an experience on our guitar.

But sometime' we would cut sugar cane in the winter months, such things as we could to get a dollar. The times was hard for a poor man. Didn't have the education to afford a better job, so we had to use it manually an' we worked through many hard trials. We endu'ed many things we didn't want to endu'e, but that was our on'iest way for subsistences. So we made it on up till now. . . . So all these things we add them together, an' you can see that my life has been a degradated life, but in dispite of all of those things, whatever the Lord holds in his stock for you, that will be yours one day, an' I'm plannin' for the future one day to have a better life than I'ze had.

Herman E. Johnson, June 12, 1961.

Since many of the blues sung by country Negroes are improvised songs which follow the flow of thought—spontaneous expressions of feeling, an examination of a large number of blues brings to light not only the singers' immediate thoughts but also a sociological picture of the yearnings, frustrations, attitudes, beliefs, and impulses typical of folk Negro society.

As in any body of popular music, most of the songs deal with love, but infidelity occurs with greater frequency in blues than in other types of American folk music. Since most country blues are sung by men, the male perspective is presented. Typically the singer presents himself as the victim of a woman's treachery:

> But the woman rocks the cradle, I declare she rules the home, . . .
> But a man rockin' other men's babies, an' the fool think he rockin' his own.[1]

Often the singer's complaint is that she won his love and then returned to her regular lover or her husband.

> You done done made me love you, now yo' man done come.[2]

Occasionally a male singer reveals his own impulses toward promiscuity:

> A man gets tired o' one woman all the time.[3]

The man's jealousy often expresses itself as an impulse toward violent punishments — beatings, mutilation, or sometimes murder:

> An' the day that you quit me, Alberta, that day you die.[4]

> Lord, you jump this time, you sure won't jump no mo'.[5]

> Walk all night long with my .44 in my han',
> I was lookin' for my woman, found her with another man.[6]

> I'm gonna cut yo' doggone head four different ways,
> That's long, short, deep, an' wide.[7]

1. Herman E. Johnson, "Crawlin' Baby Blues," No. 174
2. Butch Cage and Willie B. Thomas, "Shake 'Em on Down," No. 175A
3. Guitar Welch, "Boogie," 120B
4. Robert Pete Williams, "Alberta," No. 198A
5. Hogman Maxey, "Fiddle Blues," No. 183
6. Butch Cage and Willie B. Thomas, "44 Blues," No. 181A
7. Lemon Nash, "A to Z," No. 182

Yonder comes a man with a great big knife,
Somebody been messin' with his wife.[8]

I know she had been talkin' with her other man . . .
So evil as a man can be,
Yes, I'm a hoochie coochie (tough, powerful, and clever) man,
Don't nobody mess with me;
I look at the little woman, she could hardly see,
You talk about a man, I'm supposed to be;
I mess with your ears, I mess up your face,
I leave you with both your legs outa place.[9]

There is also the frequent statement by the man that he will mistreat her as she has mistreated him:

May be the last time, you can hear your baby say, . . .
It's your turn, little woman, but it's gonna be mine some day.[10]

Fidelity is sufficiently rare that a special point is made of having had only two romances:

I ain't never had but four womens in my life, . . .
That was my mother, an' my sister, sweetheart an' my wife.[11]

Tenderness is uncommon but occurs occasionally as in these examples:

Any time is the right time to be with the one you love, . . .
She gets up an' tells me a lot o' sweet names,
Then she lay down, turn out the light,
She cries out, "Sweet daddy, everythin' it is all right,
Yes, everythin' is all right for me."[12]

Don't the moon look pretty, shinin' through the tree, . . .
Lord, I can see my little woman, but I swear she can't see me.[13]

I love my baby, boys, I tell the world I do, . . .
She's the sweetest little ole woman in this ole roun' world to me.
Tell me, baby, what make you love me so, . . .
You call me your baby boy, God knows I call you my baby
    girl . . .

---

8. Butch Cage and Willie B. Thomas, "You Can't Get Drunk No Mo," No. 46
9. Otis Webster, "Woman Done Me In," No. 137
10. Guitar Welch, "Worried Blues" (II), No. 216
11. Charles Henderson, "Cold-Hearted Mama," No. 171
12. Otis Webster, "Night Time Is the Right Time," No. 169
13. Guitar Welch, "Don't the Moon Look Pretty," No. 11

Woh, Cora, oh-oo, woh, baby, please come on home,
Say, that'll be the day, little woman,
We gonna lock the door, throw the key away,
That'll be the day, baby, that I'll prove my love to you.
That'll be when I'll pay, baby, I'll pay the debt I owe.[14]

Even more seldom, there is an expression of unselfish self-sacrifice:

I made up my mind, baby, if you want somebody else,
Go on, may God bless you, an' have fun.[15]

Another response to infidelity, relatively common, is that of the abject lover; he is unhappy because she is being unfaithful, but he cannot help loving her:

Please don't leave me, please don't never, never go, . . .
Well, if you leave me, baby, I'm goin' crazy, yes I know.[16]

Baby, baby, please throw this old dog a bone.[17]

Some say she was out last night with Mr. Jackson,
Some say she was out with Mr. Lee,
I don't give a doggone who she was out with,
Just as long as you bring her home to me.[18]

Now looka here, woman let me tell you what you can do,
You can hook me to a log wagon, now I'll pull just like an ox;
You tell me, woman, what more you want me to do,
I love you, woman, baby, you just don't treat me right.[19]

The man also appears sometimes as the weaker of the two when he confesses his dependency on her, appealing to her maternal instincts:

Please, please, woman, please don't leave me here,
I swear I'm a poor little boy, I can't hardly see my way.[20]

The sexual relationship is often on a cash basis:

14. Roosevelt Charles, "My Baby Blues," No. 129
15. Roosevelt Charles, "Long About Midnight," No. 89
16. Clarence Edwards, "You Don't Love Me, Baby," No. 177
17. Clarence Edwards, "Please Throw This Dog a Bone," No. 161
18. Butch Cage and Willie B. Thomas, "My Wife Done Joined the Club," No. 163
19. Roosevelt Charles, "Hard Time Lovin' Blues," No. 164
20. Charles Henderson, "Cold-Hearted Mama," No. 171

You ain't got no money, man, I would rather see you go.[21]

Well, you been takin', takin' all my money in my clothes.[22]

Now stack o' dollars, stack o' dollars, just as high as I am tall, oh Lord, . . .
Now you be my baby, mama, you can have them all.[23]

Shake, shake, woman, I'm gonna buy you a diamond ring, . . .
If you don't shake, darlin',' I ain't gonna buy you a doggone thing.[24]

When she get all your pocket change, then she drive you from her town.[25]

I knocked on the door, I heard my baby say, "Who is there?"
"You know this ole gamblin' chile, baby, I been gamblin' all night long."
She says, "Don't come in here, daddy, less'n you got some money."[26]

Another ugly aspect of love, the birth of illegitimate children, is treated occasionally in blues:

Now my mother, poor thing, ain't married, Lord I have to be a bastard,
Ain't no need o' me askin' no question now sir, God knows she ought to know the reason why.[27]

Let me tell you, mama, the reason why I left home, . . .
My daddy (went) from the South, oh Lord, before I was born.[28]

The instability of family life among folk Negroes has led to heavy reliance by the children on the mother. The consequences of the death of the mother are themes of a substantial number of blues:

My poor mother lay down an' died, an' I knowed that I was down, . . .
I had nobody to be my friend like my mother did.

21. Herman E. Johnson, "Po' Boy," No. 170
22. Clarence Edwards, "You Don't Love Me, Baby," No. 177
23. Clarence Edwards, "Stack o' Dollars," No. 178
24. Robert Pete Williams, "Make Me a Pallet on Your Floor," No. 204
25. Herman E. Johnson, "The Deceitful Brownskin," No. 200
26. Roosevelt Charles, "I'm a Gamblin' Man," No. 73
27. Roy Lee Jenkins, "Bastard Child," No. 203
28. Robert Pete Williams, "Rollin' Stone," No. 88

Lord, when my poor ole mother were livin', I could take this
  world at ease, . . .
But now she is dead an' gone, freight train are my only home.[29]

Lord, a motherless child has a hard time when mother is dead.
When your mother is dead in her (grave),
Lord, and (you) ease around from do' to do',
A motherless child has a hard (time) when your mother is
  dead.[30]

Reminded constantly of the barriers set up against them
because their skin is not white, influenced by the Caucasian
tastes in beauty spread by motion pictures and television, folk
Negroes are highly color conscious; they have, as Paul Oliver
has pointed out in *Blues Fell This Morning,* an elaborate series
of distinctions in describing pigmentation—ashy black, choco-
late-brown, coffee, sealskin brown, brightskin, high yaller,
lemon, and others.[31] As happens frequently, a minority culture
absorbs the prejudices against it of the majority, a phenomenon
the sociologists call "self-hatred." There are numerous blues
praising the virtues of Negroes of a particular shade, others
rancorously attacking their faults. The black girl is presented
as variable in mood, murderous and evil:

Woh, I don't want no black woman to bake bread for me, . . .
Because black is evil, Lord, I'm 'fraid that she might poison me.
But a black woman so evil, after a while she'll want to cut
  yo' throat,
She'll lay down with a butcher knife in her right hand, a razor
  in her left.[32]

I don't drink no black cow's milk,
I don't eat nothin' no black woman cook for me,
You might get evil, an' she might poison me.[33]

I don't want no jet black woman,
Oh, to fry no meat fo' me,
Lord, black is evil, she like to kill poor me.[34]

---

29. Robert Pete Williams, "Don't You See What a Shape I'm In," No. 60
30. Robert Pete Williams, "Motherless Children Have a Hard Time," No. 58B
31. Paul Oliver, *Blues Fell This Morning,* London 1960, p. 80
32. Roosevelt Charles, "I Don't Want No Black Woman," No. 118
33. Otis Webster, "Woman Done Me In," No. 137
34. Leon Strickland, "How Long Blues," No. 132

She is also ridiculed for her futile attempts to subdue the glitter of her skin:

> Jet black woman outshine the sun,
> Lipstick an' powder don't help her none.[35]

On the other hand, the black girl is often depicted as more likely to be faithful than girls with lighter complexions. The latter would be apt to have more temptations, and sometimes to have the possibility of passing themselves off as white:

> 'Cause some crave for yellow, please give me black an' brown, . . .
> Your black gal be wit' you when your yellow gal turn you down.[36]

In contrast to this attitude toward a yellow gal is this picture which emphasizes sweetness, cheerfulness, and lovability:

> You catch a yellow gal, wake up, smilin' in the mornin',
> Call you sweet names at midnight.
> Yellow gal she gonna call you daddy all day long.[37]

The brownskin woman gets her share of abuse:

> You never know what's on a brownskin woman's min',
> She may be huggin' an' kissin' you, leavin' you all the time.[38]

In some blues the man complains of the woman's turning away from him because he has grown old:

> Now don't deny me, woman, don't deny me,
> That's all that I, that's all that I can do,
> But I want you to remember, that some day you'll be old too.[39]

> Well, you don't want me, woman, just because I done growed old, . . .
> You find you a young man, you like better than you do me.[40]

Growing old is also treated in terms of the shock a man feels when he faces the ravages of time in himself:

35. Butch Cage and Willie B. Thomas, "Shake 'Em on Down," No. 175A
36. Lemon Nash, "Please Give Me Black an' Brown," No. 119
37. Roosevelt Charles, "I Don't Want No Black Woman," No. 118
38. Cage and Thomas, "Mean Brownskin," not included
39. Herman E. Johnson, "I'm Growin' Older," No. 210
40. Robert Pete Williams, "Teasin' Blues," No. 211

I done got so ugly, I don't even know myself.[41]

Folk blues singers often attribute their misfortunes to a jinx, a malign force which plagues them:

I been havin' trouble, ever since I was two feet high, . . .
Look like blues an' trouble gonna follow me till I die.[42]

I'm tryin' to raise my little family, woh man, somethin' got
me barred.[43]

Yes, I'm worried, woman, yes, I'm worried as a man can be,
Oh, the jinx is on me, baby, why did it have to be?[44]

Seems like everybody, baby, done turn their back on me, . . .
You know bad luck in my family, little girl, an' it all done
fall on me.[45]

You know it's bad luck an' trouble been followin' me,
Ever since I was six months old.[46]

Lord, trouble, trouble follow me all my day', . . .
Lord, it seems like trouble gonna kill me dead.[47]

Sometimes the bad luck is attributed to a specific cause; the most common is having a black cat cross the singer's path:

Lord, it must have been a black cat, sure done crossed my
trail, . . .
Lord, the reason I say it, I seen where he drug his tail.[48]

In one instance, the singer blames his mother's cold treatment of him on the fact that he is a seventh child, a likely source of bad luck:

Mama, I may be yo' seventh child,
It look like I'm the odd one,
Well, I gets treated so dirty.[49]

41. Robert Pete Williams, "Ugly Face Blues," No. 212
42. Herman E. Johnson, "Happy Days," No. 70
43. Smoky Babe, "Insect Blues," No. 18
44. Guitar Welch, "Moanin' Blues," not included
45. Guitar Welch, "Sundown Blues," No. 68
46. Roosevelt Charles, "Trouble Followin' Me," No. 3
47. Hogman Maxey, "Black Cat Blues," No. 111
48. Hogman Maxey, "Black Cat Blues," No. 111
49. Robert Pete Williams, "Walk-Up Blues," No. 150

The strongest charm for regaining a wayward lover is the Black Cat Bone:

> I'm gonna buy me a Black Cat Bone, . . .
> Remember 'bout me, woman, they tell me this is all right.[50]

This is an expensive and highly valued charm, a scarce magical talisman because of the elaborate ritual of creating it. Another talisman with magic powers is the mojo hand, which is made out of personal fragments like hair from the armpits or pubic region, finger-nail parings, also fragments of underclothing, menstrual cloth, parts of night creatures like bats and toads.

> Well, I'm goin' back to New Orleans, . . .
> I'm gonna buy me a mojo hand,
> Well, I'm gonna show all you women how you oughta treat yo' man.[51]

Brought in largely by slaves from the West Indies after the revolution of 1803, voodoo is still a force of some importance in New Orleans and to a lesser degree in country sections of Louisiana.

> Oh, listen here, woman, know you can tell me no lie, . . .
> Oh, darlin', the way you smell, darlin', I know you been with the hoodoo . . .
> I want you to know in the mornin' soon,
> Pack yo' trunk, I want you to leave,
> Don't stay long, I don't want no hoodoo woman, oh Lordy,
> Oh, you know this hoodoo woman are killin' me.[52]

> You been dealin' with the devil, you better leave that man alone, . . .
> You gonna wake up some mornin', you gonna find yourself outdoor'.
> I'm goin' to the hoodoo, I'm gonna put you under my feet, . . .
> I'm gonna have you, baby, do anythin' in the world I want you to do.[53]

Sickness and death are central themes in blues:

---

50. Robert Pete Williams, "Black Cat Bone," No. 109
51. Clarence Edwards, "Goin' Back to New Orleans," not included
52. Robert Pete Williams, "Hoodoo Blues," No. 113
53. Robert Pete Williams, "The Midnight Rambler," No. 112

When I was on my feet, I could not walk down the street,
For the women lookin' at me, I'm cryin', hey, baby, that T.B.
  killin' me,
Doctor say, "Baby is dyin' by degree'."[54]

Oh, black night fallin', my pains comin' down again, . . .
Oh, I feel so lonesome, oh I ain't got no frien'.[55]

My baby used to come to the hospital, try to make me smile,
Worry 'bout my condition, she say, "Be all right after a while."[56]

Lord, I'm achin' all over this mornin', I believe I got the
  pneumonia this time.[57]

Run an' tell my mother, please come an' see the last o' me, . . .
I ran on my sick bed, God knows I'm almost dead.[58]

The sickness of dope addiction is an occasional theme; in this
example the singer stresses the effect on him of his environment:

Well, my sister used a needle, an' my brother used 'em too,
  early rider, early rider, . . .
Now when it run in the family, what you 'spect poor me to do,
  early rider, early rider.[59]

Death is depicted forcefully:

Now, don't you hear me talkin' to ya, pretty mama,
Smoke like lightnin', baby, an' shine like gol',
Since I found my gal, ooh, on the coolin' board.[60]

They took my baby, down to the buryin' groun', . . .
I love you, baby, Lord, an' I just can't keep from cryin' . . .[61]

Well, the graveyard is so lonesome, an' the blues is there to
  stay, . . .
Oh, there's so many good women driven to the graveyard by
  some no good triflin' man.[62]

---

54. Guitar Welch, "T. B. Blues," No. 49
55. Hogman Maxey, "Black Night Fallin'," No. 52
56. Hogman Maxey, "My Baby Used to Come to the Hospital," No. 53
57. Otis Webster, "Achin' All Over This Mornin'," not included
58. Robert Pete Williams, "Almost Dead Blues," No. 54
59. Moses Jones (pseudonym), "I'm Gonna Build Me a Castle," No. 55
60. Leon Strickland, "Smoke Like Lightnin'," No. 48
61. Guitar Welch, "T. B. Blues," No. 49
62. Billie Pierce, "Gravedigger Blues," No. 50

Without faith, without the religious Negro's belief in going to glory, in being welcomed by a kindly fatherly God, the thought of death summons up a bleak picture:

> Tombstone landin', baby, an' ole dry bone, . . .
> They are before (me) when I am dead an' gone.[63]

Although church-going folk Negroes almost always make a sharp demarcation between those who are "saved" (those who will sing only spirituals) and those who are depraved (those who engage in sinful activities like singing blues, unfortunate souls destined for hell), blues singers usually have been actively exposed to religion, especially through their mothers. The imagery of spirituals therefore constitutes a portion of their mental storehouse of folk phrases. While most of them have no active faith in a hereafter, they often feel that maybe there is a God and one might as well play it safe by appealing to him when there is trouble. Or sometimes the use of verses which contain reference to God is conventional. On the other hand, some singers of "sinful" songs have a deeply felt religious faith, Robert Pete Williams and Willie B. Thomas, for example.

> I know I'm black, walkin' roun' with a hungdown head,
> I ain't got nowhere, God knows the way I try,
> Everybody but the white man that I got on my side,
> Wanta know who that, that the Good Lord up above.[64]

> Woh, fell down on my knee, woh, Lord, I begin to pray, (2)
> Woh, Lord, I want you to help us, baby, oh Lord, in our wicked way.
> Woh, Lord, the sun shinin', an' a dark cloud risin' in the east,
> Mm, sun is shinin', an' a dark cloud risin' in the east,
> Woh, there ain't no use o' you gettin' scared, baby, woh, that's the chariot after me.[65]

> Children runnin' roun' here cryin' for bread,
> With bare feet, I ain't got no shoes on my feet,
> Oh Lord, I fell down on my knees,
> I believe I sendin' up a prayer,
> Oh, I ask the Lord to help me please,
> Lord, help me, please Lord, help poor me.[66]

63. Smoky Babe, "Dell on the Mountain," No. 56
64. Robert Pete Williams, "Yessuh and Nosuh Blues," No. 29
65. Hogman Maxey, "Drinkin' Blues," No. 6
66. Robert Pete Williams, "Tough Livin' Blues," No. 61

Oh, listen here, baby, baby, what I got to say to you,
Oh, oh, listen here, darlin', what I got to say to you,
Oh the Good Book tell me, you got to reap what you sow.[67]

Now, Rock of Ages, come down an' pray for me.[68]

Hate to go an' leave my mother an' father,
Hate to go an' leave my mother an' father stay,
Lord, I hope they come see me on that Resurrection day.[69]

In several of the songs the performers present a significant picture of their underlying attitudes toward the paternalistic relationship between plantation owner and Negro worker which used to be widely prevalent in the Deep South and is still not extinct. As in feudalism, in which lord and vassal each had his rights and duties, the plantation owner assumed the right to control the life of his tenant farmer, his conditions of employment, and to some extent his personal activities; it was also his duty to advance his colored sharecropper enough food and money so that he could survive until the crop was harvested, to furnish him with equipment, and to help him out if he fell ill or landed in jail. From the point of view of the plantation with a sense of *noblesse oblige,* as boss he was an autocratic but kindly father who knew what was best for the Negro farmer, whom he viewed as a wayward child. The point of view of the latter is apparent in these quotations:

My papa always told me, "Son, if you ever get with a good man stay there."[70]

The son starts out believing his father's guiding principle; the best life for a Negro farmhand can be secured by working all his days for a paternalistic planter. But when the young farmer begins to work, he finds the boss to be either reluctant to supply him with tools, or if he does, they are apt to be old broken-down implements poorly suited for the job.

Yes, you know when I begun to farm,
My old boss didn't want to furnish me.[71]

---

67. Robert Pete Williams, "Bobbie's Blues," No. 67
68. Leon Strickland, "Ordinary Blues" (I) , No. 59
69. Smoky Babe, "Bad Luck an' Trouble," No. 69
70. Otis Webster, "When I Begin to Farm," No. 27
71. Otis Webster, "The Farm Blues," No. 30

> Every time I get ready to plant,
> Old plow stop up, stop up, stop up,
> I couldn't get a stand o' seed.[72]

The farmer is cynical about the owner's attempts at economy. When the owner suggests that the more they save, the more the farmer will have for himself, he replies:

> "Yeah, sho' is more you have, but (I) ain't gonna have nothin'. I'm gonna do the work, you gonna do the spendin'."[73]

Or, more bitterly, the farmer thinks:

> He had one hoss name' Jack, an' one name' Trigger,
> All the money for him, an' none for the nigger.[74]

Also, often he feels that the boss exploits him by making him work a longer week than he had agreed to:

> Now looka here bossman, you know when I hired t'you,
> I hired for five days an' a half,
> Now you tryin' to get seven days here. That ain't right.[75]

Traditionally, during the growing season, when the farmer has no money, he comes to the boss, begging for an advance against the crop, sometimes to buy a practical item, more often to spend on having a good time.

> Yes, I went to my bossman, just for a pair o' blue jean',
> He looked at me, say, "Son, what do you do with all your money?"[76]

> "Looka here, say, Bossman, I want a few dollars,
> I gotta go out there to that ole jook joint tonight."[77]

The boss generally counters with one or more of several reasons for not advancing him any more money, one being to suggest that the farmer has everything he needs:

> "You look here. You got fertilize,
> You got poison."[78]

---

72. Otis Webster, "When I Begin to Farm," No. 27
73. Otis Webster, "When I Begin to Farm," No. 27
74. Otis Webster, The Farm Blues," No. 30
75. Otis Webster, "I Want to Tell You Bossman," No. 28
76. Otis Webster, "I Know How to Do Time," No. 13
77. Roosevelt Charles, "Mule Blues," No. 14.
78. Otis Webster, "When I Begin to Farm," No. 27

The farmer replies that he has other needs than the practical necessities for farming:

"I ain't thinkin' about what I have,
'Cause I want somethin' to spend, don't mean no car tires, neither,
I want somethin' to spend."[79]

The boss may also suggest that the farmer's desire to have a big evening will get him into trouble:

"Yeah, but son, you oughta take your time,
You get in trouble, first thing you know,
You'd be in jail, an' you'd be callin' me up. . . .
Yeah, but, son, you oughta be careful,
Don't throw all your money away."[80]

"Son, you gonna throw away all your money."[81]

"Yeah, but you better count that money,
Gonna be in debt, can't get out."[82]

In some cases the farmer expresses his reliance on the boss's coming to his aid when he gets into trouble:

"Well, boss, that's what you for, take care o' me,
I'm workin' for you, isn't I?

Well, if I can't get out (of debt), I'll always have a good job,
'Cause you won't run me off I know."[83]

Sometimes the farmer expresses his desire to spend money as he sees fit rather than in accordance with what the boss thinks is best for him:

"Well, boss, you tol' me if I made you a good hand,
You don't care what I do with the money I make."[84]

He may also rebuke the boss for his interference in his private life; he says to the boss:

"You got your wine at home."[85]

79. Otis Webster, "When I Begin to Farm," No. 27
80. Otis Webster, "I Want to Tell You Bossman," No. 28
81. Roosevelt Charles, "Mule Blues," No. 14
82. Otis Webster, "I Know How to Do Time," No. 13
83. Otis Webster, "I Know How to Do Time," No. 13
84. Roosevelt Charles, "Mule Blues," No. 14
85. Roosevelt Charles, "Mule Blues," No. 14

When the boss asks him to explain, he replies:

"Well, now wait a minute, bossman, you want to know just
    a little bit too much.
'Cause I'm turnin' these furrows, an' the rows is straight,
    ain't they?"[86]

When the cotton crop is being weighed, the Negro farmer is
likely to discover that despite his backbreaking work "from
can to cain't" (from when he can first see sunlight till when
he can't), he has earned nothing over his expenses and in fact
is in debt to the owner of the plantation:

Then here come the poor farmer comin' up to settle,
Here the bossman with his pencil,
"You raise so many bales o' cotton this year,
But you still owe me a little bit.
Try to raise a little bit more next year."
"Woh, oh, Mr. Bale Weevil, I done broke up your land,
I done planted your cotton seed, I done raised your cotton,
I done poisoned the bolls, killed the bale (boll) weevil,
Now here you come takin' it all from me."[87]

Occasionally the field hand accepts his position with resignation,
or he may take great pride and pleasure in a job well done:

I may pick some cotton, I may pull some corn,
Well, you know now, people, that field work's gotta go on.[88]

Why don't you have a team pair up like this team do?
I tell you if you ain't a mule skinner,
You don't know what to do.
Watch me when I get on this lan', you better yea.
Look at him fallin' back over there.
Boy, that's why they call me a plowhand.[89]

More frequently the farmer is bitterly disillusioned with the
boss and with the system:

Yes, I woke up, bossman, you won't do nothin' you say,
Yes, I'm gonna have to go, bossman, you won't do nothin' you
    say,
Boy, my little family done got naked, an' I can't help me no way.

86. Roosevelt Charles, "Mule Blues," No. 14
87. Roosevelt Charles, "The Boll Weevil and the Bale Weevil," No. 15
88. Smoky Babe, "Cotton Field Blues," No. 21
89. Roosevelt Charles, "Mule Blues," No. 14

You know my wife got sick, I went to the doctor,
He wouldn't wait on her at all.

I asked my boss for a treat,
He said, "Now looka here, I tell you what I'm gonna do,
If you will me everythin' in your house,
I'll do what I can for you."

Woh, bossman, you ain't the man I thought you was.[90]

Reactions against injustice may also take the form of spite:

> I'm gonna—, I'll poison him for ya,
> I ain't gonna pray I'll kill the boll weevil.[91]

The sharecropper is willing to suffer himself in order to hurt the plantation owner he feels is victimizing him. Appeals to the generosity of the boss produce results which the singers satirize with biting irony:

"Woh, bossman, please, what you gonna do 'bout me?"
He say, "Well, I got an ole suit, I'm gonna give you;
Say, the rats done cut a hole in the rear end,
An' I had it patched."[92]

Here he come a-runnin' to the door, ole pair o' khaki an' ole
    pair o' boots;
I told the ole goof that wouldn't do.
Come to the door with a ole paper sack,
An' his hand with some light bread in it,
An' some hog hocks, but they had been et off.
But I didn't throw them away.[93]

Significantly, in one instance the singer rejects the paternalistic relationship in these terms:

> Woh, you ain't got no black child.[94]

The boss is speaking in paternal fashion when he addresses the sharecropper as "son." In asserting his independence the latter denies the plantation owner's right to treat him as a child.

---

90. Otis Webster, "When I Begin to Farm," No. 27
91. Otis Webster, "When I Begin to Farm," No. 27
92. Roosevelt Charles, "The Boll Weevil and the Bale Weevil," No. 15
93. Otis Webster, "When I Begin to Farm," No. 27
94. Roosevelt Charles, "Bossin' Blues," No. 26

Protest against poor treatment may take the form of biting the lip and saying nothing because complaining is likely to produce worse trouble:

> You better be smart, you better not cry,
> You sure have trouble with the man.[95]

Unexpressed except in song or in conversation with his friends are sentiments like these:

Yassuh an' nosuh, all over there's no good place,
Oh, yassuh an' nosuh, an' all over this earth there's no place,
He may be young, he don't have to be more than sixteen
  years old,
You got to honor him at the groun'.[96]
Well a nigger an' a white man, playin' seven up,
The nigger beat the white man, scared to pick it up.[97]

When the farmer does give vent to his grievance to the boss, he usually does so humbly:

> Excuse me, Mr. Johnson, I haven't meant no harm;
> Why you knocka me down? Why you knocka me down?[98]

Occasionally a sharecropper loses control of himself and attacks the boss:

(The bossman) went to get off his horse, I opened my big
  gun, .41, . . .
I tried to pin his right leg down there.
He'll always remember.[99]

More typically, when the sharecropper has trouble with his boss, or when the crops fail, he heads for another plantation or wanders from town to town.

I'm gonna pack my suitcase, baby, an' down the road I'm
  goin'.[100]

The rolling stone motif appears in numerous blues. The wanderer may be moving in hope of finding a better boss, a more

---

95. Lemon Nash, "Early in the Mornin'," No. 24
96. Robert Pete Williams, "Yassuh an' Nosuh Blues," No. 29
97. Otis Webster, "Bottle Up an' Go," No. 31A
98. Godar Chalvin, 'Why You Knocka Me Down?" No. 25
99. Roosevelt Charles, "Bossin Blues," No. 26
100. Guitar Welch, "Boll Weevil Blues," No. 20

fertile farm, some other job; or he may be leaving town because of trouble with a woman or the law; sometimes he travels because he is possessed by a wanderlust:

Got a mind to ramble, got a mind to head for town,
Got a mind to ramble, I won't settle down.[101]

I plowed all up in Arkansas,
Would've plowed in Mississippi, but I ain't stopped by there yet,
I went out in Texas, I turned a few furrows there.[102]

To the folk Negro the train is fascinating; sometimes he finds it appealing because it is a means of escape; by riding the rods or hiding out in a boxcar, he can head on down the line and leave a repressive dull life behind. The train is also the means by which the woman who loses interest in him can make her escape. Furthermore, the train stirs his imagination with its mournful moody whistle, the furious burst of steam it emits, and the clatter of its wheels on the tracks. Consequently folk images built on the train are common.

My papa tole mama, before I was born,
You got a boy chile comin', be a rollin' stone . . .
I was standin' in my window, lookin' down the railroad track, . . .
Here come a train along, a train comin' along, puffin' along,
I'm gonna ask trainman, see would he take me along. . . .
I'm goin', goin', mama, perhaps oh for half the worl'.[103]

When the singer thinks of suicide, an appropriate end is death under the wheels of a train:

I'm gonna lay my head, baby, on some lonesome railroad line, . . .
'Cause the ole freight train comin', satisfy my worried min'.[104]

The train carries off his woman. Often the singer rushes to the station to try to prevent her from running off, but he usually arrives too late and sadly has to give up the thought of pursuing her because he does not have the money to buy a ticket.

---

101. Butch Cage and Willie B. Thomas, "Bugle Call Blues," No. 95
102. Roosevelt Charles, "Mule Blues," No. 14
103. Robert Pete Williams, "Rollin' Stone," No. 88
104. Butch Cage and Willie B. Thomas, "Heart-Achin' Blues," No. 76

Will you tell me where my easy rider gone, . . .
'Cause that train carry my baby so far from home.[105]

I couldn't buy me no ticket, baby, I walked back through
   the do',
My baby lef' town, an' she ain't comin' back no mo'.[106]

It was a great long engine, and a little small engineer,
It took my woman away along, and it left me standin' here.[107]

But sometimes the singer gets so excited by the spectacle pro-
vided by the train that his sorrow about losing his woman drops
into the background:

Well, train I ride don't burn no coal at all, . . .
She's gonna shoot way off, she's call' the Cannonball.[108]

Me, big fool, so worried an' blue,
Don' know what I wanna do.
I thought about my ole guitar, right back in a corner,
Come to playin', my babe is gone.
My baby gone—.
Lord, I know that mornin', boy, that train run so fast,
You couldn't hear nothin' but that bell on him.
Conductor run up to the engineer,
Say, "We's fifteen minutes late.
If we can't catch it up, what we gonna do?"
I wish you'd heard that train runnin' that mornin'.
But when you got t'the corner 'fth av'nue, boy!
You couldn't hear nothin' but that bell.
When they got there jus' fifteen minutes late,
I wish you could've hear them conductors,
Meetin' one another with their watches in their hand,
I wish I had them watches 't was tickin' that mornin'![109]

The general decay of small farms, mechanization of such
formerly manual operations as cotton picking and cane cutting,
the growth of opportunities in the big cities outside the South
during World War II when labor shortages opened up many
doors which had previously been closed to Negroes—all com-

105. Butch Cage and Willie B. Thomas, "Easy Rider," No. 77
106. Butch Cage and Willie B. Thomas, "Heart-Achin' Blues," No. 76
107. Herman E. Johnson, "C. C. Rider," No. 198D
108. Butch Cage and Willie B. Thomas, "Easy Rider," No. 77
109. Leon Strickland, "Train Blues," No. 78

bined to produce a migration North and West. A significant
number of blues sung in Louisiana speak with interest or
enthusiasm of Kansas City, Chicago, and California—areas to
which there has been extensive migration from the Deep South.

> Say, my home is in Mississippi, but you know I'm Chicago-
> bound.
> Well' I'm goin' to see my baby, people, she done moved all
> up there,
> I say I'm gonna work hard, I'm gonna try to get my fare.[110]

> Come on, baby, don't you want to go,
> Back to my ole city, sweet home, Chicago.[111]

> I was standin' in my back do', lookin' way over in the east, . . .
> Lord, my mind was in California, an' I was standin' here on
> the beach.
> Lord, if I was just where my min' (was), Lord, I wonder
> would things be any better with me, . . .
> Oh Lord, one day, baby, I be right where my min' was today.[112]

The appeal of more plentiful and better paying jobs in the big
cities found ready ears among those who had suffered from
poor crops and hard times in the country:

> Boll weevil knocked down all my cotton, woh people, I didn't
> make no corn.[113]

> Man, let me tell you about farmin',
> There's too many if's in farmin'.[114]

> Children runnin' 'roun' here cryin' for bread,
> With bare feet, I ain't got no shoes on my feet.[115]

> Can't go wrong, everythin' I had is gone, starvation,
> Since me an' my pork chops ain't together,
> Keep me starvin' all the time.[116]

> I ain't just all alone, there is others too,
> I'm not all alone, there is others too,
> I see both white an' black walkin' the road,
> Tryin' to find somethin' to do.[117]

---

110. Smoky Babe, "Chicagobound," No. 107
111. Smoky Babe, "Baby, Don't You Want to Go," No. 108A
112. Robert Pete Williams, "California Blues," No. 105
113. Smoky Babe, "Insect Blues," No. 18
114. Roosevelt Charles, "The Boll Weevil and the Bale Weevil," No. 15
115. Robert Pete Williams, "Tough Livin' Blues," No. 61
116. Guitar Welch, "Starvation," No. 62
117. Smoky Babe, "Hard Time Blues," No. 65

I'm lookin' for a depression in 19 and 61,
And what grieves me so bad, I can't have no more fun.
I been drivin', I been walkin',
Till my hands and feet is tired,
An' I been goin' here and yonder,
But I can't find no job.[118]

The themes of loneliness and isolation occur repeatedly. The rolling stone thinks longingly of the community he has left behind and the warmth of home and family:

> Well, I'm jus' a pore boy here,
> Long ways from home,
> I got mother, sisters, an' brothers,
> I been away too long.[119]

The farm worker who has wandered to a new area sings:

I'm sittin' a thousand miles from nowhere,
In a little ole one room little country shack, . . .
I wake up every night aroun' midnight, people, I just can't
sleep no mo', . . .
I just have the crickets an' the frogs to keep me company,
an' the wind howlin' roun' my do'.[120]

The penniless and/or sick man bemoans the fact that all his supposed friends have abandoned him in his time of need:

Yes, when I had money, I had friends for miles an' miles
aroun',
Now I have done got broke, baby, done taken down sick,
My friends even quit comin' roun', scared I'd ask them for
a favor.[121]

When a man is in trouble, it seem like he lose all his friends, . . .
My friends all forsaken me, Lord since I been born.[122]

The importance of alcohol in a folk non-religious environment is reflected in the many varied references to drinking. The singer drinks to deaden the wound caused by his woman's leaving him:

---

118. Herman E. Johnson, "Depression Blues," No. 64
119. Smoky Babe, "Long Way from Home," No. 91
120. Clarence Edwards, "A Thousand Miles from Nowhere," No 12A
121. Roosevelt Charles, "Greenback Dollar Blues," No. 66B
122. Robert Pete Williams, "Don't You See What a Shape I'm In," No. 60

Woh, been, been drinkin' all night long, . . .
Woh, I gonna just keep on drinkin' till my baby come back
home.[123]

Getting drunk is dangerous since one can get into trouble. The
singer, responding to his woman's objections, promises to lead
a better life:

Yes, I'm gone get drunk an' clown, baby, I wanta drink my
wine some more.
When I come home last night, first thing my baby said, "Daddy,
I know that you been drinkin' wine."
I say, "Ah, honey, I been drinkin' wine, wine again.
I don't want you woman, to tell me about ole Government
Street no mo'.

Government Street ain't nothin' but trouble, I'm gonna leave
ole Government Street alone,
You know I'm goin' back home, little girl, God knows I'm
gonna stop an' settle down."[124]

The anguish of the alcoholic who is vainly trying to leave
drunkenness behind and reform rings out in:

Let me go home, whiskey,
Let me go home, whiskey,
I'm gonna love my wife last (tomorrow) night,
Don't come back drunk no mo'.[125]

The reverse situation also occurs, the man criticizing his woman
because she is drunk all the time:

Now she's a whiskey-headed woman, an' she stays drunk all
the time, . . .
If you don't stop drinkin', I believe you gonna lose your min'.

Every time I see you, you at some whiskey joint,
You standin' aroun' the crowd, beggin' for one more half
a pint.[126]

Another blues about a drunk woman emphasizes her inability

123. Hogman Maxey, "Drinkin' Blues," No. 6
124. Roosevelt Charles, "Government Street Blues" (I), No. 39
125. Godar Chalvin, "Let Me Go Home, Whiskey," No. 38
126. Otis Webster, "Whiskey Headed Woman," No. 40

to co-ordinate her movements and the singer's anger at her degeneration:

> She come in drunk, talkin' all out her head,
> Reach for the foot, miss the whole durn bed . . .
>
> Well, she still drinkin' Manny an' she wants more,
> Reach for the knob, miss the whole durn door . . .
>
> Don't nothin' make me madder'n a drinkin' ole gal,
> She make me think about what she once have had.[127]

Another singer's objection to his woman's getting drunk (and his suspicion that the cause is her disappointment at being rejected by her other lover) leads to his knocking her down:

> I know you had been drinkin', baby, I had—, I just don't like
>   it woman,
> And there's no need to say I (do).
>
> I was standin' at the gate, when she looked aroun',
> Caught her by the hair an' I knocked her down.[128]

The same singer, Otis Webster, who in another blues had expressed great indignation at his woman's drinking, himself gets drunk to forget his worries:

> I'm worried baby, an' drunk alla time, . . .
> Well do nothin', nothin' to please my min.'
>
> I'm drinkin', babe, I'm drinkin', baby, on'y thing pacify
>   my min'.[129]

He also confesses that drinking caused his ending up in prison:

> Oh, whiskey an' gin is one thing I do crave, . . .
> You know that the thing that cause me here today.[130]

The pleasure of drinking is captured by:

> Let's go out an' have some fun, darlin', we gonna ball to the
>   break of day.
> If the river was wine, me an' my baby be drunk all the time.[131]

---

127. Otis Webster, "She Drunk," No. 41
128. Herman E. Johnson, "She Had Been Drinkin'," No. 44
129. Otis Webster, "Whiskey Drinkin' Blues," No. 43
130. Otis Webster, "Whiskey Drinkin' Blues," No. 43
131. Robert Pete Williams, "I'm Lonesome Blues," No. 45

Disappointment at the coming of Prohibition motivated these lines:

> Now, you can't get drunk no mo',
> You may try, you can't buy,
> You can't get drunk no mo'.[132]

One singer comments sadly that he doesn't have enough money to buy wine:

> No nickel won't buy some wine.[133]

His next remark to his woman states in effect that since she is drunk she should be ready to sleep with him.

> Now you're drunk, now, baby,
> Come on, shake 'em on down.[134]

The urge to gamble can become as irresistible as the alcoholic's craving for a drink. The drive to get money to play can drive the addict to pawn all his possessions, neglect his family and even commit crimes.

> I pawn my home, bran' new automobile,
> Just to play another game o' Georgia Skin.
>
> Oh, Georgia Skin, baby, 'll make you turn your mother down,
> Oh, Georgia Skin, woman, 'cause me to lose my baby (in) town.
>
> Yes, that's why they call it Georgia Skin, it'll make you rob
> an' steal.[135]

A substantial number of folk blues deal with crime and prison. The crime most frequently mentioned is murder.

> Say, my cousin Sonny Boy got shot, just as he was walkin'
> out the do'.[136]

> Take her down in the alley, please don't murder her here.[137]

> Been down on Angola,
> Oh, God, I've been down in a pen,

---

132. Butch Cage and Willie B. Thomas, "You Can't Get Drunk No Mo'," No. 46
133. Leon Strickland, "No Nickel Won't Buy No Wine," No. 42
134. Leon Strickland, "No Nickel Won't Buy No Wine," No. 42
135. Roosevelt Charles, "Georgia Skin," No. 74
136. Smoky Babe, "Bad Luck an' Trouble," No. 69
137. Guitar Welch, "Dark Alley Blues," No. 133

I done killed my little ole woman,
Gotta serve that time again.[138]

I'm gonna shake hands with my partner, I'm gonna ask him
  how he came here, . . .
You know I had a wreck in my family, they're gonna send me
  to the ole electric chair.[139]

Blues sung by those who have been condemned generally
attack the judge and the district attorney for unfair treatment
and/or the severe sentences.

First time in trouble, I done get no fair trial at all.[140]

"I'm gonna lock you back in jail just thirty long days."
Mean ole judge, boy, an' a lowdown D.A.,
Say, the judge passed my sentence, man, an' the D.A. wrote
  it down.[141]

You know that ole judge must been mad, . . .
When he gave me my sentence,
He throwed the book (at me) .[142]

Oh, six months ain't no sentence,
Woh, twelve months ain't no time,
Lord, they give me an' my buddy,
Fourteen to ninety-nine.[143]

Six months ain't no sentence, two years ain't no time, . . .
I got a frien' in prison now, got ninety-nine.[144]

Some got six months, some got a solid year,
But me an' my buddy, we got lifetime here.[145]

Electrocution is discussed in practical terms which emphasize
the callousness of execution:

Wonder why they electrocute a man at the one o'clock hour
  at night? . . .
The current much stronger, people turn out all the light.[146]

---

138. Leon Strickland, "How Long Blues," No. 132
139. Guitar Welch, "Electric Chair Blues," No. 141
140. Robert Pete Williams, "Some Got Six Months," No. 125A
141. Roosevelt Charles, "The Government Street Blues," (II) , No. 131
142. Robert Pete Williams, "Some Got Six Months," No. 125A
143. Leon Strickland, "How Long Blues," No. 132
144. Otis Webster, "Penitentiary Blues," No. 126
145. Robert Pete Williams, "Some Got Six Months," No. 125A
146. Guitar Welch, "Electric Chair Blues," No. 141

Locked in a cell or working on the prison grounds, the prisoner longs for his woman:

So far distant, so far distant away,
You know I can't see your face, little girl,
Lookin' at your picture all in a frame.[147]

Would you believe that I cried all night long, . . .
Said, I miss you little girl, from the time I let you in my home.[148]

Although most of the time he mournfully expects his woman to have forsaken him for another lover, sometimes he voices hope that she will welcome him back:

Oh, I know my baby sure gonna jump an' shout, . . .
When she get that letter, done roll my long time out.[149]

The prisoner complains that his woman and all his friends have abandoned him:

You know when a man is down, it ain't long before his folks
    forget all about where he is . . .
Sometime' that I sit down, I have to write my own self,
    sometime', . . .
I have to fool these yother inmate' like I'm receivin' mail
    from home.
You told me that you loved me, baby, hey, you just told pore
    Bob a lie,
After I fell in trouble, you showed me how you made behind.[150]

My baby put me down when the D.A. wrote my charge down.
You know when I was out on the streets, I had my friends all
    over town,
"Say, come on boy, let's get another drink."
But now I'm locked down in jail, my friends even quit comin'
    roun'.[151]

The perspective of friends is also expressed; they are sorry for him but feel that a person who gets into trouble persistently is not worth bothering about:

147. Roosevelt Charles, "Love Trouble Blues," No. 139
148. Andy Mosely, "Lorraine Blues," No. 134
149. Hogman Maxey, "My Baby Sure Gonna Jump an' Shout," No. 130
150. Robert Pete Williams, "Up an' Down Blues," No. 142
151. Roosevelt Charles, "The Government Street Blues" (II) , No. 131

> Oh Red, Red is in jail, . . .
> Ain't got nobody to go ole Red's bail.
>
> Pore Red, what's you gonna do? . . .
> I'm sick an' tired, foolin' roun' with you.[152]

Sometimes (this is more probably what the prisoner fantasizes about doing rather than what he actually does) he tells off the warden and other prison authorities:

> Well, warden, you know I'm mighty sick an' tired o' this job, . . .
> Well, I said that last July, I know I was only riskin' my life.[153]

The prisoner feels that he is wasting way because of his depression.

> Lord, I feel so bad sometime', seems like I'm weakenin' every day.
> You know I begin to get gray since I got here, well a whole lot of worryin' causin' that.
> But I can feel myself weakenin', I don't keep well no mo'.
> I keeps sickly.
> I takes a lot of medicine, but it looks like it don't do no good.[154]

At other times his despair overwhelms him and he longs for death or even considers suicide:

> You know a lotta time', I wisht, baby, that, I wisht that I was dead an' gone, . . .
> I'll tell you the reason why I wish that, baby, you know a criminal ain't no more'n a dog.
> Lord, my worry sho' is carryin' me down.
> Sometimes I feel like, baby, committin' suicide . . .
> I got the nerve if I just had somethin' to do it with.[155]

Anxiously he waits for the decisions of the parole board in Baton Rouge, or of the pardon board in New Orleans:

> Oh, I'm gonna cry all night this time, little girl, an' I won't cry no mo', . . .
> Because if I make parole on this September, woh, I'm goin' on from do' to do'.[156]

152. Leon Strickland, "Pore Red," No. 127
153. Cyprien Houston, "Those Prison Blues," No. 128
154. Robert Pete Williams, "Prisoner's Talking Blues," No. 2
155. Robert Pete Williams, 'Prisoner's Talking Blues," No. 2
156. Andy Mosely, "Lorraine Blues," No. 134

When there is no hope of pardon or parole in the immediate future, he is likely to fantasize about freedom and escape:

> In the mornin', 'fore the sun go down, . . .
> I'm gonna be in Montana with them long-eared houn's.[157]

In the bit of dialogue:

> "Say there, ole partner, how about let's goin' down the road
> a piece an' havin' a ball."
> "O.K., Bob, I don't care if I do,"[158]

his use of a casual tone is an ironic way of expressing his desire to follow his whims as he would if he were free. In addition to making his escape, he would like to treat the captain as an inferior to whom he is calmly condescending:

> I wake up in the mornin', partner, with the risin' sun, . . .
> Well, captain call me, I say, "Sorry, baby, gone."[159]

Most of the older country blues singers—those over forty—have had a total of only a few months of school, squeezed in over a period of two or three years in between planting and harvesting seasons. The consequences of having no education at all are suggested in the following:

> You know I'm all down an' worried, because I broke my
> mother's rule, . . .
> Been out on the solid highway, keep from goin' to school. . . .
>
> Woh, in this town, in this town, the people call me a fool, . . .
> The people all call me a fool, darlin', because I didn't go to
> school at all.[160]

Although as a child the singer (Robert Pete Williams) had rebelled against his mother's insistence that he go to school, as an adult he was saddened by the low opinion the people of his town had of him because of his inability to read and write.

In "When I Was a Little Ole Boy," the singer (Clyde Causey), who is twenty-two years old, expresses the point of view of the hopeful and ambitious members of the younger

---

157. Guitar Welch, "Levee Camp Song," No. 136
158. Guitar Welch, "Electric Chair Blues," No. 141
159. Guitar Welch, "Levee Camp Song," No. 136
160. Robert Pete Williams, "Broke My Mother's Rule," No. 218

generation of country Negroes—a rejection of the ways of the past, with their associations of degradation, and a conviction that it is possible to rise in the world and that education offers a practical means of doing so.

In the song, the singer is a child of ten sitting in a tree, watching his parents working hard picking cotton. His father tells him to watch closely how the work is done because he will have to earn his living in the same way. The son replies:

> The day way back there is over with, . . .
> Everybody got to go to school now these days.[161]

The father agrees that he is right.

> Ever since then he sent me to school
> To learn what I can in school.
>
> Well, I stayed in school round about
> Till I got round about twelfth grade,
> Then I came outa school an' I got me a little job,
> An' I start to teachin' them children.
> An' he told me, "What did you teach the children?"
> An' I told him, "I teach the children science."
> An' he told me, "Lord, you know one thing,
> You so good to my children."[162]

The song is actually the result of wish-fulfillment thinking since Clyde Causey himself did not complete high school and is unemployed except for playing at dances on weekends, but the fact that he fantasizes in these terms indicates an important new direction in folk Negro attitudes. The dream is one his parents (sharecroppers near Clinton, Louisiana) never dreamed.

While this grouping of blues verses in terms of themes offers a significant insight into the feelings of country Negroes toward their environment, at the same time the quotations tend to give a misleading expression. The emphasis is on frustration, anger, aggressiveness, sadness, oppression, hunger, suffering, faithlessness in love, restless wandering. Only occasionally is there a verse which expresses faith, hope, or optimism, feelings which surge in so many spirituals. The meaning and function of the blues in the social context within which they are performed— something which one cannot grasp adequately from seeing

161. Clyde Causey, "When I Was a Little Ole Boy," No. 219
162. Clyde Causey, "When I Was a Little Ole Boy," No. 219

the texts and music on paper—emerge more clearly in the light of these additional quotations from the remarks of country Negroes.

Georgianna Colmer, a surprisingly vigorous woman of sixty-seven, proclaims in a low-pitched resonant voice that almost makes a country shack rattle:

> Way back yonder I was a big size gal, I 'bout thirteen or fourteen old, an' I'ze learned how to plow, an' I used to go out soon in the mornin', catch my mule, go to the field an' plow. I dirt that cotton so till the white folk would stop in their car. . . . "I'm tellin' you, that gal really plowin' that cotton."
>
> I just hook my mule in the mornin' an' go. I knowed how to hook him up, knowed to put the gears an' everythin' on him, an' go out there in the field, an' plow an' dirt. Dirt that cotton up . . . an' the hoes come up behind, an' then when they hoed, I come right back, I come right back an' put that dirt to it, an' I'd lap that dirt so close roun' that cotton till people would stop an' see me plow. An' I just quit hoein' altogether. I, I plow till I got me a husband. . . . When I got him, he didn't want me to plow no mo', but I love to plow. I used to plow all the time; I never would hoe no mo', an' I just liketed that job. . . .
>
> I used to get up soon in the mornin', sometime' I'd cook, an' sometime' . . . my sister would bring my breakfas' to me an' I plowed that cotton. An' I used to go to the fiel' when cotton pickin' time an' I had a baby. An' I'd walk about a mile an' a half . . . an' I picked them 212 pounds o' cotton every day. You know had that much walkin' to do, an' pick that much cotton . . .
>
> I sing the blues an' cuss the mule out when they wouldn't walk right, sing the blues an' cuss the mule out. It was ole man told me, say, "If he don't do right, cuss him out. He'll do right if you cuss him out."
>
> An' I just go start to cussin' . . . way out in the fiel', "God damn ya, get on that row!" . . .
>
> Oh, I was young then, I could do a whole lot o' work when I was young. . . . I do anythin', eat a great big potato, 'bout that big, raw, never quit goin'. . . . I never did have the stomach ache when I was a girl. I just et anythin', peanuts, raw peanuts, just anythin' an' never did have the belly ache. . . . An' way back yonder I was a crackerjack. I never did stop hardly fo' pain in the stomach, or grippe, or nothin' like that. I just

stayed goin', just worked until my clothes be stickin' to me, just sweat, you could almost wring the sweat out, an' I felt good then, big ole chew o' tobacco in my mouth, my jaw stickin' way out; I'm spittin', ya see— I just felt so good.

When the time come, I just th'ow that sack, big ole sack, at least from here to that door. I just grab it half-way an' sling it on up there. Then long sack, people didn't pick in no little ole sack like they do now. Them sacks'd reach from here to that do', an' I just grabbed halfway, come on up with it. . . .

When I get there, I have a hundred in them, 'scusin' the sack weight. Sack weight was five pounds off an' that left me a hundred. Yas suh. I was somethin' when I was young. I was stout, good, an' strong; I love to pick up a bag weight. . . . I love to reach down an' get up a load. Yah, put on them pants an' go to that field an' I do some work.

An' so I'd raise a good garden. I had a whole lot o' chillun; I had eleven head, an' I'd raise a big garden fo' 'em, big lot o' corn. I'd go grind my meal. . . . I didn't have much to buy, but flour an' salt an' bakin' powder, an' soap an' matches an' like that. . . . I raised that big garden for them chillun an' people would ask, "What you feed 'em on? I just tell 'em, I say, "Slop." Different stuff ya know, liquor, . . . just have that pot ya know packed in with greens, somethin' to fill 'em up. Raise a lot o' peas, okra, just to keep 'm full ya know.

An' when white folks get over there, "What you feed yo' chillun on? They just as fat!" I say I just feed 'em on plenty rabbit, coon, possum, cooked 'em there mustards, an' make a few little roun' meat balls, an' drap in there, an' stir 'em, raise hogs. . . . Oh when I was in the course o' raisin' my chillun, I just had a whole lot. . . . Had good milk cows, one of 'em would give a water bucket o' milk, had two. I had my children just like a butterball, 'cause I wasn't too lazy to get out an' work for 'em.

There were times when Georgianna got deeply disturbed:

Sometime' I'd get discouraged when I done that crop, wouldn't get nothin', done work hard, ya know, an' then I'd be lookin' for somethin' at the end of May, say I come out (broke even), I'd get some discouraged then. Sometime' I'd hop out an' move, I'd leave . . . I didn't get no money, felt some disencouraged, some bad.[163]

---

163. Interview of Geogianna Colmer, June 10, 1960, recorded by Harry Oster

Her dominant point of view, however, was positive and optimistic, marked by pride in strength and in doing a job well. Managing by ingenuity and constant effort to feed her children, she lived zestfully, enjoying the hard work and buoyed up by her faith in her own power to defeat trouble. A similar joy in living despite a life of insecurity and trouble pervades most blues performances.

Georgianna summed up an important characteristic of blues singing when she remarked, "I'd sing them old moans until I got happy." Other Louisiana singers have made like observations: Robert Pete Williams, "I want you to be happy an' take the blues like me"; Hogman Maxey, "Whenever you sing the blues jus' right, why you feels like a million when you may not have a dime." These quotations suggest a function of blues like that which Aristotle attributed to tragedy, catharsis of the emotions. Singing about trouble defeats sorrow, somehow purges the heart of fear, anxiety, and depression.

A related function of blues is apparent in a line popular in Negro folksongs, "I'm laughin' just to keep from cryin'," which Butch Cage often sings, and in Willie B. Thomas's reference to "sorrowful joy." If one can make a joke out of a situation, even though it be a grim joke, if one can go through the motions of gaiety, trouble ceases to be overwhelming.

Roy Lee Jenkins suggests another facet when he says, "The blues ain't blue; it's keepin' it all to yourself. . . . Now tell 'em, guitar, 'cause they might not understand me. Maybe if you was to come out, tell 'em what you mean, they might get it." The blues feeds on loneliness. If the singer can express his depression to others, sorrow becomes bearable. An important function of blues—in fact of Negro folk music in general—is to create emotional rapport between the individual and his society. The church member shouting hallelujah, swept along by the hysteria of the preacher and the congregation, the worker in a chain gang responding to the leader's ironic chant, and the blues singer stirring up excitement among a crowd of friends in a country shack, a dingy bar, or a dance hall—all find their sufferings and frustrations easier to bear through achieving a sense of union with a group.

The positive and optimistic aspects of blues are projected through the use of lively and spirited accompaniments, through a cheerful tone of voice, through wry good humor, through

exuberant movements of the body while performing. Though
a country blues singer-guitarist usually performs sitting down,
in effect he dances the song, tapping out lively rhythms with
both feet and swaying sensuously in movements of head and
body.

Although there is a significant number of blues which express
unrelieved gloom, most blues are ultimately optimistic. While
the texts may be mournful and bursts of moody feeling may
sound in the accompaniment, most blues "are not intrinsically
pessimistic; their burden of woe and melancholy is dialectically
redeemed through sheer force of sensuality into an almost
exultant affirmation of life, of love, of sex, of movement,
of hope."[164]

---

164. Richard Wright, foreword to Paul Oliver, *Blues Fell This Morning* (London: 1960), p. ix

Chapter Four

THE BLUES AS POETRY

IN ADDITION TO THEIR SIGNIFICANCE as a reflection of folk attitudes and their functions as self-expression, catharsis of emotional disturbance, social protest, identification with society, and accompaniment to sensuous dancing, blues are also notable as folk poetry. Examining the blues in this collection, one can isolate certain central conventions of imagery, style, and structure.[1]

Personification is a favorite figure of speech. The blues is presented as something animate, a living entity, rather than as an abstract state of mind.

Oh, I woke up this mornin' with the blues knockin' on my
do', . . .
When I wake up in the mornin', blues is howlin' roun' my do'.[2]

The lines evoke the picture of sadness pounding on the door, like a fierce beast trying to force his way in to crush the singer. At other times the blues is a less fierce but still insistently menacing visitor:

Mm, tell me, blues, what in the world are you tryin' to do?
Oh, looka here, blues, what in the world are you tryin' to
do to me?
I say, tell me, blues, what in the world are you doin' here
so soon?[3]

1. See also the discussions in Howard W. Odum and Guy B. Johnson, *The Negro and His Songs* (Hatboro: 1964), pp. 269-296; Samuel B. Charters, *The Poetry of the Blues* (New York: 1963), *passim*
2. Butch Cage and Willie B. Thomas, "44 Blues," No. 181A
3. Robert Pete Williams, "Goodtime Lonesome Blues," No. 8

Most of the time such images are one element in a total picture, a touch of shadowy color, but occasionally the personification is sustained throughout, as for example in Roosevelt Charles's "Walkin' with the Blues." Blues is a constant companion who walks, talks, eats, sleeps with him, sits beside him, drags him down, destroys his rest—in short, torments him unceasingly. Desperately, pleadingly, Charles addresses the relentless monster:

> Well, go on then, blues, won't you let me take my rest.[4]

Godar Chalvin personifies his personal demon when he sings:

> Let me go home, whiskey.[5]

In similar fashion, trains are often treated as beings with feelings rather than as impersonal machines:

> Well, when I first start to hoboin', I taken the freight train for my friend.[6]

Another train, which takes away the singer's woman, appears not only mean and lowdown but also adds insult to injury by insolently blowing black smoke over him:

> Well, that mean ole, ole Frisco, an' that lowdown Santa Feel, . . .
> Taken my babe away, Lord, an' blow black air on me.[7]

Personification also occurs in the form of conversations which the singers hold with birds, animals, and insects. The bluebird is a favorite emissary of love because its color makes it appropriate for some one who has the blues.

> Bluebird, bluebird, I want you to fly down on Shannon Street,
> I don't want you to stop flyin' until you give Miss Lacybelle this note for me.[8]

A mule protests to his driver:

> Well, I cross in the saddle, the mule begin to jump,
> He looked at me, an' he bit his bottom lip;
> He looked up then, an' he had no corn,

---

4. Roosevelt Charles, "Walkin' with the Blues," No. 1
5. Godar Chalvin, "Let Me Go Home, Whiskey," No. 38
6. Roosevelt Charles, "Freight Train Blues," No. 87
7. Otis Webster, "Mean Ol' Frisco," No. 83
8. Otis Webster, "Bluebird Blues," not included

He say, "Ah, you can't ride me,
'Cause we can't get along."[9]

Another mule, himself working too hard with inadequate equipment, expresses his sympathy for his driver:

The mule drove four feet, an' the poor thing ask me how I feel.[10]

The boll weevil is personified as an ostensibly weak creature who is fiendishly devious and superhumanly tough. For example, in one of Otis Webster's songs, the insect lulls the sharecropper into a false sense of security, suggesting that there is no need to try to poison him since he is such a weak creature:

He walk in the square, he hid his head,
He said, "Cotton Man, I'm most dead."[11]

Acting humble and servile, the weevil worms his way into the farmer's fields. Finally, supported by his large powerful family, the weevil crows sadistically over the ruin of his simple gullible foe:

I clean out the crop, everythin' I thought I (you) had,"
He said, "I got every doggone thing you had."[12]

An important part of the appeal of such songs lies in the identification of the singer with the trickster weevil, who is essentially like the weak but cunning monkey and rabbit of Negro folktales. In picturing the triumph of a tricky little creature over apparently stronger enemies, the singer engages in wish-fulfillment fantasy.

More common than personification is the use of metaphors and similes, especially those in which humans are compared with animals, birds, insects, or fruit; the point is usually sexual or romantic.

Blacksnake blues killin' me, mm, mm, black snake crawlin'
in my room, . . .
Somebody give me these blacksnake blues.[13]

---

9. Otis Webster, "You Oughta Heard My Grandma," No. 10
10. Otis Webster, "Gettin' Late in the Evenin'," No. 35
11. Otis Webster, "Boll Weevil Blues," No. 16
12. Otis Webster, "Boll Weevil Blues," No. 16
13. Robert Pete Williams, "Black Snake Blues" (II). No. 159B

The black snake is obviously the woman's lover, and the image also has overtones of the temptation of Eve by the Devil. More basically it represents a phallus. In the following two examples, the sting of the ant and the snout of a hog grubbing hungrily for food have a similar significance. "Rootin'" is a common metaphor for fornication.

> Well, you know I'm a little crawlin' ant, baby, gonna crawl up on your hand,
> Well, when I sting you, baby, well you won't let me be.[14]

> Now looka here, little girl, you caught me rootin' when I was young,
> Told me I was the man you love,
> Now come to find out you in love with some one else,
> I'm a prowlin' ground hog, an' I prowl the whole night long;
> I'm gonna keep on rootin', baby, until the day I die.[15]

The following metaphors are less earthy and more romantic in tone:

> I wish I was a catfish, swimmin' in the deep blue sea,
> I'd have all you pretty women, fishin after, sho' 'nuff after,
> I's glad after me, an' after me.

> I wish, wish I was a jaybird, flyin' right up in the air,
> I'll build my nes' in some o' you brownskin,
> Declare you brownskin, sho' 'nuff you brownskin, you brownskins' hair.[16]

Animal metaphors are often used to express the theme of the abject love, the male who loves a woman generally mean or unfaithful:

> Baby, baby, please throw this old dog a bone.[17]

> You got me way down here,
> In a rollin' fog,
> An' treat me like a dog.[18]

> I so long for wrong, baby, been your dog, . . .
> 'Fore I do it again, baby, I sleep in a hollow log.[19]

14. Roosevelt Charles, "I Wisht I Was an Ant," No. 158
15. Roosevelt Charles, "I'm a Prowlin' Ground Hog," No. 157
16. Mary Sassafras, "Catfish Blues," not included
17. Clarence Edwards, "Please Throw This Dog a Bone," No. 161
18. Guitar Welch, "Baby, Please Don't Go," No. 192A
19. Percy Strickland, "I Won't Be Yo' Lowdown Dog No Mo'," No. 205

The dog image is apt but trite. A fresher one for the submission of an abject lover is:

> Now looka here, woman, let me tell you what you can do,
> You can hook me to a log wagon, now I'll pull just like an ox.[20]

The man who refuses to be cuckolded sings:

> Now ain't no monkey, don't climb no tree,
> No woman don't make no fool outa me.[21]

Although in some contemporary Negro folklore the monkey is a trickster hero, in the context of the above blues lines, the word connotes a weak ridiculous servile creature, who runs away from trouble instead of manfully crushing it.

Riding is used metaphorically to describe the sex act:

> I want you to ride me, baby, till I say that I got enough, . . .
> I got a coal black mare, you know she sure can saddle along,
> She can ride me a while until I be right where (I belong.)[22]

The use of horseback riding as a sexual metaphor is relatively archaic. Possessing an automobile is of special importance to Negroes; barred by social and economic barriers from satisfying jobs and from living in decent housing, the Negro male loves big heavy automobiles. Driving his old Buick or Cadillac he is swift, powerful, graceful, manly, irresistible; he finds a partial substitute for gratifications of comfort, importance, and power. By extension, a man about to have an orgasm is racing furiously along the highway, a rival lover is another driver at the wheel, a fickle woman is a cheap decrepit car, a desirable lover is a smooth chauffeur.

> Well, I'm a highway man, hollerin' hoo, baby, don't block the road, . . .
> Well, I'm lickin' cool one hundred, now baby, hoo, Lord, I'm lookin' boun' to go.[23]

> You had a good little car, too many drivers at your wheel . . .
> Woh, some folks say she's a Cadillac, oh I say she must be a T-Model Ford, . . .

20. Roosevelt Charles, "Hard Time Lovin' Blues," No. 164
21. Otis Webster, "Been out West, Headed East," No. 79
22. Robert Pete Williams, "Rock Well Blues," No. 194
23. Smoky Babe, "Terraplane Blues," No. 152

Oh, she got a shape all right, man, she just don't carry no
heavy load.[24]

Wants you to be my chauffeur, . . .
Yes, I want you to drive me,
I want you to drive me roun' town,
Well, I drive so easy, I can't turn him down.[25]

The respect for an old woman who can still make love is
expressed in automotive terms:

You may be old, ninety-eight years,
You ain't too old to shift them gears.[26]

When the woman he has been sleeping with is in bad shape as
a result of drinking rotgut whiskey, one blues singer remarks:

Oh, yeah, somethin' wrong with my little machine,
Well, my baby sho' got standard carburetor, put in bad
gasolene.[27]

A powerful image of rejection drawn from the automobile is:

I asked for water, she gave me gasolene.[28]

This would be a particularly vivid image for Negroes who have
worked in filling stations or who have tinkered with old cars.
Such a familiarity is illustrated by an incident I shared. In
August, 1961, I was driving through Mississippi with Smoky
Babe when a fuel line in my 1955 De Soto developed a bad
leak. I stayed with the car while Smoky, who has worked as a
grease monkey and mechanic, hitch-hiked to Clarksdale to get a
new line. When he had replaced the line, pumping the gas
pedal failed to draw gas into the carburetor. I was stumped,
but Smoky quickly disconnected one end of the fuel line, sucked
gasolene into his mouth, and spit it into the carburetor. The
motor started right up.

Riding a train is also used as a sexual *double entendre*. Annabelle Haney sings:

He's a railroad man, sho' do love to ride, . . .
If it ain't ridin' that Santa Feel, sho' ain't satisfied. . . .

24. Hogman Maxey, "Drinkin' Blues," No. 6
25. Charles Henderson, "Wants You to Be My Chauffeur," No. 165
26. Otis Webster, "Bottle Up an' Go," No. 31A
27. Smoky Babe, "Somethin' Wrong with My Machine," No. 151
28. Smoky Babe, "Lowdown Woman," text not given

When the train in the station, he sho' do fool aroun', . . .
He got a sweet-lovin' mama, he sho' won't put me down.[29]

Another series of sexual images comes from cooking and baking:

Roll your belly like you roll your dough.[30]

Well, now I can tell by the way she roll her dough,
She can bake them biscuits once mo'.[31]

Roll me, mama, like you roll roll yo' dough,
Oh, I want you to roll me, roll me over slow.[32]

Jelly roll, jelly roll, rollin' in a can,
Lookin' for a woman ain't got no man,

Chorus: Wild about jelly, crazy about sweet jelly roll,
     If you taste good jelly, it satisfy your weary soul. . . .

Ain't been to hell, but I been tol',
Women in hell got sweet jelly roll. . . .

Reason why grandpa like grandma so,
Same sweet jelly she had a hundred years ago.[33]

Jelly roll is a pastry twisted into a roll; there is an implied comparison with the motions of sexual intercourse.

The female sex organs are compared to fruit and the sex act to picking it:

Well, you've got fruits on your tree, mama, an' lemons on
    your shelf,
I know lovin' well, baby, you can't squeeze them by yourself.

Please let me be your lemon squeezer, Lord, until my love
    come down,
Now let me be your lemon squeezer until your love come down.

Lord, I saw the peach orchard, the fig bush too,
Don't nobody gather fruit, baby, only like I do.[34]

Dancing also supplies metaphors for sexual relations:

---

29. Annabelle Haney, "He's a Railroad Man," No. 166
30. Butch Cage and Willie B. Thomas, "Shake 'Em on Down," No. 175A
31. Smoky Baby, "Biscuit Bakin' Woman." No. 155
32. Hogman Maxey, "Rock Me, Mama," No. 154
33. Butch Cage and Willie B. Thomas, "Jelly Roll," No. 153
34. Otis Webster, "Fruits on Your Tree," No. 156

You been slippin' out on me all night, doin' a lowdown
boogie woogie.[35]

In addition to the many images involving a comparison between fornication and driving vehicles, carrying on household
activities, picking fruit, and dancing, there is an abundance of
metaphors and similes built on imaginatively pictured parallels
between the singer's feelings or situation and other familiar
elements of the country Negro's environment, such as the
frustration of the gambler who loses, observation of the sun,
moon, and stars, the isolation of a prisoner, the depressing
surroundings of a homeless wanderer. A favorite metaphor
drawn from gambling is:

Just keep on bettin' an' your dice won't pass,[36]

a colorful way of saying, "Just keep on playing around, just
keep on pursuing other lovers and sooner or later you will
lose out." Celestial bodies appear in the tender line:

She got a light in her mouth, shine like the mornin' star,[37]

and in the contemptuous:

Oh, jet black woman outshine the sun,[38]

which in its context is derogatory; the singer is jeering at her
shiny black skin which glistens despite attempts to tone it down
with lipstick and powder. Because of the usually honorific
connotations of "outshine the sun," here the image takes on
ironic overtones. The setting of the sun and the coming of
darkness lend themselves readily to metaphorical use:

Oh, black night fallin', fallin' roun' me, . . .
Now here I am, tryin' to feel my way along.[39]

Despair is aptly compared to some one groping in the dark
trying to find his way.
   The unhappiness of a prisoner is poignantly evoked in the
lines:

35. Robert Pete Williams, "Goodtime Lonesome Blues," No. 8
36. Smoky Babe and Sally Dotson, "Your Dice Won't Pass," No. 75
37. Otis Webster, "Night Time Is the Right Time," No. 169
38. Butch Cage and Willie B. Thomas, "Shake 'Em on Down," No. 175A
39. Hogman Maxey, "Black Night Fallin'," No. 52

Lord, all late in the evenin',
I hear somebody say, "Where in the world you workin' at?"
"You know, way across over yonder."
"Way across over where?"
"Way on the other island on the other side,
Sounds like I can hear my baby callin' me."[40]

As a prisoner in Angola, the singer is in a sense on an isolated island shut off from the island of the normal world in which his woman is.

The sadness of the lot of the down-and-out wanderer is memorably suggested in:

Tombstone is my pillow, an' the fairground is my bed.[41]

Lord, ever since my mother been dead, . . .
Lord, the rocks been my pillow, Lord the cold groun' been my bed.[42]

The loneliness of the homeless penniless loveless wanderer is also vividly captured in:

When a man all alone, you know just how it feel,
Ain't got nobody to keep him company, make him feel just like a lost bird.[43]

A recurrent and still fresh metaphor expressing the feelings of rolling stones is:

I was sittin' here wonderin' would a matchbox hold my clothes,
I ain't got very many matches, but I got many miles to go.[44]

Like the best folk metaphors, this one uses a familiar everyday object in a startlingly incongruous text. Usually blues singers refer to suitcases and trunks, e.g., "My suitcase is packed and my trunk is already down the line." Thus there is an implied comparison which is strikingly ironic. On the one hand it is startling to think of a matchbox in the same breath with a suitcase, but at the same time the container which will hold

40. Roosevelt Charles, "My Baby Blues," No. 129
41. Robert Pete Williams, "Thousand Miles from Nowhere," No. 12B
42. Leon Strickland, "Ordinary Blues" (I), No. 59
43. Robert Pete Williams, "Lonesome Blues," No. 180
44. Robert Pete Williams, "Highway Blues," No. 72

almost nothing is not too small for the man who has no possessions.

In making use of such clever, richly evocative figures of speech, blues singers rely heavily on conventions of rhetorical structure. In both talking blues and blues which are more rigid in structure most lines are made up of two sections of approximately equal duration with a caesura (a pause) in between, more or less in the middle. Often there is a striking contrast between the first half of a line and the second half, and/ or between the opening line of a verse and the last line. The result of these elements in combination is a quotable verse, complete in itself, often aphoristic, rhythmically appealing as the words trip easily off the tongue and readily remembered— roughly analogous to the heroic couplet of the eighteenth century, if we disregard the repetition of a line in the blues.

> True wit is nature to advantage dressed,
> What oft was thought, but ne'er so well expressed.

The final line completes the thought initiated by the first, in a way which is clever, witty, dramatic, or strikingly imaginative. Since such a verse or line is a satisfying unit in itself, a singer who is making up a song as he goes along by free association can fit into the mood of what he is saying a stock aphoristic or clever verse which deals with the situation on his mind, lines like:

> When you see me comin', baby, raise yo' window high, . . .
> When you see me leavin', hang yo' head an' cry.[45]

Comin' contrasts with *leavin'*, *raise yo' window high* has meanings on several different levels; since he enters by the window, the man is a secret lover. It also is an active image for welcome though ironically different from flinging a door open in welcome. Finally, it has sexual overtones; the window through which the male enters is a vagina symbol. All the connotations which go with *raise yo' window high* are contrasted with *hang yo' head an' cry.*

---

45. Charles Henderson, "She Was a Woman Didn't Mean No One Man No Good," No. 188

Hey, when you see me comin', put yo' black dress on, . . .
I swear the graveyard gonna be yo' restin' place, an' hell
    gonna be yo' home.[46]

Here the arrival of the lover is ironically different from what it
is in the previous example. The woman has been unfaithful to
him, rather than to her regular lover. The only contrast is an
implied ironic one between dread, fear, and gloom at the approach of the lover and the joy which a woman should feel at his
arrival. Fundamentally the verse is composed in terms of
balance; the idea in the first line, get dressed for mourning
and death, parallels the ideas in the final line, *graveyard* is
balanced by *restin' place, hell* by *home;* rhetorically, the effect
is movement toward a climax, a progression in importance
from adopting a garb suitable for death, to resting in the graveyard, to suffering for all eternity.

Death is presented with similar grimness in the lines:

Tombstone landin', baby, an' ole dry bone, . . .
They are before me, when I am dead an' gone.[47]

The graveyard is presented in highly specific and forbidding
terms, *tombstone landin'* and *ole dry bone,* which are the ob-
jective correlative of the abstract *dead an' gone.* In this instance,
the usual order of an abstract statement followed by a concrete
image is reversed. The effect is less exciting.

In another blues the singer (addressing his woman, who is
dying of T.B.) presents a horrifying scene:

Graveyard ain't nothin', Lord, but great lonesome place, . . .
You can lay flat on your back, little woman, and let the sun
    shine in yo' face.[48]

Nothin' is balanced with *great lonesome place;* the first line,
which is relatively abstract, is balanced with a concrete picture
in the second, and the second line is balanced within itself.
The last line begins with a phrase which has pleasurable connotations—"lay flat on your back" suggests either rest or love-
making, but the end of the line twists the meaning ironically
toward a dreary painful isolation in which her only companion
is the South's hellishly hot sun.

---

46. Charles Henderson, "61 Highway," No. 102
47. Smoky Babe and Sally Dotson, "Dell on the Mountain," No. 56
48. Guitar Welch, "T. B. Blues," No. 49

Robert Pete Williams moans in his most moving song:

> Yes, I'm goin' down slow, somethin' wrong with me,
> I've got to make a change while that I'm young,
> If I don't I won't never get old.[49]

The vagueness of the first line is appropriate since the ailment is not any particular physical disease but is the psychological and emotional effect of hopelessness and despair in prison. Making a change and being young are contrasted with not doing so and not growing old. The effect is aphoristic and witty.

A clever verse dealing with love for another man's wife runs:

> Lord, I love you, baby, but I'm scared to call your name,
> Lord, you're a married woman, I love you just the same.[50]

The first half of each line is contrasted with the second. In the proper order of climax, the stronger idea comes at the end.

Equally clever and tightly constructed is another verse dealing with infidelity:

> Woman rocks the cradle, I declare she rules the home, . . .
> But a man rockin' other men's babies, an' the fool think he
> rockin' his own.[51]

Woman's position is presented in the first line, man's contrasting one in the second. She is strong and sinful, he is weak and gullible. The final statement, *the fool think he rockin' his own,* is rhetorically powerful.

Since the proper order of climax is movement upward in the scale of importance or dramatic impact, the following achieves a comic effect through the use of anti-climax:

> Now I have pawned my shoe', I even down an' pawned the
> suit off my back,
> I woulda pawn my sock', but they got holes in 'em.[52]

In poetic terms the lines are stronger, more stirring to the imagination because they occur in a context in which the humor is tinged with sadness; since the singer is a compulsive gambler, the lines take on ironic overtones.

---

49. Robert Pete Williams, "Prisoner's Talking Blues," No. 2
50. Hogman Maxey, "Fiddle Blues," No. 183
51. Herman E. Johnson, "Crawlin' Baby Blues," No. 174
52. Roosevelt Charles, "Georgia Skin," No. 74

An example of wit is:

> I ain't gonna tell you what the Dago tol' the Jew, . . .
> Don' like me, baby, be sure don't like you.[53]

The impact stems largely from the clever construction of the stanza, as does much of the effect in the following:

> It was a great long engine, an' a little small engineer,
> It took my woman away along, an' it left me standin' here.
> But if I just had listened unto my second min',
> I don't believe I'd been here, wringin' my hands an' cryin'.[54]

These lines are full of balanced contrasts, the *great long engine* and the *little small engineer*, the woman who leaves her lover and the lover who is left behind, his first impulse to love and trust her and his second, probably not to have anything to do with her.

The same singer speaks of the coldness of his woman in a homely but memorable image drawn from farming:

> But there is no mo' potatoes, you see the frost have killed
>   the vine,
> An' the blues ain't nothin' but a good gal on your min'.[55]

Among the poor, potatoes are one of the foods which are the staff of life. The two portions of the first line balance well, and the metaphor appropriately and poetically suggests that her coldness has killed what he needs for sustenance. In epigrammatic fashion the final line sums up his situation and amplifies the meaning of the first line.

In describing his alcoholic woman, Otis Webster sings:

> She come in drunk, talkin' all out her head, . . .
> Reach for the foot, miss the whole durn bed. . . .
>
> Well, she still drinkin' Manny, an' she wants more,
> Reach for the knob, miss the whole durn door.[56]

In these verses there is not only an internal balance within lines, but also the two stanzas have a parallel structure. The

53. Charles Henderson, "Rock Island Blues," No. 96
54. Herman E. Johnson, "C. C. Rider," No. 198D
55. Herman E. Johnson, "C. C. Rider," No. 198D
56. Otis Webster, "She Drunk," No. 41

effect is to emphasize in vivid and precise, easy to visualize terms, the clumsy actions of a drunken woman.

Another drunken woman is made memorable in these arresting lines:

> Heyah, heyah comes that woman, oh Lord, she's so bad drunk
>   again,
> Lord, her pocket full o' money, an' her belly full o' gin.[57]

The second line strikingly expands and makes specific the implications of the first. The combination of both a full pocket and a full belly raises the nasty suspicion of prostitution, a thought which is cleverly suggested rather than crudely stated.

The wanderlust finds eloquent expression in:

> One day I was walkin' out on the career,
> Lookin' at the birds, how they were treadin' the mighty air,
> I looked at automobile', how they was runnin' the track,
> It looked sweet to me, decide' I better run the highway.[58]

Coming from a talking blues, these lines are more conversational in their flow than most verses in blues of more classical structure, but there are caesuras in three of the lines, and *how they treadin' the mighty air* and *how they was runnin' the track* are completely parallel, but at the same time there is the contrast between the sky and the earth. *Treadin'* is used in a metaphorically fresh way since it suggests a solid purposeful movement in contrast to the soaring and swooping movement usually associated with birds on the wing.

Another striking statement of the urge to hit the road is:

> When the moon jumps on the mountain, Lord, I'm gonna be
>   on my way,
> I'm gonna be on this ole highway until ole dollar a day.[59]

Although both lines are complex sentences (that is have an independent and a dependent clause), the order is reversed in the final line, contrary to the impulse toward parallelism, but whoever coined this verse in this form originally had a keen instinct for poetic effect. (Although it is possible that the form resulted from a desire to find a rhyme for *way*, the lines are so

57. Leon Strickland, "How Long Blues," No. 132
58. Roosevelt Charles, "Trouble Followin' Me," No. 3
59. Leon Strickland, "Key to the Highway," No. 104

clever, I doubt this was the reason.) *When the moon jumps on the mountain* like *birds treadin' the mighty air* in the previous example uses a verb which is startlingly in contrast to those generally associated with the moon. The moon would more typically *come, glide,* or *rise,* all smooth and unstartling movements; *jump* fits the mood of the singer, his yearning for quick motion, for getting rolling right away. *I'm gonna be on my way* and *I'm gonna be on this* highway deal with movement, though not notably, and then, in contrast to the three previous clauses until *ole dollar a day,* an elliptical, compressed and colorful way of suggesting that sooner or later the wanderer is going to have to stop somewhere and plod through a dull job.

In most blues it is customary though not invariable for the opening line of a stanza to rhyme with the final line. The tendency in Negro folk speech for all the vowels to be close to each other in sound and the practice of dropping consonants not only at the ends of words but also in the middle of them make it easy for a singer to create rhymes even in the course of original improvisation. Sometimes too there is rhyme by assonance, that is the singer uses near rhymes, e.g.: time . . . min (d), joint . . . pint, say . . . here (heyah) , gol (d) . . . boa (r)d, tone . . . gone, bone . . . gone, sign . . . town, frien (d) . . . man, train . . . name, gone . . . town, and min' . . . cryin'.

In the more archaic blues, especially those by Robert Pete Williams, and in talking blues, rhyme occurs only occasionally, in the latter most often when the singer slips from speech into song. In Smoky Babe's "Car Trouble Blues," for example, when he is carrying on the spoken part, he uses no rhymes, but when he begins to sing, he makes the lines rhyme, not difficult for an *ay* sound even during improvising:

I was glad I was with him, trouble we had on the way,
Well, his automobile got broke, we had to find some place
   to stay.

When he starts to sing about the cities for which the road is *bound,* predictably the rhyme which pops into his head is *town:*

Then we started travellin Highway 82, we was Chicago boun',
Well, a good thing about it, we was in this ole Mississippi
   town.[60]

60. Smoky Babe, "Car Trouble Blues," No. 99

In essence the blues form makes use of many of the same devices as art poetry. Abstract states of mind like a sad mood are presented through concrete images; inanimate objects and non-human creatures following blind instincts are given personalities and values so that man can literally communicate (usually futilely) with the forces which dominate his life. The images are drawn from the environment of the singer, *the farm:* mules, boll weevils, dogs, horses, hogs, birds, bees, snakes, fish, crops, rivers and ponds; *domestic life:* cooking, baking; *travel:* trains, automobiles, highways, boats, rivers; *recreation:* sex, drinking, dancing, and gambling; the *heavenly bodies:* sun, moon, and stars.

The blues verses which enter folk tradition and are widely used have characteristics much like the heroic couplet and the epigram of more sophisticated literature; they make use of carefully balanced phrases and ideas or balanced contrasts; the words are combined in such a way that they have rhetorical impact and are rhythmically appealing; the idea in a verse is usually one oft thought "but ne'er so well expressed."

Since the basic elements of most blues, verses like those discussed above, are standardized bricks which can be used to construct a wide variety of buildings, it is revealing to discuss the creative process at work and to describe the circumstances in which songs were composed and sung, and to examine how individual performers of varying creative abilities handle their raw materials.

The first song Hogman (Matthew) Maxey (a blues singer I recorded extensively at Angola) sang for me was "Drinkin' Blues."

 6. *Drinkin' Blues*

1. Lord, I got a woman, oh Lord, she lives down 'cross the way,
Mm, I got a woman, woh Lord, she lives out 'cross the way,
Woh Lord, she just well a-quit me, woh Lord, I know she
  ain't gonna stay.

2. Lord, I come in last night, Lord, I found my baby gone,
Woh Lord, come in last night, woh Lord, I found my baby gone,
Woh Lord, I begin to wonder, wonder what's been goin' on
  wrong.

Spoken: Now play that for me.

3. *Sung:* You ever had the blues, Lord, you know just how I feel,

Mm, mm, mm, you ever had the blues, you know just how I feel,

Boys, you had a good little car, too many drivers at your wheel.

4. You ever love me, baby, why don't you tell me so?

You ever love me, baby, why don't you tell me so?

Lord, if you don't love me, baby, you just as well to let me go.

5. Mm, been drinkin' so long, now stay drunk night an' day,

Mm, been drinkin', stay drunk night an' day,

Woh, I got to stop my drinkin', Lord, I'm gonna drive my baby away.

6. Too many women, oh Lord, is on my min',

Mm, too many women, oh Lordy, is on my min',

Oh Lord, I got to stop my drinkin', Lord, I got to blow this town.

7. Woh, some folks say she's a Cadillac, oh, I say she must be a T-Model Ford,

Mm, some say she's a Cadillac, oh Lord, I say she's a T-Model Ford,

Oh, she got a shape all right, man, she just don't carry no heavy load.

8. Standin' on the corner, look two blocks an' a half, (2)

Woh Lord, I didn't see my baby, Lord, I sure heard her laugh.

9. Operator, operator, what time your next train leave goin' east? (2)

Woh Lord, I gotta leave this town, Lord, I never see no peace.

10. Woh Lord, I woke up this mornin', woh, my min' out in the West,

Woh, woke up this mornin', woh, my min' out in the West,

Woh, I had to leave this town, baby, women won't let bad Maxie rest.

11. Woh, fell down on my knee, woh Lord, I begin to pray, (2)

Woh Lord, I want You to help us, baby, oh Lord, in our wicked way.

12. Woh Lord, the sun shinin', an' a dark cloud risin' in the east,

Mm, sun is shinin', an' a dark cloud risin' in the east,

Woh, there ain't no use o' you gettin' scared, baby, woh, that's the chariot after me.

13. Standin' on the corner, woh Lord, I heard my bulldog bark,
Standin' on the corner, baby, woh, I heard my bulldog bark,
Woh Lord, it was barkin' at my baby, barkin at my sweetheart
in the dark.

14. Babe, don't ever quit me, darlin', oh Lord, I don't care
what I do,
Oh, don't, don't ever quit me, baby, woh Lord, I don't care
what I do,
Woh Lord, if that's the way I been follerin', you maybe do
the same ole thing too.

15. Woh, I told you, baby, Lord, I ain't gone tell you no mo',
Mm, told you, baby, an' I ain't gone tell you no mo',
Woh, before I be worried with you, baby, woh Lord, I'm
gonna let you go.

16. Woh, don't worry, baby, oh, this is my last go roun',
Mm, don't worry, woh baby, this is my last go roun',
Woh, if you don't treat me no better, woh Lord, I got to
put you down.

17. Woh, been, been drinkin' all night long,
Mm, been drinkin', baby, been drinkin' all night long,
Woh, I gonna just keep on drinkin' till my baby come back
home.

Vocal and guitar, Angola, Feb. 2, 1959.

When Maxey sang "Drinkin' Blues" for me, he was apparently excited about having a good guitar to play (mine), and stimulated by the fact that it was a 12-stringer, a type he started to play in 1936. In the grocery shop in Camp H where I set up my equipment he started to sing and was enjoying himself so much that at the end of fifteen minutes when some customers started to come in during their break for lunch he was still singing away at the same song. Since this blues is improvised and is much longer than most blues available for study, an analysis of its structure discloses significant facts as to how blues are composed in the natural folk process within the framework of traditional form and content.

Maxey is a singer who is thoroughly steeped in blues tradition, but he is not notably creative or imaginative; he is a synthesizer rather than an innovator. Consequently, in singing blues, even though he improvises freely, he is essentially stringing together standard verses from folk tradition and from records he has heard, most of them a long time ago. It is revealing to summarize the stanzas.

1. My woman might as well leave now because she certainly will before long.
2. I come home and find my woman gone.
3. She was a good woman to have, but she had too many lovers (expressed in terms of a car with too many drivers).
4. If the fourth stanza makes sense in this sequence, we must assume that his woman returned. He complains, "If you don't love me, why don't you let me go?"
5. I've been drinking constantly (the link is perhaps that trouble with his woman makes him seek solace or escape in drink); if I don't stop this drinking my drunken excesses will drive her away. (This latter part is not consistent with what went before.)
6. I have too many women on my mind (not consistent with the worrying about one woman in earlier verses); I had better leave town. (One suspects the influence of wish-fulfillment thinking; he would like to be troubled by having too many women, instead of as at present none at all; he would love to have the chance to head elsewhere.)
7. My woman (the sort of woman he had in the past) is not a slick, expensive, reliable vehicle, but a cheap, ordinary model, shapely but unreliable. There is also the suggestion that she is not sexy enough, not responsive enough to intense passion. (The thought of movement in the previous verse perhaps leads by association to the thought of a car, which in turn leads to a metaphor in which his woman is compared to a car.)
8. I heard her laughing loudly several blocks away. (The implication is that he thinks she is having a good time with someone else.)
9. I must find out when the next train is due to leave for the east because I will never find peace until I go away from this town.
10. I woke up thinking about heading for the west; women won't let bad Maxey rest. (The implication is that he plays around himself and mistreats women.) The shift from east to west would be natural for someone whose impulses fluctuate; also, an affection for juxtaposing contrasting elements or ideas is, as we have noted, a traditional device of expression.

11. I began to pray; please help my baby and me to abandon our wicked ways. (The guilt consciousness in the previous stanza leads to thoughts of turning to God for His help.)

12. Although the sun is shining, there is a dark cloud rising in the east, but don't get alarmed, baby, it's only the chariot coming after me. (Presumably it is a vehicle sent by God to take him to Hell. The image of the chariot and part of one line were suggested by a spiritual like "Swing Low Sweet Chariot.")

13. Standing on the corner, I heard my bulldog barking at my sweetheart in the dark. (In many blues the male sets a bulldog on guard to scare away rival lovers, as for example in Blind Boy Fuller's "Bulldog Blues." The implication is that his woman is being unfaithful.)

14. Please don't leave me; I will do anything to keep you. (He is expressing the point of view of the abject lover so common in blues.) You have been engaging in the same sort of bad actions I have.

15. For the last time I am warning you to behave, or I will leave you.

16. This is your last chance; if you don't treat me any better, I will drop you.

17. I've been drinking all night, and I'm going to keep on drinking until my woman returns.

In spinning out these verses Maxey was expressing his underlying preoccupations, yearning for a woman, a desire for freedom, occasional guilt feelings, hope for help and fear of punishment from God, a thirstiness for liquor mixed with a feeling that drinking tended to get him into trouble. These ideas he has embodied in what are mostly blues clichés, as for example "too many drivers at your wheel," which appears in Smokey Hogg's "To (o) Many Drivers" (Mod 2532); the second car comparison, which appears in Lightnin' Hopkins "Ida May" (Score SLP 4022), the barking bulldog, which appears in Blind Boy Fuller's "Bulldog Blues" (De 7878). Maxey may have picked up these images from these records, from numerous other records which have used the same images, from other folk performers who learned them from records, or from a tradition older than the recordings common both to Maxey and to professional performers who drew on and expressed their own folk environments. Although there is a discernible thread of association linking the ideas, internally there are often logical inconsistencies. However, when one is listening to the blues, one feels the key ideas without being aware of the departures from precise organization.

 7. *Brownskin Woman*

1. Got a mind to ramble, got a mind to settle down, (2)
Gonna leave this town, I'm gonna be Alabama boun'.

2. My mama told me, papa told me too, (2)
Brownskin woman gonna be the death of you.

3. I can't count the time' I stole away and cry, (2)
My baby she don't love me, and I can't see why.

4. She's long and tall, she's six feet from the groun',
Oh, baby, she's long and tall, she's six feet from the groun',
She's strictly tailor-made, and she ain't no hand me down.

5. She got eyes like diamonds, teeth shine just the same, (2)
She got sweet ruby lips, she got hair like a horse's mane.

6. Well, I asked the ticket agent how long the train had gone,
Well, the same old train, my baby left me alone.

7. I didn't have no money, I walked back through the door, (2)
Say my baby is gone, she won't come home (no more).

8. If I had wings like a jaybird in the air, (2)
I would find my woman if she's in this world somewhere.

Willie B. Thomas, vocal and guitar, Scotlandville, Oct. 5, 1960. (For a recording of this performance, see *Country Negro Jam Sessions,* FL 111, 1960.)

"Brownskin Woman" was recorded in a jam session at the house of Butch Cage. In terms of the social context of the performance, the musicians were affirming their identity with the group, enjoying the interaction between themselves and their friends, who laughed, shouted encouragement, clapped their hands, and sometimes danced. The music essentially expressed a feeling that they were glad to be alive. In this song, Willie B. Thomas, like Maxey, is essentially a synthesizer although in his speech he shows impressive fluency and color. With the single exception of the last part of the opening line, which would typically be "got a mind not to settle down," all the stanzas are standard in Negro tradition; this particular combination, however, is Willie's for it took shape spontaneously as he was singing. Later, although he was aware that he had produced an excellent song, he could not repeat it but had to listen to the tape recording to find out just what he had sung. Frequently I have found that blues singers have only a rough idea of what they have just sung, and when I ask them what they would like to call the song, they wrinkle their brows in perplexity, and on occasion give any name that happens to occur to them.

Like most blues, "Brownskin Woman" is not a directly personal statement though the themes of conflict between an impulse to wander and a duty to maintain a home, adulation of a tall woman and fear of losing her are reflections of Willie's impulses and problems. Although he loves his wife Martha and their seven children (three by his current marriage, four by her previous one), the burden of supporting this large family, making the monthly payments on the shack and the car, and the violent but suppressed resentment he feels toward his boss in the engineering firm where he works as a janitor, lead to his fantasizing about rambling freely from town to town.

Although he and Martha get along fairly amicably during the week, Willie generally gets howling drunk on weekends; when he is sober, Willie is most engaging and likable, but when he has had too much to drink, his frustrations and hostilities express themselves in violence—fights in bars, even attempts to stab his wife. Since she is often on the brink of leaving him, his fear of losing Martha is intense. This insecurity is compounded by the fact that she is twenty years younger than he is (he was born in 1912), still a buxomly attractive woman, tall and shapely, whereas he is plain (he describes himself as "ugly"), undersized (4'10" in height compared to her 5'7"), and as a result of a childhood accident, slightly hunchbacked. The stanzas which rose to his tongue in the course of improvisation express his underlying feelings in blues clichés rather than in his own words.

Although the verses are blues standards, there is a clear and consistent logic in their sequence, unlike Maxey's "Drinking Blues." "Brownskin Woman" includes the impulse to ramble, the reason—trouble, as his parents had predicted, with a brownskin woman, his grief in the past over her failure to love him, a description of her beauty, his trying to follow her when she had taken the train out of town, but giving up because he has no money for a ticket, and finally a wish to have wings like a jaybird so he can find her.

Similar principles of organization are apparent, among others, in Robert Pete Williams' "Goodtime Lonesome Blues" and "Bulldog Blues," Otis Webster's "You Oughta Heard My Grandma," and Guitar Welch's "Don't the Moon Look Pretty."

 8. *Goodtime Lonesome Blues*

1. Now looka here, baby, tell me what you tryin' to do,
Oh, looka here, baby, what in the world is you tryin' to do
to pore black – – – –.

2. You been slippin' out on me all night,
Doin' a lowdown boogie woogie.
Oh, baby, you got some lowdown dirty way'.

3. I'm gonna tell you what I'm gonna do, baby,
I'm gonna get out an' start goin' the same way,
That's just what I'm gonna do.

4. Oh, looka here, woman, I ain't gonna let you get nothin'
on me,
Oo, weeh, I know (what) she's up (to) today,
I'm gonna ball all night long, me an' that ole gal o' mine,
Oh, baby, behin' your back.

5. Mm, tell me, blues, what in the world are you tryin' to do?
Oh, looka here, blues, what in the world are you tryin' to do
to me?
Tell me, blues, what you doin' here so soon,
I say, tell me, blues, what in the world you doin' here so soon?

6. I'm goin' away to leave you, darlin',
I want you to take care o' yourself,
I'm goin' away to leave, darlin',
I want you to take care o' yourself.

7. Good mornin', baby, how you feel today?
Good mornin', baby, baby, how in the world you feelin'?

Robert Pete Williams, vocal and guitar, Baton Rouge, July 30, 1961.

In "Goodtime Lonesome Blues" the singer begins by condemning his woman for slipping out and sleeping with another man ("Doin' a lowdown boogie woogie"). This leads to his insisting that he will get even with her by playing the same game. He is, however, too attached to his unfaithful woman to escape his depression through such a course. The blues overwhelm him. He thinks of resolving his conflict by leaving her, but at the same time has concern for her well-being. This unselfish impulse (or one might say the attitude of the abject lover) carries over into the last verse, in which he accepts her back on the following morning with an expression of concern for her welfare.

 9. *Bulldog Blues*

1. You know I'm gonna buy me a bulldog, I want to watch you whiles I'm gone,
I'm gonna buy me a bulldog, darlin', I want to watch you whiles I'm gone,
I'm gonna tie him in my front yard so he won't let nobody in.

2. Well, I want you to tell me, baby, is you got in your mind to treat me right?
I want you to tell me, darlin', is you got in your mind to treat me right?
Well, (if) you ain't, baby, we just want to part right now.

3. If I could holler just like a mountain jack, (2)
I'd get up on the mountain, God knows I'd call my baby ———.

4. I go up on the mountain so high, I seen grass growin' on a dollar bill,
I been on the mountain so high, I seen grass growin' on a dollar bill,
I wanta tell you, woman, you know I was dead on your trail.

Robert Pete Williams, vocal and guitar, Angola, Feb. 10, 1959.

In "Bulldog Blues" the singer's first thought is to try to keep his woman faithful by stationing a bulldog in the yard to frighten lovers away. Then he threatens to leave her if she won't be true, but with a twist of thought characteristic of the blues, he wants her back again. The image he uses is powerful;

if he had the wild scream of a mountain jackass to express his anguish, he would climb high above the world and summon her. The reference to a mountain leads to another image which includes a mountain, this time embodying a shift from abject despair to vindictive pursuit. Instead of being a mournful wailing animal, he is a beast of prey with superhuman keenness of vision. Thus he has cleverly extended his metaphor. The rhetorical exaggeration of "on the mountain so high I seen grass growin' on a dollar bill" is freshly imaginative. This fanciful image may well be an inspired reworking of the relatively commonplace lines in one of Leroy Carr's later versions of "How Long, How Long" (Vo c. 1934):

I can look and see the green grass growin' up on the hill,
But I haven't seen the green back of a dollar bill,
For so long, so long, baby, so long.

 10. *You Oughta Heard My Grandma*

1. You oughta heard my grandma when she got my grandfather tol', (20)
She say, "Give it away, ole man, 'cause you know you done got too ole."

2. When my baby left the station, she left me a mule to ride, (2)
When the train pull off, my mule lie down an' died.

3. Well-a flat on his back an' a ear gone in my pocket, (2)
Well, he raised his head, you oughta see that saddle joggin'.

4. Well, in 1929, my baby come inside, (2)
She say, "Now wake up, daddy, my baby is almost died."

5. Now, do you wanta tell me, baby, (3)
I don't care, don't care, I don't care what you do.

6. Sometime', baby, I get up slap my han',
I know my baby got another man,
She walk up an' hug me tight,
Says, "Daddy, I want you to treat me right."

7. Now my baby got somethin' I can't tell,
One time walkin', an' I can yell,
Now, baby, don't you wanna go, (3)
I don't wanna tell you no mo'.

8. Jumped up, tell me two by four,
Well, she cryin', "Daddy, I can't go no mo',"
She cryin' out, tell me, "Darlin', one by two,
Look, daddy, wanta begin like you."

9. Now my baby, my baby, tell me,
I'm gonna tell my baby, she got a mule to ride.
Well, I cross in the saddle, the mule begin to jump,
He looked at me an' he bit his bottom lip,
He looked up then an' he had no corn,
He saya you can't ride me, 'cause we can't get along.

10. She left a mule to ride, yeah she left me a mule to ride,
When the train pull' off, my mule lay down an' died.

Otis Webster, vocal and guitar, Angola, Nov. 19, 1960.

Otis Webster's "You Oughta Heard My Grandma" consists mostly of images of rejection, loosely connected by association, though some stanzas are confused and do not appear to make sense in the context, a result of improvisation. The grandmother jeers at her husband because of his loss of potency. The singer's girl leaves him, and ironically, the mule she gives him is short-lived like her love; it collapses under him. His girl hugs him, and her saying that she wants him to treat her right is ironic since he knows she has another man. The exuberant next two verses probably have some association with the exciting and satisfying passion they once shared. The mule comes up again as a symbol. Like the girl, he refuses to be ridden, symbolic of the girl's rejection of the singer's passion. The mule's complaining that he doesn't have corn implies that the singer can't hold onto the woman because he doesn't have enough money.

 11. *Don't the Moon Look Pretty*

1. Don't the moon look pretty, shinin' down through the tree, (2)
Lord, I can see my little woman, but I swear she can't see me.

2. Me an' my baby, goin' walkin' down that highway side by side,
Lord, if the boat don't bring me my companion, it's gonna jump overboard an' drown.

3. I guess I'll have to try the woods a while,
Yes, I guess I'll have to try the woods a while,
'Cause the girl I been lovin', Lord, caught that southboun' train.

Spoken: Play it now, man.

4. *Sung:* Lord, goodby, little girl, you know it's time to go,
Goodby, little girl, you know it's time to go,
You know if my min' don't change, little woman, I'll never
come there no mo'.

Guitar (Robert) Welch, vocal and guitar, Angola, March 21, 1959.

Guitar Welch's "Don't the Moon Look Pretty" begins with a
tender thought—a memory of a sweet moment when he watched
his woman unobserved under the light of the moon. The second
stanza contains two thoughts—the recollection of the pleasure
of walking with his girl, then a suicidal impulse if he can't
see her soon—particularly poignant in the context of the
singer's position as prisoner at Angola. His frustration leads
to the thought of trying to escape, and then the song ends
ironically. Although he doesn't have freedom of action and
she has probably found herself another lover, he speaks as
though he has the liberty to abandon her, and, if he has the
whim, to accept her again—wish fulfillment expressed in
bravado.

One of the most haunting country blues is "One Room
Country Shack," recorded by Texas singer, Mercy Dee (Mercy
D. Walton), Sp 458, c. 1953. Several of the performers I have
recorded follow the original closely, Snooks Eaglin, Hillary
Blunt, Clarence Edwards, and Andy Mosely. Except for
Hillary Blunt, who is about fifty, all of these are under thirty.
Such imitation is common among younger blues singers, oc-
casional among older ones who inherit a tradition of improvi-
sation. A typical text is Hillary Blunt's:

 12A. *A Thousand Miles from Nowhere*

1. I'm sittin' here a thousand miles from nowhere, in a little
ole one room little country shack,
Yes, I'm sittin' here a thousand miles from nowhere, in a
little ole one room little country shack,
Whiles all in my worldly possession is a ragged eleven foot
cotton sack.

2. I wake up every night aroun' midnight, people, I just can't sleep no mo', (2)
I just have the crickets an' the frogs to keep me company, an' the wind howlin' roun' my do'.

3. I'm leavin' soon in the mornin', baby, 'fore I go outa my min', (2)
I'm gotta fin' me some kind o' companion, even if she deaf, dumb, crippled an' blin'.

Hillary Blunt, vocal and guitar, Scotlandville, Feb. 21, 1960.

 12B. *Thousand Miles from Nowhere*

1. Thousand miles, thousand miles, thousand miles from nowhere, (2)
Say, runnin' roun' here, darlin', in a little ole one horse town.

2. Well, I'm all out an' down, runnin' roun' here from do' to do', (2)
Well, I'm a thousand miles from nowhere, darlin', runnin' aroun' in this little ole one horse town.

3. Well, I've got no place to go, woman, I got nowhere to lay my worried head tonight,
Well, I took a stroll away from home, an' my mother lay down an' died.

4. Tombstone is my pillow, an' the fairgroun' is my bed,
Tombstone is my pillow, fairgroun' is my bed,
Lord, since my mother lay down an' died, Lord, look what a shape I'm in.

5. Lord, looka here, darlin', where the sun has gone, Lord, look what a shape it catchin' me in,
Look where the sun gone, baby, look what a shape it catchin' me in,
Lord, I'm gonna lay right here, use this tombstone for my pillow, an' this fairgroun' for my bed.

Robert Pete Williams, vocal and guitar; Denham Springs, Sept. 25, 1960. (The recording may be heard on *Free Again,* PrB 1026, 1960.)

When I asked Robert Pete Williams if he knew the song beginning "Sittin' a thousand miles from nowhere in a little country shack," he replied that he did not, but he immediately

began to sing a blues improvised around the ideas in the line
I had quoted. The text is not so polished and symmetrical as
Mercy Dee's, but it has a raw power of its own. The only
ideas Robert Pete has used are being "a thousand miles from
nowhere" and a general sense of isolation, not the isolation of
the sharecropper, but the isolation of a rolling stone whose
last reliable refuge disappeared when his mother had died
during one of his absences, a theme which occurs in several of
his blues. He draws on a standard blues line in "Tombstone
is my pillow, fairgroun' is my bed," a brilliant image for the
dreary position of the homeless drifter. *Tombstone*, hard, cold,
symbolic of the unbroken sleep of death, is in ironic contrast
to *pillow*, with its soft, comfortable connotations; *fairgroun'*
is desolate and bleak in contrast to the cozy bed of someone who
has a home. The last stanza presents his sense of desperation as
the sun sets, leaving him in darkness with only the tombstone
pillow and the ground bed.

Although Robert Pete approximates the form of the classical
blues, his treatment of it is fluid and unrigid.

In Otis Webster's "I Know How to Do Time" the unifying
theme is an extended ironic comparison between two types of
country Negroes, an ironic interplay between two frames of
reference—one of an Uncle Tom type, a childlike old-fashioned
plantation Negro who has faith in the paternalistic benevolence
of his boss, the other of a worker who thinks for himself, whose
fault is that "he just don't know how to do time," that is he
refuses to accept a way of life which is like being in prison.

 13. *I Know How to Do Time*

1. *Spoken:* Yes, you know, boy, I'm a raggety,
I ain't never had no good clothes,
The man I used to work for, you know,
He used to give me my room an' boa'd.
You know I thought that was a good man to work for me;
He asked (me) to go out, find another boy like me.

2. The first thing he holler, "What that man pay?"
"Oh, partner, don't worry 'bout the pay,
I guarantee you be satisfied."
"I don't know whether I be satisfied or not,
'Lessn (unless) I know what I'm gettin'."
"Oh, you silly, son, you don't know like I do;

I didn't know what I was gonna get either
Till I went there. I tell you,
Give him a day an' a half, two days,
See how you like it."
"Well, I believe I'll go down there an' try him one time."

3. *Sung:* My mule won't pull my plow, oh Lord, he's reined up
   too tight,
Say, my mule won't pull my plow, oh, the captain say he reined
   up too tight,
Lord, I begin to look at my next partner over there, he seem
   to be doin' all right.

4. *Spoken:* You know last night me an' that new boy went out
   to have some honeymoon,
He didn't know what drinkin' was.
I says, "Son, now get yourself a half pint o' wine now."
"They don't sell no half pints o' wine."
"Oh, you don't know what you talkin' about, you green!"
"Yeah, you be green 'fore you do this time."
"Yeah, that's all right, don't worry about my time, do yours."
"That's a fine way to be!"

5. Our boss told him, "Gonna give you about two and a half
   a day,
You reckon you worth that an' boa'd?"
"I don't know about that boa'd proposition. What you got to
   eat?"
"Oh, we have a few rice, beans, 'taters, cucumbers, onions—"
"What you mean name all that kind o' stuff?
Tell me what you got to eat."
"If you don't want that, you know what you can do."

6. *Sung:* Oh, bossman, I believe I got you another man
   again, (2)
Ain't but one thing I found wrong with him, he just don't
   know how to do time.

7. *Spoken:* Yes, I went to my bossman, just for a pair o' blue
   jean',
He looked at me, says, "Son, what do you do with all your
   money?"
I say, "Boss, I blow that stuff in."
"Why don't you do like that boy over there?
He got good clothes."
"Ain't been on long, long as I is."

"Yeah, but you better count that money,
Gonna be in debt, can't get out."
"Well, if I can't get out, I'll always have a good job,
'Cause you won't run me off, I know."

8. *Sung:* Sometime' I wakes up in the mornin', baby, I just
   can't eat for cryin',
Well, I wakes up so early in the mornin', baby, little woman, I
   just can't eat for cryin';
Well, you talk about a wise man know, I declare I know how to
   do time.

Otis Webster, vocal and guitar; Angola, Nov. 21, 1960.

The singer presents himself as a naive farm worker; though
ragged and impoverished, he is unaware that he is being
victimized; in fact, he thinks he has an excellent job. The
potential new worker is skeptical; he insists, unlike the singer,
on knowing what his wages will be, and what the board will
consist of. He is scornful of the board when he learns the fare
is merely cheap fruit and vegetables. In plowing the singer
has trouble getting his mule to pull his plow; the mule, like
the singer himself, is reined too tight, too rigidly imprisoned.
The other farmhand, who thinks for himself, is more successful
in plowing. When the two of them go out drinking together,
the singer, accustomed to trying to enjoy himself on little or no
money, suggests his companion order half a pint of wine. The
latter is dubious; he doubts that wine is sold in so small a
quantity. The implication is that he is not accustomed to the
kind of constant pennypinching the singer is.

When the old hand goes to the boss for some money to
buy blue jeans, the boss points out that the new boy has good
clothes. The reason, says the singer, is that he is new on the
job. When the boss counsels his faithful retainer to avoid
squandering his money—ironic since he has no money to
squander—the singer replies that he won't worry about getting
into debt he knows he can always depend on the boss for a
good job.

The song ends in the last three lines with a burst of anguish
from the singer, "Sometimes I wakes up in the mornin', baby,
I just can't eat for cryin'." The conclusion suggests an advance
from naive acceptance of his position to bitter recognition of
the nature of his servitude.

Another talking blues of impressive artistry is Roosevelt Charles's "Mule Blues."

14. *Mule Blues*

1. *Spoken:* Looka here, I got to go out there,
See what this ole mule gonna do.
Boss tole me I got to lay off them rows,
An' I got to lay 'em off straight.
You know I can't have no strangers aroun',
'Cause my mule is scared;
If that mule start to clown,
There's gonna be trouble here.

2. I went down to the lot this mornin' to catch a pair o' mules.
An' I couldn't find nothin' left but these two.
That is Dot an' Carry.
Now you know good an' well, they don't stand no jive.
I went all over the career, tryin' to find a mule to shoulder with,
Everywhere I went thei' shoulder was so',
Or either he was lame in one leg,
So I guess I'll have to try to make the day with these two.

Lord, I plowed so long.   Lord,   I can tell the squares a day.

3. *Sung:* Lord, I plowed so long. Lord, I can tell the squares a day.

Spoken: Well, you know when a man can tell the squares a day,
He must be a regular ole plowhand.
Now you know that's right, ain't it?
Yes, yes, that's right.

Well,   my mule is gait-ed down,   Boy, I walked the field

all day long,   Lord, I'm gon-na plow this field, ba-by,

Lord, and I ain't gon-na plow no more.

4. *Sung:* Well, my mule is gaited down,
Boy, I walked the field all day long,
Lord, I'm gonna plow this field, baby, Lord, and I ain't gonna
plow no more.

5. *Spoken:* Looka here, you know one thing, I searched this
whole river bottom over,
An' I ain't found another mule no where, man, plow like these
mule plow.
I'm gonna hang up my line, an' I'm gonna talk to 'em from here
on out.

6. "You better yea there just a little bit tighter, tighten up
on 'em now."
Boy, we sure movin' on along, ain't we.
Go on an' turn that furrow, boy;
Look at that plow cuttin' through that san'!
I wouldn't have a mule on earth that wouldn't tear up like
this one.

7. *Sung:* Well, I'm gonna plow on baby, woh, I'm gonna make
this day,
You know the sun is sinkin' low, man, an' my team is done got
slow.

8. *Spoken:* Boy, they walk like this all day, I got it made,
ain't I?
It's early in the mornin', about half past seven,
Looka there, boy, they gaited down,

9. Say, man, what's you runnin' across over there?
Why don't you have a team pair up like this team do?
I tell you if you ain't a mule skinner,
You don't know what to do.
Watch me when I get on this lan', you better yea,
Look at him fallin' back over there.

10. Boy, that's why they call me a plowhand.
I plowed all up in ole Arkansas,
Would've plowed in Mississippi, but I ain't stopped by there
yet;
I went out in Texas, I turned a few furrows there,
Everywhere I go they don't want me to turn my team a-loose.

11. "Looka here, say, Bossman, I want a few dollars,
I gotta go out there to that ole jook joint tonight."
"Son, you gonna th'ow away all your money."
"Well, Boss, you tol' me if I made you a good hand,
You didn't care what I do with the money I make."

"Well, you know winter time is comin'.''
"That's all right, I'm gonna be prepared for the winter.
Just give me a few dollars, I got to have me a little wine.
You got your wine at home."
"What yo' mean?"
"Well, now wait a minute, Bossman, you want to know just
    a little bit too much.
'Cause I'm turnin' these furrows an' the rows is straight,
    ain't they?"

12. *Sung:* Oh, it's gettin' late in the evenin', Lord, I feel like
    blowin' my horn,
Yes, it's gettin' late over in the evenin', baby, Lord, I feel
    like blowin' my horn.

13. *Spoken:* I wonder what the madame got for my supper
    tonight.
I know she got some red beans an' rice on the table,
But, boy, these two mules sure has got me tired, tired, tired.

*Roosevelt Charles, vocal; Otis Webster, guitar; Angola, Nov.
19, 1960.* (The recording may be heard on *Blues, Prayer, Work
and Trouble Songs,* VRS 9136, 1964.)

"Mule Blues" is unified by the dramatic presentation of
central elements in the life of the country Negro farmhand—
the feeling of affection for his mule, a craftsman's pride in a
job well done, the practice of wandering from job to job, the
turning to the boss for a few dollars in advance for a big blast,
the boss's urging that the plowman be judicious and save his
money for the winter, the yearning for letting off steam in a
jook joint after a long hot day in the fields, and finally return
to the basic Louisiana diet of red beans and rice.
    The singing and playing follow the development of the
ideas sensitively; as he gains control of the mules and man and
animals begin to function like a precise machine, one can feel
freely flowing movement and irresistible momentum; in the
dialogue with the boss, Roosevelt begins sounding servile, the
boss fatherly; then he is proud and insolent when he rebukes
the boss. Finally, as the working day comes to an end, as it
gets late in the evening, the singer projects a twilight mood
as his voice shifts into a tone of weary relaxation.
    The true blues singer improvises as easily as he speaks,
sometimes more easily. The musical and poetic structure of

the blues, its heavy reliance on standard verses and phrases, and the singer's possession of a mental reservoir of blues verses which flow into consciousness with the fluidity and often disorder of thought, in combination make improvisation a natural and simple act for the singer who has absorbed the tradition since childhood. The result may be simply a mélange of traditional verses, inconsistent in combination, or it may be an effective synthesis held together by an emotional logic of association. Most blues singers are essentially imitators; the end product of the improvisation is original primarily in the particular combination of standard parts the singer has hit upon—a patchwork quilt made of already fabricated pieces the maker has put together in a pattern which suits his impulses. Such singers, as for example Butch Cage and Willie Thomas, are not sufficiently creative to express their own lives directly in images and events fashioned from their own personal experiences, but they voice their feelings obliquely, reflecting the basic elements and attitudes of the folk Negro environment rather than specific events in their own lives. The gifted and imaginative blues singers, on the other hand, often put into words and music their own experiences and feelings; they are directly autobiographical; although they draw on standard verses and phrases, they use their raw materials cleverly, coming forth with songs which have traditional elements and at the same time original and poetically exciting turns of phrase and thought—artistic creations which have the impact and vividness of deep personal involvement. Such are the best songs of Robert Pete Williams, Otis Webster, Roosevelt Charles, and Herman E. Johnson.

In general, both creative and non-creative blues singers perform some songs essentially as they have heard them, usually songs which are to them thoroughly satisfying as they are—classics like "Trouble in Mind."

The tendency in recent years, especially among blues singers under thirty, has been toward more and more rigidity; their impulse is to learn a particular blues on a record as an entity and follow the original as precisely as they can. The tradition of improvisation in country blues is disappearing as folk Negroes become less folk and better educated.

1. Murderers' Home

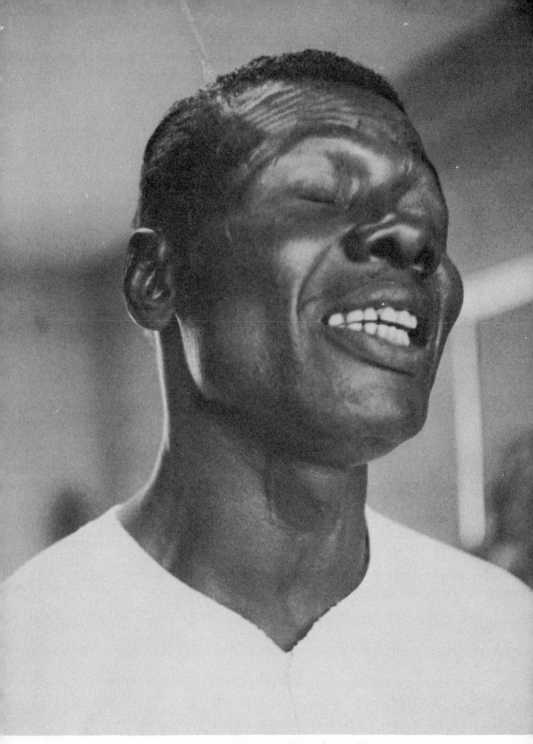

2. *Dreamin' of the Other Island*
   Roosevelt Charles

3. *Blue as a Man Can Be*
Andy Mosely

4. *Black Night Fallin'*
Hogman Maxey and Friend

5. *Got a Lifetime Here*
Robert Pete Williams

6. *Woman Done Me In*
   Otis Webster

7. *Shake 'em on Down*

103

8. *A Fiddler's Magic:*

Butch Cage and a New Generation

9. *Wonder Where My Easy Rider's Gone*

10. *Red Hot Mama*
   Billie Pierce

11. *Live By My Sweet Mama*
Sally Dotson and Smoky Babe

12. *Long Tall Woman Make a Preacher Lay His Bible Down*
Willie B. Thomas and Family

13. *Come Here, Baby, Sit Down on Your Daddy's Knee*
Leon Strickland

14. My Mother Taught Me How to Pray

15. *The Sun's Gonna Shine in My Back Door Some Day*
Herman E. Johnson

Chapter Five

THE SONGS

THIS CHAPTER IS MADE UP OF THE ANNOTATED TEXTS OF SONGS, arranged thematically. The section heading is usually a line or phrase from a blues which epitomizes the subject.

BOLL WEEVIL AND BALE WEEVIL–THERE'S TOO MANY IF'S ABOUT FARMIN' is concerned with responses to the special problems of black cotton farmers, principally their relationships with feudally paternalistic bosses and the generally futile process of trying to ʌake a living raising the crop.

MEN AND MULES gives instances of hostility and rapport between plowmen and their main source of power.

LET ME GO HOME, WHISKEY touches on the pleasures and problems of drinking.

MY PAINS COMIN' DOWN AGAIN–TOMBSTONE LANDIN' AN' OLE DRY BONE presents typical reactions to sickness and death.

BAD LUCK AN' TROUBLE–WILL A MATCHBOX HOLD MY CLOTHES deals with the death of parents, poverty, economic depression, fair weather friends, and the wanderlust of the impoverished.

I'M A GAMBLIN' MAN gives a picture of the compulsive gambler.

SHE DONE CAUGHT THAT MEAN OLD TRAIN AN' GONE centers on a frequent situation in blues, the singer's being abandoned by his woman and her choice of a train as the vehicle of escape.

In I TAKEN A FREIGHT TRAIN FOR MY FRIEND, penniless wanderers also turn to the train as their principal avenue of escape. The singer often yearns to return to his original home.

SETTIN' OUT ON THE HIGHWAY, ATLANTA, GEORGIA TO THE GULF OF MEXICO emphasizes the appeal of the open road, often as a means of reaching exciting cities like New Orleans and Chicago.

HOODOO WOMAN ARE KILLIN' ME is concerned with magic.

DARK CLOUD RISIN' deals with natural disasters, lightning, flood, and hurricane.

BLACK, BROWN, AND YELLOW reflects the extent to which folk blacks are brain-washed by American white culture to hate their own blackness and to make elaborate color distinctions.

WHEN I SAY, 'BOOGIE,' EVERYBODY BOOGIE reflects the importance of dance in Afro-American life. Even the ritualized insults of "The Dirty Dozen" are often expressed in a rhythm and form appropriate for dancing.

ME AN' MY BUDDY GOT A LIFETIME HERE covers the principal preoccupations of prisoners, thoughts of how they got into trouble, a feeling that the judge threw the book at them, yearning for a woman, dreams of escape, depression at being abandoned by everyone, concern with the problems of pardon and parole.

I'M A FULL GROWN MAN deals with the assertion of independence by a young man against the impulses of his parents to continue to order him around.

PEACHES, JELLY ROLL, GROUNDHOGS, AND MACHINES presents examples of favorite sexual metaphors based on fruit, baked goods, animals, insects, reptiles, automobiles, and trains.

TROUBLED LOVE includes a wide variety of responses to love and sex ranging from tenderness to murderous rage.

GOT TO GO TO SCHOOL NOW reflects a recognition of the vital importance of schooling in the modern world.

And then, of course, there is MISCELLANEOUS, which includes an attack on the draft of World War II and a celebration of a job in a filling station.

BOLL WEEVIL AND BALE WEEVIL
THERE'S TOO MANY IF'S ABOUT FARMIN'

15. *The Boll Weevil an' the Bale Weevil*

1. *Spoken:* Man, let me tell you about farmin',
There's too many if's about farmin',
You got to har (row) it off,
Then you got to build it up,
Then you go an' get this cotton seed,
An' you plant them in the ground;
It got to come up,
Then you got to raise it,
You got to chop your cotton.
Then 'long come the boll weevil,
He gone knock your square.
Then come the bale weevil, he gone take the bale,
You hear that ole bale weevil holl'rin' to that boll weevil,

2. *Sung:* "Woh, Mr. Boll Weevil, please don't take it all from me,"
Then you hear the farmer cry,
"Yeah, Mr. Bale Weevil, please don' knock me in the head with the pea."

3. *Spoken:* Then here come the poor farmer comin' up to settle.
Here come the bossman with his pencil,
"You raise so many bales o' cotton this year,
But you still owe me a little bit.
Try to raise a little bit more next year."
Then you hear that poor farmer holler,

4. *Sung:* "Woh—oh, Mr. Bale Weevil, I done broke up your land,
I done planted your cotton seed, I done raised up your cotton,
I done poisoned the bolls, killed the bale weevil,
Now here you come takin' all from me."

5. *Spoken:* Oh, too many if's in raisin' that cotton,
I ain't shuckin' man.
Looka here, I want to tell you, Christmas time hear that ole boss man holla,
"Woh, Bossman, please what you gonna do 'bout me?"

He say, "Well, I got an ole suit in the house, I'm gonna give you,
Say the rats done cut a hole in the rear end,
An' I had it patched."
Hear that ole farmer holla,
"Woh, that ain't no way to treat me."

Roosevelt Charles, vocal; Otis Webster, guitar; Angola, Nov. 19, 1960.

With his characteristic flair for coining original and apt metaphors, Charles calls the owner of the plantation the "bale weevil," the creature who takes what is left after the boll weevil has ruined most of the crop. Significantly, he makes a Freudian slip, a mistake which reveals his underlying feelings when he sings, "I done poisoned the bolls, killed the bale weevil." Although this is essentially an original song, the sentiments and the idiom are traditional. Similar thoughts were expressed in apparently authentic fragments of Negro songs used by writers of novels, travel books, and slave autobiographies before the Civil War. In *Clotel, or The President's Daughter, A Narrative of Slave Life in the United States,* written by a fugitive slave, William Wells Brown, 1853, p. 138, a slave, ordered to entertain, sings:

> The big bee flies high,
> The little bee makes the honey.
> The black folks make the cotton
> And the white folks get the money.

In *My Bondage and My Freedom,* by Frederick Douglass, 1855, p. 252, the following is given as an example of an improvised song:

> We raise de wheat,
> Dey gib us de corn;
> We bake de bread
> Dey gib us de cruss;
> We sif de meal
> Dey gib us de huss;
> We peel de meat
> Dey gib us de skin,
> And dat's de way
> Dey takes us in.
> We skim de pot
> Dey gib us the liquor
> And say dat's good enough for nigger.

Burlin, *Negro Folksongs,* III, 10-12, gives several examples of such a point of view by Negro sharecroppers shortly after Emancipation:

> I's been workin' in er contract
> Eber since dat day
> An' jes' found out dis year,
> Why hit didn't pay. . . .

> When Boss sol' dat cotton
> I ask fo' ma half.
> He tol' me I chopped out
> Ma half wid de grass. . . .

> Boss said, "Uncle Billy
> I t'ink you done well
> To pay yo' debts wid cott'n
> An' have yo' seeds to sell.

For a recording of Charles's performance see *Blues, Prayer, Work and Trouble Songs,* VRS 9136, 1964.

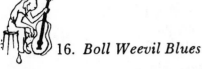

16. *Boll Weevil Blues*

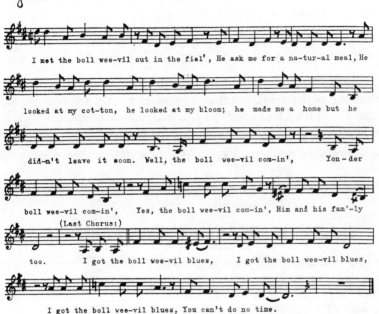

I met the boll wee-vil out in the fiel', He ask me for a na-tur-al meal, He

looked at my cot-ton, he looked at my bloom; he made me a home but he

did-n't leave it soon. Well, the boll wee-vil com-in', Yon-der

boll wee-vil com-in', Yes, the boll wee-vil com-in', Him and his fam'-ly

(Last Chorus:)

too. I got the boll wee-vil blues, I got the boll wee-vil blues,

I got the boll wee-vil blues, You can't do no time.

1. I met the boll weevil out in the fiel',
He ask me for a natural meal,
He looked at my cotton, he looked at my bloom;
He made me a home but he didn't leave it soon.

Chorus: Well, the boll weevil comin',
Yonder boll weevil comin',
Yes, the boll weevil comin',
Him an' his family too.

2. Well, the boll weevil told me I didn't have to poison cotton,
He had a way of pickin', didn't have to know nothin',
He walked in the square, he hid his head,
He said, "Cotton man, I'm most dead.

Chorus: Ain't no need o' you pausin',
Ain't no need o' you pausin',
'Cause it won't do me no good."

3. Well, the boll weevil he smart as a bee,
He knows how to eat, but he never get me,
He look at his family, begin to laugh,
He said, "Foolish man, tryin' to poison my — — —."

Chorus: You know the boll weevil blues,
      I got the boll weevil blues,
      I got the boll weevil blues,
      Pickin' my cotton an' — — — —.

4. *Spoken:* Yes, I went out there with my poison gun,
I shot the boll weevil, an' that scoundrel got up an' run;
He said, "You's a fool think you gonna give me somethin' to eat,
I don't eat a thing, I just punchin' the square."

Chorus (Sung): Because I'm on the dare,
      I'm on the dare,
      While I'm on the dare,
      He's punchin' on my square.

5. Well, I sent up to my bossman for several minutes,
He said, "You ain't go nothin', boll weevil got your rent."
Look at the bossman, begin to laugh,
"Son, you better leave town, make you some cotton fas'."
I look at my bossman, look so funny,
He say, "You got goobers, ain't got no money."
Look at the bossman one more time,
"Now you gotta make another crop an' do your time."

Chorus: Now the boll weevil blues,
      I got the boll weevil blues,
      I got the boll weevil blues,
      I can't do no time.

6. Well, the boll weevil got his hat an' shoes,
He say, "I'm so glad I done move off you,
I clean out the crop, everythin' I thought I had."
He said, "I got every doggone (thing) you had."

Chorus: I got the boll weevil blues,
      I got the boll weevil blues,
      I got the boll weevil blues,
      You can't do no time.

Otis Webster, vocal and guitar; Angola, Nov. 12, 1960.

In 1862, coming in from Mexico, the boll weevil crossed the Rio Grande at Brownsville, Texas. By 1903, leaving a grim trail of ruined cotton farmers in its wake, it had reached west Louisiana.

Some time around the turn of the century, probably in Texas, the most durable boll weevil song made its appearance, "The Ballet of the Boll Weevil," the central plot of which has the weevil moving onto a farm, looking for a home; no matter what the poor farmer does to destroy the insect, the weevil cheerfully makes himself at home and ruins everything. White, *American Negro Folk-songs*, p. 352, suggests that the line "Jes' a-lookin' for a home" came from a spiritual; in Fenner, *Religious Folk Songs of the Negro*, 1901, p. 8, there is a spiritual line, "I'm a-huntin' for a home, home." Alan Lomax has expressed his belief that "the Negro tenant farmers and farm laborers, who were also 'looking for a home,' felt some kinship with the 'little black bug.'" (Note to 16B.2 "Boll Weevil Blues," Library of Congress recordings.) Oliver, p. 19, has written that "Negroes even paradoxically found some sympathy as they saw their own unbreakable spirit symbolized in its invincibility." There are certainly occasional suggestions, as I have mentioned in the introduction, when Negro farm workers have felt a malicious pleasure in misfortunes which befell plantation owners even though they themselves were ruined. Resentfully feeling that the boss gets all, himself nothing, Otis Webster, in "When I Begin to Farm," sings:

> I'll poison him for ya,
> I ain't gonna pray I'll kill the boll weevil.

This kind of cutting of the nose to spite the face is apparent in an incident which took place on a plantation near Louise, Mississippi thirty years ago as described by Georgianna Colmer, July 31, 1961:

> An' we stayed on a man's place one; he was pretty cruel. They called him Harry Weisinger. He was tough. Call him Harry Weisinger. An' the people don't do nothin' but watch him. They didn't do much work. Watch him; when he go to town, they always go home an' go off to another place an' drink and jook. They turn the graphahorn on, it was grapha-horn in them days, yeah, record players them was in them days. An' the people would make the whiskey an' go to another house, wouldn't do nothin' but watch his car. An' when he

leave, they all lump up in one house an' dance an' drink. An' when he come back, when they see him comin' back, they get half bent, runnin' to them sacks. They pick hard so when he come back they have somethin' in there. My old man would be a month pickin' a bale. People wouldn't do nothin' but watch him. Heyah they come, half bent, watchin' the sacks, some of them done got half drunk, be out there just fumblin' at the cotton, fumblin', fumblin' roun' at the cotton.

An' sho' nuff, after a while, here he come on his red horse, got his horse all saddled up. Everyone in the field. (He) standin' up over 'em on that horse an' the people down there on their knees, peepin' through the cotton, watchin' him, peepin' through the cotton watchin' him, 'cause he cuss 'em out, he come to that field cuss 'em out.

"How come you ain't—? What you been doin'?"
"Ah been pickin'."

They been doin' nothin' but watchin', an' out there to another house, dancin'. An' so that the way they used to do that man.

He couldn't get by them people. He was tough but he couldn't get by them people.

These sharecroppers were active in causing the boss to lose money even though their action meant ruin for themselves.

Otis Webster's "Boll Weevil Blues" is a member of the "looking for a home" family of songs, which, as White points out, p. 351, "seems to be largely confined to the more southern cotton-producing states, since no songs of this cycle appear in Perrow, Talley, or Odum, whose songs are mostly from the more northerly states which were not so heavily dependent on cotton." Examples of the cycle are Huddie Ledbetter, "The Boll Weevil," Mus 226, Stin SLP 51, New York City, April 1, 1939; Vera Hall, "Boll Weevil Blues," Library of Congress, 16B 2, Alabama, 1940. Among the numerous printed texts are White, pp. 352-353; Scarborough, *On the Trail of Negro Folk-Songs*, pp. 76-79; Sandburg, *The American Songbag*, p. 252 and 8ff.; John A. and Alan Lomax, *American Ballads and Folk Songs*, pp. 112-117.

As mentioned in Chapter III, there was a boll weevil song in roughly standard blues form as early as around 1903, quoted by Handy, *Father of the Blues*, p. 75.

Among the recordings of boll weevil blues in more or less standard blues form are Ma Rainey, "Bo-Weavil Blues," Para

12080, Chicago, Dec. 1923; Bessie Smith (the same version as Ma Rainey's), "Boweavil Blues," Co 14018-D; The Masked Marvel, "Mississippi Boll Weevil Blues," Para 12805, c. 1929; Kokomo Arnold, "Bo Weavil Blues," De 7191, Chicago, 1936.

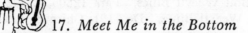

17. *Meet Me in the Bottom*

Chorus: Baby, meet me in the bottom, bring-a my boots an'
shoes, oh, Lordy, mama,
Great-a-God a-mighty, meet me in the bottom, bring
me my boots an' shoes,
You can tell, my baby, ain't go no time to lose.

1. Well, the boll weevil jumped 'cross my side,
He said, "Looky here, in fact, we gonna have a fight,"
He said, "Looky here, in fact, we gonna have a fight,"
I looked at the boll weevil, got my poison gun,
He jumped up, got in front of me and begin to run.

Chorus: Meet me in the bottom, etc.

2. Well, I rise with the sun, sit up with the moon,
Boll weevil rise, say, "I got soon."
He jumped on the poison pourin' machine,
Say, "What you poisonin' for?
You don't know what you mean."

Chorus: Gonna move here in the bottom, etc.

3. Well, the boll weevil got me because he couldn't get all he
had;
Well, he flew down an' he punch the square;
He said, "Balloon a-comin', I'm gonna move there,"
Say, "I'm gonna stop this old cotton from makin', sho'."

Chorus:

4. Well, I don't never, I can't see,
Why the boll weevil tryin' to trick poor me,
I got my poison gun, an' my poison bag,
He say, "Too late, I got everythin' you had."

Chorus:

5. Ain't no need o' me pausin',
'Cause boll weevil got my blues,
Well, the boll weevil quit, up come the boll worm,
Come on every boll he 'cern,
He looked at the boll, he puncha the square,
Boll weevil been here, everythin' is bare.

Chorus:

   Otis Webster, vocal and guitar; Angola, Nov. 12, 1960.

The same tune and general framework occur in Bumble
Bee Slim, "Meet Me at the Landing," Vo 03384, Nov. 4, 1936,
and the chorus occurs on the reverse side of the same record.

18. *Insect Blues*

1. Boll weevil knocked down all my cotton, woh peoples, I
didn't make no corn, (2)
Lord, I say my family an' my little wife jus' could not get alon'.

2. I say the worms cut my greens, we had all in search right
away,
I say the worms cut down my greens, we had trouble that year,
When I say me and my wife, family, you know we's all here.

3. Well, we gotta do better, do better, peoples, I know,
We gotta do better, we gotta do things better, people, I know,
Well, I don't want my wife an' family goin' from do' to do'.

4. Well, I say now that's all right, things be better after a while,
I say, it's all right, people, things be better after a while,
Say, my wife she's in good health, but I got one pore little
afflicted chil'.

5. I didn't raise me no cotton, I didn't raise no corn,
I didn't raise me no cotton, I did not raise no corn,
It must have been one o' them ole bad crop years, 'cause the
boll weevil did come along.

6. You know I'm talkin' about work now, woh people, that sho'
is hard,
I'm talkin' about work now, peoples, you know that sho' is hard,
I'm tryin' to raise my little family, woh man, somethin' got me
barred.

*Smoky Babe (Robert Brown), vocal and guitar; Scotlandville,
March 27, 1961.*

For a recording of Smoky Babe's performance, see *Hottes'
Brand Goin'*, PrB 1063, 1961.

19. *Boll Weevil Blues*

1. Oh, hard as me an' my baby work, boll weevil is eatin' up
all my cotton an' corn, (2)
Well, I done did all in the world I can, baby, an' the boll weevil
won't leave me 'lone.

2. Woh, I'm goin' downtown, see can I find me some Paris
Green,
Woh, I goin' downtown, see can I find me some Paris Green,
Woh, some people tell me, Paris Green make away with the boll
weevil blues.

3. Oh, I'm tire' o' workin' so hard, boll weevil won't leave
me 'lone,
Woh, oh baby, boll weevil won't leave me 'lone.
Woh, if the boll weevil keep botherin' me, God knows gonna
leave this town.

4. Woh, oh, I'm leavin' soon, darlin' you done better make up
your min' an' go too,
Woh, I'm leavin' soon, woman, you done better make up in
your min' an' go too,
Boll weevil's so bad, darlin', they won't leave us alone.

5. Well, the boll weevil done worried me so much, they forgin
to give me the blues,
Woh, the boll weevil done worried me so much, darlin', they
forgin to give me the blues.

*Robert Pete Williams, vocal and guitar; Denham Springs,
March 8, 1961.*

20. *Boll Weevil Blues*

1. Boll weevil's here, baby, boll weevil's everywhere,
Boll weevil's here, mama, boll weevil's everywhere,
Well, I would go to Arkansas City, Lord, boll weevil's over there.

2. Boll weevil, boll weevil, cut down all my cotton an' corn,
Yeah, boll weevil done cut down all my cotton an' corn,
Well, I'm gonna change my mind an' down the road I'm goin'.

3. You know my baby got ways, Lord, I just can't understan',
Yes, my baby got ways I just can' understan',
Well, she mistreat me, Lordy, Lord, done found her another man.

4. I'm gonna pack my suitcase, baby, an' down the road I'm goin',
Yay, gonna pack my suitcase, baby, an' down the road I'm goin',
Well, oh, Mr. boll weevil cuttin' down all my cotton an' corn.

Guitar (Robert) Welch, vocal and guitar; Angola, March 21, 1959.

Welch's recording of this song may be heard on *Southern Prison Blues*, ISD SLP 125, 1962.

21. *Cotton Field Blues*

1. I might pick some cotton, baby, an' I might pull some corn, (2)
I say I'm way up here in ole Mississippi, I'm up here on Mr. Walter's farm.

2. *Spoken:* But one thing about it, people, the work is so hard, looka here now, peoples, somebody done got me barred.

3. I work hard every day, I get me plenty o' res',
Looka here, peoples, I'm gettin' tired of this ole cotton-pickin' mess,
I say, I may pick some cotton, now I may pull some corn,
Looka here now, peoples, I'm way up here on Mr. Walter's farm.

4. I see my mother, she raise sweet potatoes, what it is she got,
She got a garden planted all aroun' her house,
Looka here, I'm tellin' you, peoples, I just can't be without;
I ain't gonna go hungry, I might not wear no clothes,
We have food an' water, she got a shelter to go.

5. *Sung:* I may pick some cotton, I may pull some corn,
Well, you know now, people, that field work's gotta go on.

Smoky Babe (Robert Brown), vocal and guitar; Vance, Mississippi, Aug. 10, 1962.

22. *Worried Life Blues*

1. People call me lazy, I'm just only tire', (2)
Says I work so hard, baby, water run down my — — —.

2. The reason why I work so hard, baby, keep your feet outa
   ice an' snow,
Reason I work so hard, baby, keep your feets outa that cold
   ice an' snow,
Keep you in firewood, woman. . . .

3. Lord, I never, Lord I never satisfie',
Since I worked out of town, ain't nothin' but worrie'.

4. Tell me, baby, what you got on your min'?
I say, tell me, baby, what you got on your min'?
Look, you worrie', woman, an' you never satisfie'.

5. Got the blues for you, baby, I been had 'em all day long, (2)
I won't be satisfie', till I seen your smilin' face.

*Robert Pete Williams, vocal and guitar; Baton Rouge, March
12, 1961.*

23A. *Thousand Miles from Nowhere*

1. Sittin' a thousand miles from nowhere, in a one room
country little shack, (2)
All I need in world possession is a ragged eleven foot cotton sack.

2. I wake up early every mornin', people, I just can't sleep no
mo', (2)
All the crickets an' frogs to keep me company, an' the wind
howlin' roun' my do'.

3. I wake up early every mornin', people, I'm about to go out
o' my min', (2)
I'm gonna find me some kind o' companion, boy, if she dumb,
deaf, crippled or blin'.

*Snooks Eaglin, vocal and guitar; New Orleans, January 21,
1958.*

Born in 1936 in New Orleans, Snooks Eaglin is typical of
his generation's approach to blues. Snooks, who is a highly
gifted musician, in fact one of the best guitarists living, usually
learns the blues he sings from the radio or from records, later
performing the texts as he heard them, rather than improvising
freely as do blues singers who are steeped in the old-time
tradition.

23B. *A Thousand Miles from Nowhere*

1. Just sittin' a thousand mile' from nowhere, bein' in a little
ole one side country shack,
Yes, I'm just sittin' a thousand' mile from nowhere, in a little
ole one side country shack,
Yes, I got my cotton sack hangin' on my back,
Baby, an' my trouble on every hand.

2. Lord, I don't know whicha way to go, no one talk an' carry
me on,
Just sittin' a thousand mile' from nowhere, baby, in a little ole
one side country shack,
Baby, I have a burden hangin' on my back, baby,
My baby way on down the line,

3. *Spoken:* Yes I just go on an' bring her back, man.
Mm, mm ———————————————————————————————————,
Baby, I'm worri', bother', baby, an' I don't know where to go,
But there will be one day, baby, I will come on back to the light.

Roosevelt Charles, vocal and guitar; Angola, Nov. 19, 1960.

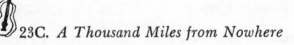

23C. *A Thousand Miles from Nowhere*

1. I'm sittin' here a thousand miles from nowhere, in a little ole
one room country little shack,
Sittin' here a thousand miles from nowhere in a little ole one
room country little shack,
Lord, an' I have no one to bring (my troubles to), no one to
say hello.

2. I'm gonna leave here early in the mornin', baby, I'm 'bout
to go outa my min',
I'm leavin' so early in the mornin', I'm 'bout to go outa my min',
Oh, an' I have no one to feel my sympathy, no one call my own.

*Clarence Edwards, vocal and guitar; Cornelius Edwards,
guitar; Butch Cage, fiddle; Zachary, Oct. 27, 1959.*

These blues, as well as 12A and 12B in Chapter IV, are folk
variants of "One Room Country Shack," words and music by
Mercy Dee Walton, (c) copyright MCMLIII, Venice Music,
Inc., 8300 Santa Monica Boulevard, Hollywood, California
90069, used by permission, all rights reserved.

The pertinent recording is Mercy Dee, "One Room Country
Shack," Sp 458, 1953.

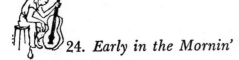

24. *Early in the Mornin'*

Well that's old song. One time I got into a tough job in Arkansas, an' it took about two years to get away from there, a place they call Osceola, Arkansas, in a levee camp. An' I was sittin' down one time, an' every time a fella'd come an' grumble about the food why the bossman'd beat him all up, so I sit down an' made that song all up.

Lemon Nash

1. Well, it's early in the mornin' when the ding-dong ring,
There's nothin' on the table but the fork an' pan,
Don't ever say anythin' about it, you sho' have trouble with the man.

2. Cook an' the flunky a-must ha' been so,
Put no sugar in my dodolojoe,
You better be smart, you better not cry,
You sure have trouble with the man.

3. Oh, boss, I'd like for you to tell me,
When you gonna pay me off,
'Cause I'm a long way from home,
An' I must have some dough.

4. I've got a letter from my mother,
I got a letter from my brother,
I got a letter from my cousin,
That they must have some dough.

Repeat 1 and 2.

Lemon Nash, vocal and ukelele; New Orleans, Oct. 15, 1959.

The first stanza occurs frequently in worksongs, particularly those on prison farms. See, for example, "Early in the Mornin'", *Prison Worksongs*, LFS A-5, Angola, 1959, and "De Midnight Special," Lomax, *American Ballads and Folk Songs*, p. 72; a non-prison variant is "Grade Song," in Odum, *The Negro and His Songs*, p. 253.

25. *Why You Knocka Me Down?*

Ex-cuse-a mé, Mis-ter John-son, I have-n't meant no harm. Why you

knock-a me down? Why you knock-a me down? You knock me ov-er the line.

1. Excuse-a me, Mr. Johnson, I haven't meant no harm.
Why you knocka me down? Why you knocka me down?
You knock me over the line.

2. Excuse me, Mr. Johnson, I haven't meant no harm,
Why you knocka me down? Why you knocka me down?
You knock me to the riverside, you knock me over the line.

Godar Chalvin, vocal and Cajun accordion; Abbeville, Feb. 10, 1956.

Although the singer has been beaten without just cause, he is humble and polite in asking for an explanation.

On the other hand, in the following song, "Bossin' Blues," the singer speaks up vigorously for the comfort of the field hands, with the predictable result that he had to get "out on the track, hoboin', an' skippin' an' dodgin' every whichaway back."

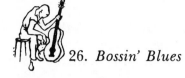

26. *Bossin' Blues*

1. *Spoken:* Well now, this is the way that I got out on the
   track,
Hoboin' an' skippin' an' dodgin' every whichaway back,
I was out on a plantation where my sister-in-law an' brother-
   in-law was,
They was choppin' cotton.
The bossman didn't 'low the womenfolks to knock off till 12.
"That's no time o' day to fix no man no meal to eat.
An' a man git tired o' fried friz, an' overturn' hotcakes.
He wants boiled food sometime', especially when he's plowin'
   all day."

2. I told my little sister, "Carny," I say,
"Look, sister, why don't you go an' fix yo' husband a little bit
   to eat, somethin' with meat?"
"Buddy, they don't 'low the women to knock off here until
   12 o'clock,
The same the men do."
I says, "Sister, "What time do you have to cook your husband
   a meal?"
She say, "Well, I fry him a hoe cake, fry him a piece o' salt meat,
Maybe fry him a egg." I say "That's the very reason you look
   so pore today.
You go on ahead to the house, I'm here on my vacation."
I say, "I can chop enough cotton in yo' place."
Well, she say, "Well, okay, Buddy, but it's gonna be a little
   humbug there."
I say, "Well, I take care o' your situation."

3. Here go my sister, she goin' on to the house.
Look at that girl walkin' out 'cross that field;
After a while I look 'cross the field,
Here come an old red horse,
With a white man on his back;
The old horse was trottin', look at him trottin' on out the way,
Boy, he's in a hurry too, ain't he?

4. I said, (*Sung:*) "Oh, Bossman, tell me what you on yo'
way?"
Spoken: After a while he got there to say, I say, "Yeah."
"Where that woman supposed to be here choppin' cotton?"
I say, "She go to the house to fix me an' my brother-in-law a
meal to eat."
He say, "Well look, you ain't doin' nothin',
You don't run nothin' on this 'ation;
Say, I tell these women to knock off,
When the men knock their mules off,
The women drop their hoes, go to the house, an' cook a little
bit to eat."
I say, "That ain't no time for no cook to cook no meal in
thirty minutes,
Which you do know, an' you want 'em back in the field at 1,
I say they don't get off until 12."
He say, "Don't you know, I get off this horse,
An' I build a shoe-shop in yo' you-know-what."

5. I looked at him an' told him, "My good man,
Sung: Yeah, foots is made to walk on,
Don't you ever try to kick poor me."
Spoken: He say, "Don't you tell me what to not to try to do."
Huh, I looked at him, I said, "I'm tellin' you 'bout this o' mine."
He went to get off his horse, I opened my big gun, .41,
Let me hear it cry one time.
Boy, listen to that .45 cryin', I ain't shuckin',
Listen at it.
I tried to pin his right leg right down there.
He'll always remember.
Sung: Woh, you ain't got no black child,
You ain't got no business kickin' me.

*Roosevelt Charles, vocal; Otis Webster, guitar; Angola, Nov.
19, 1960.*

27. *When I Begin to Farm*

1. *Spoken:* Yes, you know when I begin to first farm,
I didn't know a thing about raisin' nothin.'
My papa always tol' me, "Son, if you 'ver get with a good man,
  stick there."
I didn't know how it went along in them days,
That was olden time.

2. I went to the bossman to get me some cottonseed;
I had my land broke well.
Every time I get ready to plant,
Old plow stop up, stop up, stop up;
I couldn't get a stand o' seed.

3. I went back an' asked my bossman,
"You oughta buy a planter, you want me to farm for you."
Said, "We can get by cheaper, the more you have again."
"Yeah, sho' is more you have, but I ain't gonna have nothin'.
I'm gonna do the work, you gonna do the spendin.'
That's all right too. How about borrowin' a little money
  this evenin'?"
"Now look here. You got fertilize',
You got poison." "I ain't thinkin' about what I have,
'Cause I want somethin' to spend, don't mean car tires neither,
I want somethin' to spend."

4. "Well, I'll tell you what you do.
Come on up to the house, there we'll get together."
"Uh, uh, come on let's get together here.
You get up there, you ain't comin' out."
"Well, come on up there, we do somethin'."
"Well, all right then, Captain, I'm comin' up;
I want to borrow five dollars from you,
Want to borrow me some money,
I got a pretty good crop.
Now it comin' on good, you know it look good, don't it?"

5. "Yeah, it looks good, but you know the boll weevil—"
"I ain't got nothin' to do with the boll weevil now,
I ain't askin' him for that,

I'm gonna—I'll poison him for ya;
I ain't gonna pray I'll kill the boll weevil.
You ain't got as much sense as I is."

6. I wanted to get tough with the man,
Ole lady standin' out there with her ole apron on.
"Say, boss, look here, my old lady needs some clothes tomorrow,
Ah, I want to get some money to get her some clothes too."
"Oh, get some of these fertilize'—"
"Uh-uh, that won't do to wear to no church,
Come on, treat me right now,
To get together you got to do somethin'."

7. *Sung:* Yes, I woke up, bossman, you won't do nothin' you
say,
Yes, I'm gonna have to go, bossman, you won't do nothin' you
say;
Boy, my little family done got naked, an' I can't help me no way.

8. *Spoken:* You know my wife got sick, I went to the doctor,
He wouldn't wait on her at all;
I asked my bossman for a treat;
He said, "Now looka here, I tell you what I'm gonna do,
If you will me everythin' in your house,
I'll do what I can for you.
Sung: "Woh, bossman, you ain't the man I thought you was."

9. *Spoken:* Here he come a-runnin' to the door, ole pair o'
khaki an' ole pair o' boots;
I told the old goof that wouldn't do.
Come to the door with a old paper sack,
An' his hand with some light bread in it,
An' some hog hocks, but they had been et off.
But I didn't throw 'em away.
That's the size o' that story now.

Otis Webster, vocal and guitar; Angola, Nov. 19, 1960.

28. *I Want to Tell You, Bossman*

1. *Spoken*: You know I went to my bossman' house,
Just to get me a little change.
He looked at me an' told me,
"Son, this ain't pay day."
An' I begin to look at my bossman,
Talk to him a little bit.

2. "I want to go out for a spin."
He says, "Son, the best thing for you to do tonight,
Is try to stay in."
I say, "Boss, you don't know like I do.
You got yours at home, I gotta go hunt mine."
"Yeah, but son, you oughta take your time;
You get in trouble, first thing you know.
You'd be in jail, an' you' be callin' me up."

3. "Well, boss, that's what you fo', take care o' me,
I'm workin' for you, isn't I?"
"Yeah, but son, you oughta be careful,
Don't throw all your money away."
"I ain't throwin' it away, boss.
You all let me out at night,
An' I do all your work, an' I do it good;
You pleased at my work, you told me you was."
"Well, I am, I am, I know you a good worker."

4. *Sung:* "But I just wanta tell you, bossman, I just want to
   have me some fun at night,
I just wanta tell you, bossman, oh Lord, oh like to have some
   fun at night."

5. *Spoken:* He (I) said, "Now looka here, bossman, you know
   when I hired t'you, I hired for five days an' a half,
Now you tryin' to get seven day' here, that ain't right."
"Now looka here, boy, let me tell you somethin'—"
"You don't wanta stop me from gettin' my money?
Oh, bossman, you talkin' now, you talkin' kinda funny;
You oughta come along, let's get along, we can get along.
I don't know where to go but here.
You raised me, an' now, what you want to run me off?

6. *Sung:* Please, Mr. Bossman, please give me one more try
again,
Please, Bossman, please give me one more try again;
You know I ain't got no peoples here, an' I taken you for my
frien'."

Otis Webster, vocal and guitar; Angola, Nov, 26, 1960.

29. *Yassuh an' Nosuh Blues*

1. Well, on my way a-goin' along, I got no success at all,
I go to my bossman' house, walkin' in, forget to reach for my hat;
When I forget, leave it on my head,
'Cause he likely to get him a club an' knock it off my head.

2. Oh, if you forget, tell you, "Nigger, what's wrong with you?"
"What you mean, boss?" "I want you to get that hat off yo' head!"

3. Yassuh an' nosuh, all over there's no good place,
Oh, yassuh an' nosuh, an' all over this earth there's no place;
He may be young, he don't have to be no more than sixteen or seventeen years,
You got to honor him at the groun'.

4. Well, they treat me so dirty, they jus' don't know how to treat no black man,
Boy, if they let the Negro alone, everythin' gonna be all right.
I heard the Governor man one day, if they let the Negro alone, everythin' gonna be all right,
But all this politics is for the sake o' the black man.

5. I know I'm black, walkin' roun' with a hungdown head;
I ain't got nowhere, God knows the way I try.
Everybody but the white man that I got on my side;
Wanta know who that? That the good Lord up above.

Robert Pete Williams, vocal and guitar; Denham Springs, Nov. 12, 1960.

In describing the typical upbringing of a boy on a plantation, Willie B. Thomas remarked:

When boy was ready for long pants, old man was call him in an' go to talk to him. Mama settin' down there. "Now you gettin' to be a young man . . . I want you to know how to treat these girls, an' always remember your mammy an' daddy an' the trainin' we brought you up. An' stay out the jailhouse, don't steal from nobody.

An' let these white folks alone. Honor the white folks, honor 'em, yassuh an' nosuh. You have to do that. See that was a great honor in those days. . . . Great honor to be obedient. You sho' had to be obedient to white people. That's taught from the fire hearth trainin' up. You see, when a white man walk up, you surely had to get plumb out the way.

Interview, Baton Rouge, June 5, 1961.

Robert Pete's point of view is a mixture of resentment at the traditional subservience to whites and at the same time a fear of changes in the status quo.

30. The Farm Blues (I)

1. I used to farm, I used to farm, baby,
When I met you, now you found out my job,
How, honey, you won't, you won't wanna do;
You oughta make up your little mind, girl,
An' try one more time.

2. I learned how to work hard, baby, long long time ago,
Now the way you love me, baby, nobody know,
Make it up in your little mind, that's one more time.

3. *Spoken:* Yes, you know when I begin to farm,
My old boss didn't want to furnish me,
He had one mule name' Jack, an' one name' Trigger,
All the money for him an' none for the nigger.
You know that's a shame,
You try to make a livin',
When your boss won't give you no kind o' break,
But still he call you chicken.

4. *Sung:* Let me tell you, baby, what I'm gonna do,
I'm gonna run away from here, baby,
I'm gonna make an arrangement for you,
I have found out we can make it thisaway.

5. *Spoken:* She told me that night, you know, when I first
met her,
"Say, looka here, Daddie, you don't have to work,
You can wear diamonds every day,
'Cause all my men, they do what I say,
You don't have to pay no rent,
Either buy nothin' to eat,
Because I got a swing
In old boss' yard that hit can't be beat."

6. *Sung:* "You is the woman that I been lookin' for, you is the
one I dearly love,
Lord, make it up (in) your little mind, baby, honey, try one
more— — — —.
Spoken: I believe this is it."

Otis Webster, vocal and guitar; Angola, Nov. 26, 1960.

Here the girl he wants is reluctant to live with him because he has a lowly job working on a farm. He comments bitterly on the futility of his position, "All the money for him, an' none for the nigger," a line common in Negro worksongs (White, p. 253) and other Negro songs (Perrow, "Songs and Rhymes from the South," JAF, 1915, p. 140; Talley, *Negro Folk Rhymes,* p. 207; Scarborough, p. 228.) Then Otis engages in a flight of wish fulfillment, imagining that his woman is a wealthy lady who can support him in style so that he can wear diamonds every day—a favorite fantasy of his. Similar lines occur in several of his blues.

31A. *Bottle Up an' Go*

Chorus: Gotta bottle up an' go,
Gotta bottle up an' go,
Now them high-powered woman sho'
Gotta bottle up an' go.

1. Tole my baby, just a week before last,
Guess she had lived just a little too fast,

Chorus:

2. Now looka here, woman, where you stay last night?
None o' your business, you ain't doin' me right.
Spoken: Baby, what you got to do?

Chorus (sung):

3. You may be old, ninety-eight years,
You ain't too old to shift them gears,
Spoken: You got to do what?

Chorus (sung): Now then etc.

4. Well a nigger an' a white man, playin' seven up,
The nigger beat the white man, scared to pick it up.
Spoken: He had to bottle up an' do what?

Chorus (sung): He had to go, bottle up an' go, etc.

5. My mama killed a chick, she thought it was a duck,
She put it on the table, both legs stickin' up,
Spoken: She had to do what?

Chorus (sung):

 Otis Webster, vocal and guitar; Angola, Nov. 5, 1960.

31B. *Bottle Up an' Go*

1. Nigger an' a white man, playin' seven up,
Nigger beat the white man, an' scared to pick it up,

Chorus: You got to bottle up an go,
  You got to bottle up an' go,
  High powered women,
  Sure got to bottle up an' go.

2. My gal got a chicken, thought it was a duck,
Put him on the table with his legs stickin' up,

Chorus:

3. Repeat 1.

4. Looka here, baby, what you gonna do.
You got way there, by my view.

  Robert Pete Williams, vocal and guitar; Baton Rouge, June 28, 1961.

31A and 31B are folk variants of "Bottle It Up and Go," words and music by Robert Brown, (c) Copyright MCMXL, MCMLXIII by Music Corporation of America, 322 West 48th Street, New York, N.Y. 10036, used by permission, all rights reserved.

31C. *Gotta Shake 'em Up an' Go*

Chorus: Gotta shake 'em up an' go, (3)
  Time begin to windin' up.

1. Well, I run out on the streets,
Begin to catch a trolley,
He jump an' he told me to walk out in a hurry.
My money played out,
I just had a dime,
He told me, "You gotta catch the back,
You got to ride clean behin'."

2. I'm gonna move yonder, baby,
I'm gonna move on, baby,
I'm gonna move on, baby,
Move on out your town.

3. Well, I wonder what's the matter,
I can't get no mail,
A black cat jumped across my trail,
I wonder what's the matter, don't get no time,
My baby ducked under an' put me down.

Chorus:

4. Well, the woman I got she's cherry red,
She keep me thinkin' all outa my head,
She drunk, man, begin to spin,
Take your time 'cause you's goin' with other men.

Chorus: Goin' shake etc.

5. I got somethin' to tell you, you may not like,
Quit me this time, I don't want you back,

Chorus:

6. Some drink whiskey, an' some drink wine,
Gin, doggone, baby, I'm treatin' you fine,
You get up in the mornin', claim you can't cook,
Every time I look at you, begin to rook.

Chorus:

Otis Webster, vocal and guitar; Angola, Nov. 5, 1960.

Making use of the "Bottle Up and Go" framework and tune, Webster has improvised freely.

The first two variants resemble the Tommy McClennan "Bottle It Up and Go," Bb 8373, 1939, which includes the outspoken stanza about the game of seven up.

Among many other recordings are Blind Boy Fuller, "Step It Up and Go," Vo 05476, Cq 9344, Co 37230, 30011, March 5, 1940; Huddie Ledbetter, "Bottle It Up and Go," Fkwy FP241, New York City, Sept. 1948. The card game also occurs in recorded blues with the Negro represented by a monkey, the white man by a baboon, as for example in Dirty Red, "Mother Fuyer," Ald 194A, Chicago, 1946. Stanzas dealing with a Negro and a white man playing seven up appear in White p. 385; Odum, JAF, XXIV, 255 (the same quoted in Odum, *The Negro and His Songs*, p. 227); Scarborough, p. 180, this last referring to a monkey and a baboon.

The old lover who can still shift gears also appears in Ida Cox, "Four Day Creep," Vo 05298, PaE Rs974, New York, Oct. 31, 1939.

The difference in attitude between country and city Negroes toward the use of word "nigger" was dramatically illustrated by what occurred when Big Bill Broonzie brought Tommy McClennan to a party after his first recording session. When McClennan started to sing his "Bottle Up and Go," Big Bill got worried. In Mississippi at that time it was part of the every day speech of both white and colored, but Bill was well aware that nobody up North in Chicago wanted to hear it. He tried to warn his friend, but McClennan lost his temper and shouted, "The hell with them, I'll sing my song anywhere I want to." As Bill had expected, a riot ensued. He managed to get McClennan out the window and the two raced for shelter in a friend's house. Around McClennan's neck still dangled all that was left of his guitar, the cord and a piece of the neck. (Broonzie, *Big Bill Blues,* pp. 108-109.)

MEN AND MULES

32. *Cultivator Blues*

1. *Spoken:* Lord, it wasn't on Tuesday, man, it was early one
   Friday mornin',
Man, done got started out to farm, to scratch that ole corn
   down the road,
You know everythin' about Lou Berta bein' 'cross the line,
Boys, I couldn't be on time, come to breakfast that mornin',
If I hadn't been lucky, I wouldn't got there at all;
You know that somethin' came up behind me like a bolt o' heat,
   an' a streak o' lightnin',
One mule went south an' the other one went north;
Well, Jack, I'm gonna tell you, I thought there was lightnin'
   there too.
Looka here, man, I went hangin' on like one o' the wild boys
   from the West,
I heard somebody say, "You ain't like the rest."
"But that's all right, I'm gonna hang here."

2. There's a ole bread truck sittin' in front o' me,
Man, that was somethin' to see;
I look over an' seen that mule head out over that bread truck
   wheel,
Like a streak o' lightnin' an' a bolt o' heat,
I fell away from that mule,
Mule goin' north, one south,
The cultivator turn upside down,
An' there I was layin' dead on the groun',
Look back across my shoulder,
You know my baby wasn't nowhere roun',
An' come to think about it,
If I hadn'ta been lucky an' swift myself,
My baby wouldn'ta seen me alive no mo'.

3. Boy, looka here, I went stumblin' an' staggerin' across the
   career.
Some one hollered, "Is you hurt?"
I said, "I ain't hurt, I just so nigh dead,
I don't know what to do, I'm more dead than alive."
Somebody say, "What all that blood doin'?

Where it comin' from?"
I say, "It must be comin' offa me."
I say, "I ain't hurt that bad, I know."
You know, after a man get near killed,
He don't feel it hurt until after he seen what happened.

4. I went trackin' 'cross the road,
I call one mule an' whale him 'cross the head with a single-tree;
Man holler, "Don't brutalize 'im thataway!"
"Well, he done brutalize me, done nearly kill me,
What else do you expect for me to do?
I ain't gonna pat 'em an' hold 'em in my han',
Ain't gonna give him no milk bottle either."
He say, "Well, you better go on cross an' check with the doc."
Says, "The croaker he might have his habits on too,
I better go on over there with the greatest of ease."

5. I went an' knocked on the door;
The doc say, "Who is that?"
I say, "Well, this is ole bronco from across the road."
"What done happen to you?"
"Well, man, don't come shootin' that line o' jive at me,
Askin' me what's wrong with me,
An' I'm here more dead than I is alive."
"What's the matter, man?"
"Listen, man, do you know them two mules near about killed
    me?"
"Near about killed you?"
"Listen, man, don't come here shuckin', do somethin' an' do it
    quick,
Just before I pass out."
"Before you pass out? Where you goin'?"
I say, "I might be goin' to the graveyard,
If another snap like that come today."

6. I walked on in the clinic;
He looked at me an' say,
"Mm, that's a little bitty scratch."
"Man, you talkin' about a scratch, an' here's a hole
In my leg you can drive yo' fist through."
"Man, I say that's just a little ole scratch."
An' you know how long it taken that little scratch to get well?
It taken exactly one month an' three days.

Boy, that was bad, wasn't it?
An' then, the next day, after that Friday,
That Friday week, I went limpin' out on the line.
The man say, "You think you can make it?"
I say, "I'm gonna make it if you try.
I'm sorta like the song—

7. *Sung:* You can make it if you try,
Now if yo' baby tell you,
That you is goin' wrong,
Don't you go out singin' the blues,
An' feelin' kinda bad,
You know you can make it, if you try."

8. *Spoken:* Man, I ain't gonna get drunk an' clown no mo',
An' I swear I ain't gonna get my baby deep down on my min'
   no mo',
Not on Friday mornin', say that's right,
Tomorrow is Friday too, ain't it? Good night.

*Roosevelt Charles, vocal; Hogman (Matthew) Maxey, guitar;
Angola, Oct. 10, 1959.*

An original and autobiographical song about an incident
which had occurred several weeks before he performed it. The
remark about lightning in the eighth line is a reference to
Maxey's almost getting killed by a bolt, an incident Maxey had
made up a song about earlier in this same recording session. See
"Lightnin' Blues," No. 114.

33. *The Ole Mule Breakin' Blues*

1. Woh, rider, I want to ride a mule right off yo' fiel',
I want to break him on down in my hands.
You ain't got nothin' but deadheads in yo' lot,
They don't know right from wrong;
I want two mules to walk where I tell 'em move on down the field.
I want a brand new middle buster too,
I want a Yellow Jacket turnin' plow.

2. I'm gonna broadcast my lan',
Gonna lay off my row;
Gonna plow the mule the whole year through,
Because I wanta holler, yay, mule;
Gonna name one Lightnin', gonna name the other Thunder,
Gonna cross this man's land;
I'm gonna holla, whoah, now,
You know the sun is sinkin' low.

3. That's what I say about a young team, man,
Lord, how cool they is, look at them deadheads you got there,
They almost gone, that's why I wanted mine, right off the green.
"Why don't you yay over there, Lightnin'?"
An' when I hollah, "Haw, Thunder!" somethin' gotta break.
That's the reason I named them two black mules like that.

4. We gonna plow all day, an' when night comes,
An' early in the mornin', gonna have to break 'em all over again,
'Cause they full o' mustang;
I don't like nothin' but young stuff,
Because I done growed too old to fuck with old head';
That's why I don't want a pair o' old mules.
"You better yay, Lightnin', get over haw, Thunder,
Break a trace, whoah now, haw there. Hold it. Don't move!"

Roosevelt Charles, vocal; Otis Webster, guitar; Angola, Nov. 5, 1960.

Charles expresses great pride in doing a job well and an affection for his mules, despite occasional incidents like the one

154 Living Country Blues

described in "Cultivator Blues." At the same time he uses the situation humorously as a metaphor for his zest for fiery young women.

A *middle buster* is the hardest plough to control on a farm. (Broonzy, p. 35.)

34. *Mule Blues*

1. *Spoken:* Let me get out here an' try to work these mules,
I'm workin' with four o' them.
You know what a four mean?
That's a fourspot;
I'm gonna try to do the best I can,
I haven't worked that many mules,
But I believe I can do it.

2. *Sung:* Oh, you know I'm workin' so hard, look here, buddy,
   you know I'm almost burned out,
Oh, buddy, I just can't hardly catch my wind,
Oh, gal, oh, gal, wonder why you treat me so mean,
Oh, you know, buddy, this pair o' mules is 'bout to carry me
   down.

3. *Spoken:* Hey now, get away, Red, get over there, Red.
Come back here, Red.
Gee, gee, haw, yeah, back!"

4. *Sung:* Oh, Lord, ain't but one thing worryin' me, four pair
   lines in my han',
There ain't but one thing I need, four pair lines in my han', (2)
These four mules, they 'bout to pull a pore boy down.

5. *Spoken:* You know I'm down here in these ditches,
Tryin' to build this highway,
I do that kinda work all my days;
Mules that I'm workin', I got 'em well trained,
I can work 'em without a line if I wanta.

6. *Sung:* Mm, way down, boy, gonna build this levee for this
   man.
Looka here, good gal, here way down on the bottom,
Workin' out on the good road, tryin' to build this levee for
   this man.

7. *Spoken:* "Gee, here, get over there, Red,
Yeah, haw, come on back there!"
I use mules just the way I like 'em. It's all right.

   *Robert Pete Williams, vocal and guitar; Baton Rouge, July
31, 1961.*

35. *Gettin' Late in the Evenin'*

Get-tin' late in eve-nin', sun is al-most down, I can

hear my bud-dy cal-lin' way a-cross the coun-try-side, "What you got to plow

down?" Say my mule done got weak, he can't make it to the end;

You know fod-der won't do to feed no mule, It takes corn to

car-ry 'em on. Well, I went to my boss-man, told 'im, "I got to have a

sweet ten inch duck bill, That's the on-ly thing I can find, Take this

groun', where I can build me a lit-tle hill, The groun' done got so hard

my plow won't go in. It ain't do-in' a thing in the world but

kil-lin' your men. Oh, cap-tain, please do some-thin' for me." He say,

"Well, I'm goin' to town to-mor-row, I will bring you some-thin' will take

the groun'." He brought me a mule bus-ter, It was load-ed with steel, The

mule drove four feet, an' the poor thing ask me how I feel; I be-

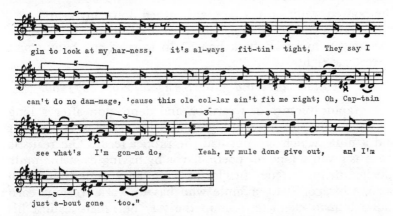

gin to look at my har-ness, it's al-ways fit-tin' tight, They say I

can't do no dam-mage, 'cause this ole col-lar ain't fit me right; Oh, Cap-tain

see what's I'm gon-na do, Yeah, my mule done give out, an' I'm

just a-bout gone 'too."

1. Gettin' late in the evenin', sun is almost down,
I can hear my buddy callin' way across the countryside,
"What you got to plow down?"
Say, my mule done got weak, he can't make it to the end;
You know fodder won't do to feed no mule,
It takes corn to carry 'em on.

2. Well, I went to my bossman, told 'im,
"I got to have a sweet ten inch duck bill,
That's the only thing I can find,
Take this groun', where I can build me a little hill,
The groun' done got so hard my plow won't go in.

3. It ain't doin' a thing in the world but killin' your men.
Oh, captain, please do somethin' for me."
He say, "Well, I'm goin' to town tomorrow,
I will bring you somethin' will take the groun'."

4. He bought me a mule buster, it was loaded with steel,
The mule drove four feet, an' the poor thing ask me how I feel;
I begin to look at my harness, it's always fittin' tight,
They say I can't do no damage, 'cause this ole collar ain't
fit me right;
"Oh, Captain, see what's I'm gonna do,
Yeah, my mule done give out, an' I'm just about gone too."

5. Here my wife brought me some water, I was too glad to
drink;
The first swallow I taken, God knows I like to faint;

She poured water on my face, an' bathed down my arm,
Say, "Soon's you get up an' come to yourself man,
I want you to go on back home," so worried my baby won't
  treat me right.

Otis Webster, vocal and guitar; Angola, Nov. 26, 1960.

A graphic picture of weariness and depression after a long
day spent in plowing hard ground with inferior equipment
and a mule which has not had the proper feed. The realistic
scene is given a fanciful poetic flavor by having even the mule
touched by his fatigue. In Florida Kid, "Lazy Mule Blues," Bb
8625, Chicago, 1940, a mule who has to work without corn
shows human characteristics in the way he rebels against his
master.

36. *Hay Cuttin' Song*

1. *Spoken:* Man, I'm gonna tell you my story, just what I been
   doin',
You know, I been balin' hay all the week,
Seven days a week, man, you don't believe me, do you?
You know they have one hay baler out there,
An' not too many men;
An' you know what they did?
Sent out, got another one,
Say we wasn't workin' fast enough,
An' sweat droppin' down like balls o' rain.

2. I tell you one thing—
I was sorry that I ever was born a man,
I wisht I was born a woman,
Work out in the hayfield until sun go down,
An' you know what I got to do when I come in?
Got three or four cow' to milk, man,
When I milk them cow', well, I gotta milk the cow',
Looka here, boy, what tickle me,
Have to go to that house an' wash up a lot o' dishes;
After I wash them dishes, got to go out there an' feed the dog
   there,
Got a couple o' calf then, got to feed 'em at the barn,
Raisin' 'em by hand.
Be night when I go home,
I have to carry my flashlight with me.
Why? 'Cause I know walkin' at night I be scared I might step
   on a snake,
Man, I'm scared o' them things.

3. I say, looka here, some day I swear to God I sure look to
   get away from this place.
I be so tired sometime', I ask my ole lady,
I say, "Looka here, gal,
If you was able, I'd ask you to go
Get somebody to go to bed with you,
That just how tired I may get, gal."
She said, "You shouldn't work so hard."

"How in the world can I help that?"
"Tell the man that you're tired," she say.
I say, "I tell him that, but he don't pay that no min'.
He hear me blowin', he say, 'What the matter?'
I say, 'Man, I'm tired an' hot now,'
He say, 'Let's get it, boy.' "

Robert Pete Williams, vocal and guitar; Baton Rouge, Oct. 10, 1960.

Although "Hay Cuttin' Song" describes the dreary round of backbreaking endless toil, Robert Pete presents his feeling in the laughter-through-tears idiom of many folk blues. In this case, the laughter lies in the jolly tone with which he describes a bitter state of affairs. Making a joke out of a grim situation is a healthy psychological release, a form of expression of folk Negroes which gives outsiders the mistaken idea that they are always carefree and unworried. The surface gaiety is often an alternative to depression, psychosis, or violence.

For a recording of Williams' performance, see *Free Again,* PrB 1026, 1960.

37. *Lay by the Corn*

1. *Spoken:* You know what that man tole me, said, "Looka
   here, Pete,
I want you to take that mule, go out there,
An' I want you to lay by that corn."
I say, "Yes suh."
No sooner I fetch the other work up there,
He say, "I want you to do it good," I say, "Yes suh."

2. I hook that mule up, here go me an' that mule,
"Come on here, mule."
I go in that cornfield, I lay down by the corn.
I look back at the mule, I say, "Well, lay down."
That mule throw one his ears up, an' one down on me,
Look like to me he wanta kick me.
I got up, I say, "You ain't gonna lay down?
I'll tell you what to do."

3. I went back there, I took that singletree,
Hit that mule 'side of the head, knocked him down, 'side the
   corn,
Boy, he fell like a log.
An' then I knocked off for dinner, you know.

4. Went on in, he said,
"Well, Pete, how you do today?"
I say, "I did all right."
"Where the mule?"
I say, "He out there in the fiel'."
"Why didn't you bring him?"
I say, "He still layin' by the corn."
"Layin' by the corn?" "Yes suh."
"Oh, you don't mean to tell me that mule layin' by the corn
   itself?"
I say, "Yes, he is." He say, "Now look now—"
I say, "You tole me to go out there an' lay by the corn, didn't
   you?"
He say, "Yeah."

5. I say, "I tole the mule to lay down. He wouldn't.
I'm gonna tell you what I did.
I got up, an' I got that singletree,
Went up 'side that mule' head."
"Well, where he at now?" "Down in that field.
He could be daid, I don't know."
"Wait a minute, you don't tell me that.
Wait till I come back."

6. That man he stepped in the house,
Come out there with a shotgun,
An' one more thing you call a buggy switch,
You ever seen that?
That one o' them buggy switches that sets up in a buggy.
"Oh, looka here, Boss, I'm just jokin',
I'm gonna get that mule right now, here I go."

7. I got out o' shootin' distance o' that man,
You know, him an' that buggy switch;
Boy, went up there with my back turned on that man,
I was just like one o' these jets, just took off.

   Robert Pete Williams, vocal and guitar; Baton Rouge, June 22, 1961.

   This numbskull account is based on an actual event which took place in 1936.

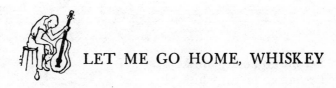 LET ME GO HOME, WHISKEY

38. *Let Me Go Home Whiskey*

Let me go home, whis-key!   Let me go home, whis-key!

I'm gon-na love my wife last night,   Don't come back drunk no more.

Let me go home, whiskey!
Let me go home, whiskey!
I'm gonna love my wife last night,
Don't come back drunk no more.

Godar Chalvin, vocal and Cajun accordion; Abbeville, Feb.
10, 1960.

Chalvin sings blues in both French and English. Like many
of the present day inhabitants of southwest Louisiana, he is
bilingual though more at home in Cajun French than in English.

39. *Government Street Blues* (I)

1. I believe I stop by Big Four, baby, get me a little shot o'
   wine, little girl,
You know I'm gonna get drunk an' . . . clown on Government
   Street,
Baby, I've got them ole Government Street blues.

2. I seen my baby, comin' up one mornin', man, on 14 an'
   Government soon,
I said, "Looka here, little girl, tell me what in the worl' you
   doin' up here?"
I was down in the bar room, I was way down on Government
   Street,
Well now, if you wanta get drunk an' clown, please drop aroun'
   ole Government Street.

3. You know you can get a shot o' wine for fifteen an' a dime,
Man, I want you to think you're thirty twice, after that ole
   thunderbird.

4. Yes, I'm gone get drunk an' clown, baby, I wanta drink my
   wine some more."
When I come home last night, first thing my baby said, "Daddy,
   I know that you been drinkin' wine."

5. I say, "Ah, honey, I been drinkin' wine, wine again.
I don't want you, woman, to tell me about ole Government
   Street no more.

6. Government Street ain't nothin' but trouble, I'm gonna
   leave ole Government Street alone,
You know I'm goin' back home, little girl, God knows I'm
   gonna stop an' settle down."

*Roosevelt Charles, vocal, unaccompanied; Baton Rouge, May
12, 1959.*

When Charles was paroled in the spring of 1959, he got a
room in Baton Rouge on 14th Street, a few houses from Government Street in the heart of a large Negro community. The
bars on Government Street are always mobbed and police
cars patrol the area constantly, waiting for the inevitable fights.

For another blues by Charles describing more serious trouble in the same part of Baton Rouge, see "Government Street Blues" (II), No. 131 in this collection.

40. *Whiskey Headed Woman*

Chorus: Now she's a whiskey-headed woman an' she stays drunk
all the time, (2)

If you don't stop drinkin', I believe you gonna lose your min'.

1. Everytime I see you, you at some whiskey joint,
You standin' aroun' the crowd, beggin' for one more half a pint,

Chorus: Now you's, etc.

3. I come in in the mornin', you all layin' drunk,
You know you ain't treat me right, little woman, what you goin',

Chorus: Now you's, etc.

4. You done got to the place where you don't do nothin' you
say,
I don't need you, woman, 'cause you ain't got no business here,

Chorus: 'Cause you's, etc.

5. You don't need no steam rod aroun' your bed,
You got a little man, you keep your cherry red.

6. You don't love me thataway, you don't love me thataway,
You don't love me thataway, baby, you gonna lose your job.

7. Well, I woke up last night, an' the night befo',
The thing you been doin', you ain't gonna do no mo'.

8. You don't love me thataway, you don't love me thataway,
You don't love me thataway, baby, you gonna lose your job.

9. What you want with a rooster, when he won't crow for day,
What you want with a woman, won't do nothin' she say.

10. You don't love me thataway, you stay drunk all the time.

Otis Webster, vocal and guitar; Angola, Nov. 12, 1960.

The first two stanzas are essentially identical to, the third
and fourth stanzas similar to those in Tommy McClennan,
"Whiskey Head Woman," Bb 8373, Chicago, Nov. 22, 1939.

41. *She Drunk*

Chorus: She drunk, she drunk, she drunk, oh, she drunk.

1. Well, she drink that ole whiskey, an' she drink that ole wine,
She think she goin' out, she havin' a time,
She come in drunk, talkin' all out her head,
Reach for the foot, miss the whole durn bed.

Chorus:

2. Well, she still drinkin' Manny an' she wants more,
Reach for the knob, miss the whole durn door.

Chorus:

3. Don't nothin' make me madder'n' a drinkin' ole gal,
She make me think about what she once have had,
Gets up in the mornin' an' tries to cook,
She can't do a thing but primp in her look (s).

Chorus:

4. Well, I find she didn't have no shoes,
I taken her in, man, an' quiet her blues,
Now she done got smart an' thinks she's grown,
She gets up shakin', ain't got no home.

Chorus:

5. I don't like no woman drinks all the time,
She don't do a thing but give you a time,
You goes in, man, think you gonna be all right,
She stays up all night, she ain't treatin' you right.

Chorus: Now she's, etc.

6. Well, I got one woman, hair like horse's mane,
I got another, hair like drops o' rain.

Chorus:

7. When I found this girl, she is in this worl',
But she got smart, thinkin' she gonna do me bad,
I hugged an' kissed her, on the side,
Believe she think I ain't treat her right.

Chorus: She drunk, she drunk, drunk,
That all night drinkin' gal.

8. I done tired, woman, foolin' with you,
Because you found out you won't do,
Best thing for me to do is carry you back home,
I found out, honey, we can't get along.

Chorus: Well, you drunk, you drunk,
You's drunk, want no drinkin'.

Otis Webster, vocal and guitar; Angola, Nov. 5, 1961.

Webster's song has a structure and ideas similar to Champion Jack Dupree, "You Been Drunk," Joe Davis 5106. Perhaps both variants come ultimately from an older record, certainly from a tradition older than Champion Jack's record.

Manny is Manischewitz wine, a sweet syrupy Jewish wine originally designed as a ceremonial drink for holy days. Mogen David, another brand of the same type, is also popular among folk Negroes.

42. No Nickel Won't Buy No Wine

1. No nickel won't buy some wine, (2)
Now you're drunk now, baby,
Come on, shake 'em on down.

2. No nickel won't buy some wine, (2)
Now get drunk now, woman,
Just shake 'em on down.

3. *Spoken:* Yeah, yeah, shake 'em on down.
No nickel won't buy some wine.
Bring that bottle to me,
Where you goin' with that pint?

4. *Sung:* No nickel won't buy some wine, (2)
Now you're drunk now, baby,
Come on, shake 'em on down.
Spoken: That's what I'm talkin' about.

Leon Strickland, vocal and guitar; Killona, Nov. 27, 1959.

Strickland has taken one stanza of "Shake, Shake, Mattie" and expanded it mostly through repetition into a whole blues. His tune and guitar accompaniment are the same as in his rendition of "Shake, Shake, Mattie," No. 167C.

43. *Whiskey Drinkin' Blues*

1. I'm worried, babe, an' drunk alla time,
I'm worried, baby, an' I drink all the time,
Well, don't do nothin', nothin' to please my min'.

2. Oh, whiskey an' gin is one thing I do cra(v)e, (2)
You know that the thing that caused me here today.

3. Well, I drink a little wine, but I'm fool about my beer,
I drinks a little wine, but I'm fool about my beer,
You know when I go up on that Pardon Board, I'm gonna try
    an' get away from here.

4. Well, I wrote the judge a letter, he didn't give me no
    'sideration,
He tol' me I had to stay a few more years,
I can tell the time will be one day.

5. One more drink, baby, I will tell it all.

6. Find me a whis', find me a gin,
Find me a man that don't drink (wine),
I get drunk sometime' begin to jump.
Tell my baby, "Don't you wanta fight?"

7. I'm goin', baby, I'm drinkin', babe, on'y thing pacify my min'.

8. You know if you got a woman she love to drink,
You gotta a man't don't do you no thing,
She's always primpin' by my side, she don't do a thing but
    stays out all night.
She drinks, babe, don't you drink, babe, don't you drink, babe,
    'cause we can't get along.

9. I went out to the pool hall to rack some ball,
Tole me, "You go, daddy, this is all."

10. I come back with ten, fifteen dollars in my han',
I know you been gamblin', baby, 'cause doin' with other men,
'Cause I'm goin', babe, goin', baby, don't you wanna go.

11. I'm goin' back, try one more time,
I can't satisfy you, baby, keep from cryin',

My baby made up to treat me right,
Say, "Too late, honey, I'm gonna put you out."
I'm goin' back, babe, I'm goin' back, babe,
I'm goin' back, babe, to try it one more time.

Otis Webster, vocal and guitar; Angola, Nov. 5, 1960.

In a somewhat confused rambling fashion, which is often typical of improvised blues, especially fast ones like the above song, where the singer has little time to think up lines, Webster reveals a good deal about his inner feelings—he is worried and concerned about his failure to win a concession from the Pardon Board; although conscious that drinking brings out quarrelsome impulses in him and gets him into trouble, in fact led to the violent action which landed him in jail, he has a strong craving for alcohol to pacify his mind. The woman he is singing about has disturbed him by her primping and infidelity, but he also reveals that his gambling and drink annoyed her. Despite a strong desire to be rid of her for good, he feels a contrary impulse to try living with her again.

44. *She Had Been Drinkin'*

1. I know you had been drinkin', baby, I had– – –, I just don't
like it, woman,
And there's no need to say I – – – –.

2. I was standin' at the gate, when she looked aroun',
Caught her by the hair, and I knocked her down,
'Cause she had been drinkin', mama had – – – – – –
I just don't like it, woman, I – – – – – – – – –.

3. She got away from me, beat me to the door,
She and I tumbled all over the floor,
Because she had been drinkin', mama had been – – –
I just don't like it, baby I don't – – – – –.

4. You been givin' me lots of trouble, runnin' aroun'
That man you used to love, he must've put you down,
Is that why you're drinkin', then I am – – – – –,
I don't like it, woman, – – – – – – – –,
I know you had been drinkin', then I had – – – –,
I just don't like it, woman, an' there's no need to say I – – – –.

*Herman E. Johnson, vocal and guitar; Baton Rouge, May 27,
1961.*

Here Johnson is using the archaic practice of Blind Lemon
Jefferson and Blind Willie Johnson (common in folk circles
when they were recording) of omitting words or portions of
lines and letting the guitar complete what was unsaid.

45. *I'm Lonesome Blues*

Lord, look-a here, ba~by,   Oh,   dar - lin',

what you want   pore Bob   to do?   Oh,   babe,

what you want pore Bob   to do?   You must want

me, ba — by, Lord,   For to lay down an' die for   (you).

1. Lord, looka here, baby, oh, darlin', what you want pore Bob to do?
Oh, babe, what you want pore Bob to do?
You must want me, baby, Lord, for to lay down an' die for (you).

2. If you ever been down, baby, you know just how this pore (boy feel),
If you ever been down, woman, you know how it is.

3. Wonder why, woman, you wanna treat me this way,
Oh, I wonder why, baby, you wanna treat me this way.

4. I'm worried, woman, I ain't got no place to go;
Let's go out an' have some fun, baby, we gonna ball all night long,
Let's go out an' have some fun, darlin', we gonna ball to the break o' day.
If the river was wine, me an' my baby be drunk all the time.

Robert Pete Williams, vocal and guitar; Angola, Feb. 22, 1959.

In Negro folksongs collected before records became important there are numerous examples of lines like Williams' final ones; see, for example, White, pp. 368-369:

If de ribber was booze,
An' I'se a mallard duck;
I'd dive to de bottom, boys
An' I'd neber come up . . . ,

If de river was whiskey,
En if I was er duck,
I'd go down and never come up.

If de blues was whiskey,
I'd stay drunk all de time.

Such lines (apart from the mention of blues) come from the folksongs of whites in the southern mountains, ultimately from the British Isles.

See also Sleepy John Estes, "Diving Duck Blues," Vic V-38549, Bb B 7677, Memphis, Sept. 26, 1929.

For a recording of Williams' performance, see *Angola Prisoners' Blues*, LFS A-3, 1959.

46. *You Can't Get Drunk No Mo'*

1. All them women used to walk the street,
The law done moved them off the street.

Chorus: Now you can't get drunk no mo',
    You may try, you can't buy,
    You can't get drunk no mo'.

2. Way up yonder on Dago Hill,
The Law done moved the gal
That lived there still.

Chorus: You can't, etc.

3. Yonder comes a man with a great big knife,
Somebody been messin' with his wife.

Chorus: Now he can't get drunk no mo',
    He may try, he can't buy,
    He can't get drunk no mo'.

   Butch (James) Cage, vocal and fiddle; Willie B. Thomas, vocal and guitar; Zachary, Oct. 10, 1960.

   The song is in a style associated with the records of Tampa Red. Dago Hill was a center of Italian bootleggers in St. Louis. A recording on a similar theme is Tampa Red and Georgia Tom, "You Can't Get That Stuff No More," Vo 1706, Ban 32799, Mel M-12732, Or 8245, Per 0248, Rom 5245, New York, Feb. 4, 1932.

47. *The Piano Blues*

What a piano blues come from, long time ago befo' the piano blues came out, we used to play these jazz bands, we had 'em on the plantation, mos' every plantation had its ban', but after the whiskey went out, then you couldn't drink this liquor free like you could befo', an' then we had the liquor, we had the bootlegger slippin' in the alley, so we had a piano joint; we played the piano, an' that's where these blues come from, in the same time. The blues come from when the liquor went out; we so sorry it went, we sung:

> So long, highball, so long, gin,
> Tell me when yo' comin' back agin,
> I got the blues, I got the alcoholin' blues.

The "Piano Blues" come along just behind that, what the piano man played.

—Willie B. Thomas interview

1. Mama tol' sister, close the piano down, (2)
She didn't have no blues, but she hated to hear them soun'.

2. Come here, pretty mama, I want to whisper in your ear,
Come here, pretty mama, let me whisper in your ear,
I got somethin' to tell you I don't want no one to hear.

Herman E. Johnson, vocal and guitar; Baton Rouge, Nov. 3, 1960.

MY PAINS COMIN' DOWN AGAIN
TOMBSTONE LANDIN' AN' OLE DRY BONE

48. *Smoke like Lightnin'*

1. Oh, smoke like lightnin', baby, an' shine like gol',
Now don't ya hear me talkin to ya, pretty mama,
Smoke like lightnin', baby, an' shine like gol',
Since I foun' my gal on the coolin' board.

2. Well, I can't go down that big road by myself,
Now don't ya hear me talkin' to ya, pretty baby,
I can't go down that big road by myself,
If you don't go—ooh, I guess myself I ooh somebody e—eeh.

3. I stop an' listen as the bell is tone',
Now don't ya hear me talkin' to ya, pretty baby,
Now stop an' listen as the bell is tone',
Lord, I had a sweet little woman, but she dead an' gone.

4. I'll follow my baby to the buryin' groun',
Now don't ya hear me talkin to ya,
I follow my baby to the buryin' groun',
She ain't comin' back, eeh, eeh, no mo'—oh, no mo'—oh.

5. I stopped an' listen at the bellin' tone,
Now don't ya hear me talkin' to ya, pretty baby,
I stopped an' listen at the bellin' tone,
I want my baby, but she dead an' gone.

Leon Strickland, vocal and guitar; Killona, Nov. 27, 1959.

The tune and second stanza resemble those in Tommy Johnson, "Big Road Blues," Vic 21279, Feb. 3, 1928. There is also a similar use of falsetto.

The "coolin' board" is a death bed.

 49. *T.B. Blues*

1. Woh, baby, the T.B.'s is killin' me,
Lord, baby, T.B.'s is killin' me,
Bad luck in my family, Lord, you done all fell on me.

2. When I was on my feet, I could not walk down the street,
For the women lookin' at me, I'm cryin', hey baby, that T.B.
   killin' me,
Doctor say, "Baby is dyin' by degree'."

3. You know it's a mean mistreater that doin' me thisdaway,
It's a mean mistreater, Lord, that been doin' me thisdaway,
That's all right, baby, I'm gonna see you some old day.

4. I went an' asked the doctor, "Save her if you can,"
Yeah, asked the doctor, "Please save her if you can,
Give her anything, baby, any drugstore would buy."

5. They took my baby, down to the buryin' groun',
Taken my baby, down to the buryin' groun',
I love you, baby, Lord, an' I just can't keep from cryin'.

6. Graveyard ain't nothin', Lord, but great long lonesome place,
You can lay flat on your back, little woman, an' let the sun
   shine in your face.

7. Just a good girl gone, ain't that a cryin' shame, (2)
Just a good girl gone, oh baby, way down in Shady Lane.

   *Guitar (Robert) Welch, vocal and guitar; Angola, Feb. 27,
1959.*

   The first two stanzas resemble lines in Victoria Spivey, "T.B.
Blues," OK 8494, St. Louis, April 27, 1927. See also Willie
Jackson, "T.B. Blues," Co 14284-D, New York, Jan. 21, 1928,
which is essentially the same as the Spivey recording.

   White, p. 391, quotes lines collected in 1918 which resemble
Welch's sixth stanza:

      Well the grave-yard must be an awful place,
      Lay a man on his back an' throw dirt in his face.

The same thought in slightly different words is expressed in
Handy, *Blues: An Anthology*, p. 15.

50. *Gravedigger Blues*

1. Well, the graveyard is so lonesome an' the blues is there to stay, (2)
Oh, there's so many good women driven to the graveyard by some no good triflin' man.

2. Let me be yo' little bulldog, till yo' main dog come,
Let me be yo' little old bulldog, till yo' main dog come,
Well, I will do somethin', daddy, that yo' main dog ain't never done.

3. When I had my big money, I had friends for miles aroun',
When I had my big money, baby, I had friends for miles aroun',
Since my money done give out, I can't find no friend o' mine.

4. Well, I wished I had, baby, my whole heart in my han', (2)
'Cause I can show these peoples how my trouble stan'.

5. When you see two women runnin' han' to han', (2)
I will bet you my las' dollar, the other one goin' with the other one's man.

6. Don't never take no woman, no woman to be yo' frien', (2)
She will sit down an' laugh, an' talk with you, an' she'll be tryin' to take yo' man.

7. Well, I ain't goodlookin', it's not the clothes I wear, (2)
I got a sweet disposition, take me most of anywhere.

8. I'm gonna sing these blues to you, daddy, like yo' mama never sung befo', (2)
Ah, yo' mama is leavin' you, daddy, an' I ain't comin' back no mo'.

Billie Pierce, vocal and piano; De De pierce, trumpet; New Orleans, Feb. 15, 1960.

The stanzas are all standard ones which wander freely from blues to blues.

"Gravedigger Blues" is included in this collection as an example of city blues. See Chapter II for a general discussion of city blues.

51. *Dig My Grave with a Silver Spade*

1. Well, dig my grave with a silver spade, (3)
You may let me down with a golden chain.

2. Have you ever heard a church bell tone? (3)
Then you know that po' boy's dead an' gone.

3. Well, it's two white horses in a line, (2)
Well, it's two white horses is in a line,
Gonna take me to my buryin' groun'.

4. Have you ever heard that church bell tone? (3)
Then you know that po' boy's dead an' gone.

5. Will you see that my grave will kept clean, (3)
Then you know that po' boy's dead an' gone.

6. It's a bad wind have never change', (3)
Then you know that po' boy's dead an' gone.

7. Well, dig my grave with a silver spade, (3)
You may let me down with a golden chain.

8. Well, it's two white horses in a line, (2)
Well, it's two white horses is in a line,
Gonna take me to my buryin' groun'.

9. Have you ever heard a coffin' soun'? (3)
Then you know that po' boy's dead an' gone.

Tom Dutson, vocal; Robert Pete Williams, guitar; Angola, June 5, 1959.

Originally a Negro spiritual, this evocative picture of funeral ritual was first widely popularized by Blind Lemon Jefferson, "See That My Grave Is Kept Clean," Para 12608, Feb. 1928. See also Smith Casey, "Two White Horses," Library of Congress 17A, Brazonia, Texas, 1939; Lightnin' Hopkins, "One Kind Favor," RPM 346, Houston, c. 1951.

For a recording of Dutson's performance, see *Angola Prison Spirituals*, LFS A-6, 1959.

52. *Black Night Fallin'*

1. Oh, black night fallin', my pains comin' down again,
Oh, oh, black night fallin', my pains comin' down again,
Oh, I feel so lonesome, oh, I ain't got no frien'.

2. Oh, oh, just another pain, oh Lord, it hurts so bad,
Mm, just another pain, oh Lord, oh, it hurts so bad;
Lord, I feel so lonesome, baby, lost the best friend I've ever had.

3. Oh, sheets and pillow cases torn all to pieces, baby, blood
stain all over the wall,
Mm, sheets and pillows torn all to pieces, baby, and blood stain
all on the wall,
Oh, Lord, I wasn't aimin' when I left, baby, and the telephone
wasn't in the hall.

4. Oh, Rocky Mountain, that's a lonesome place to go,
Mm, Rocky Mountain, that's a lonesome place to go,
Oh, I'm goin' up on the mountain, knock upon my baby's do'.

5. Take me back, baby, try me one more time,
Oh, take me back, baby, try me one more time,
Oh, Lord, if I don't treat you no better, I'm gonna break my
back a-tryin'.

*Hogman (Matthew) Maxey, vocal and guitar; Angola, March
2, 1959.*

For a recording of Maxey's performance, see *Angola Prisoners' Blues,* LFS A-3, 1958.

53. My Baby Used to Come to the Hospital

1. My baby used to come to the hospital, try to make me smile,
Worri' 'bout my condition, she say, "Be all right after a while."

Chorus: She's the one, yeah, yes an' she is the one,
      Yes, she's so sweet, she the only one for me.

2. Lay down on the bed, baby, body full o' wrackin' pain,
Baby come to see me every day, she have to come in the rain.

Chorus:

3. Take me back, pretty mama, babe, where I belong,
I'm worried about you, baby, been gone so long.

Chorus:

   *Hogman (Matthew) Maxey, vocal and guitar; Angola, Feb.
27, 1959.*

54. *Almost Dead Blues*

1. Run an' tell my mother, please come an' see the last o'
me, (2)
I ran on my sick bed, God knows I'm almost dead.

2. Don't run for no doctor, oh, doctor can't do me no good,
Don't get no doctor, baby, doctor can't do me no good,
I'm gonna make up my min', darlin', it seem can't do me no
good.

3. Run here, little ole wife, sit down on my worried bed,
Run here, wife, sit down my worried bed,
Sit down on my bed, darlin', an' rub my worried head.

4. I want you to know, baby, yo' po' husban' almost dead,
I'm almost dead, darlin', been on my bed since the last o' May.
Mm, mm, mm, – – – – – – – – – – – – – – – – – – –.

*Robert Pete Williams, vocal and guitar; Denham Springs,
Feb. 10, 1960.*

The song ends with moaning, an occasional feature of blues,
more common in spirituals.

For a recording of Williams' performance, see *Free Again*,
PrB 1026, 1960.

55. *I'm Gonna Build Me a Castle*

1. I'm gonna build me a castle on that ole far off jubilee,
   early rider, early rider, (2)
I'm gonna 'vite all you dope fien's to come an' stay with me,
   early rider, early rider.

2. Well, my sister used a needle, an' my brother used 'em too,
   early rider, early rider,
Well, now my sister used a needle an' my brother used 'em too,
   early rider, early rider,
Now when it run in the family, what you 'spect poor me to do,
   early rider, early rider?

3. I got two dope fien' brothers, an' I can't tell them apart,
   early rider, early rider, (2)
Well, now one is my brother, an' the other one is my blood,
   early rider, early rider.

Moses Jones (pseudonym), unaccompanied vocal, during music therapy session at Louisiana State Mental Hospital in Jackson, April 16, 1961.

As one would expect of a schizophrenic who is not completely separated from reality, Jones (a patient in his early twenties) sang a blues which has a certain logical coherence though the images are surrealistic. "Castle" and "jubilee" fancifully suggest a remote stronghold in which he and his friends can indulge their dope addiction happily, shut away from the condemning world. Though he is sorry for himself, he justifies his addiction as inevitable in a family where both his brother and his sister are "dope fiends." The second dope fiend brother, "his blood," is apparently himself. The antiphonal refrain, "early rider," suggests metaphorically that he began to ride the dope habit at an early age. Possibly also, it is a variation on the familiar "easy rider," in which case he could have meant that he was a youthful lover of the drug.

Champion Jack Dupree's "Junker Blues," OK 06152, Jan. 28, 1941, Chicago, has one line which resembles the first line of the second stanza:

My brother, my brother used a needle, and my sister sniffed cocaine.

56. *Dell on the Mountain*

Sally:

1. Oh, Dell on the mountain, cravin' on the Santa Feel, (2)
That's the place in the bend, place I crave to be.

2. I got three little puppies an' two little shabby houn',
Got three little puppies an' two little shabby houn',
They call them dog' for to run my baby down.

Smoky:

3. Tombstone landin', baby, an' ole dry bone',
I say tombstone landin', babe, an' ole dry bone',
They are before when I'm dead an' gone.

Sally:

4. Well, it's C.C. rider, see what you done done,
Well, C. C. rider, see what you done done,
You made me love you, now your man done come.
Spoken: All right play.

5. *Sung:* Oh, little Dell on the mountain, cravin' on the Santa
Feel, (2)
It's a place in the bend like one (where I crave to be).

Smoky:

6. I'm goin' back up the river, baby, an' I won't be back for
long,
I'm goin' back up the river, baby, won't be back for long,
That's where I'll be when I'm dead an' gone.

Smoky Babe (Robert Brown), vocal and guitar; Sally Dotson, vocal; Scotlandville, Feb. 25, 1960.

During a taped private interview with Francis Smith, an important English collector of blues records, Little Brother Montgomery performed the "Santa Fe Blues," which includes a stanza like the opening one of "Dell on the Mountain," except that from his explanation it was apparent that the phrase he was singing was "Oakdale on the Mountain," that is a city lying along the Missouri Pacific Railroad, whereas in Sally Dotson's variant, which sounds essentially the same, a girl named Dell, who lives on a mountain, yearns to travel to a place on the Santa Fe Railroad. His earliest recording of the song was Bb B-6811, New Orleans, Oct. 16, 1936.

The opening stanza of Arthur "Big Boy" Crudup, "Death Valley Blues," Bb 8858, Chicago, c. 1941, contains an image like the one Smoky Babe uses in the third stanza:

I went down in Death Valley, nothin' but tombstones an' dry bones, (2)
That's where a poor man be, Lord, when I'm dead an' gone.

BAD LUCK AN' TROUBLE
WILL A MATCHBOX HOLD MY CLOTHES

57. *My Mother 'n Father Are Gone*

Mm– – –hm– – – (*moaning*)
My mother 'n father both are dead now,
My mother are in heaven I know,
No one to, oh, hear me, to hear me when I groan.
I wish't I had a mother here,
I, oh, wish't I, I had a, a mother, oh, here,
So she could hear me when I groan,
So she could, oh, hear me when I groan.
But my mother an' my father both are gone,
My mother, oh, an', an' father both are gone,
No one to hear me when I groan,
No one to hear me when I groan.

Georgianna Colmer, unaccompanied vocal; Port Allen, June 10, 1961.

This field moan is typical of an early form of blues, an improvised expression of sadness in which the rhythm is quite free and almost every word is melodically ornamented.

58A. *Motherless Children* (I)

1. Motherless children has a hard time when mother is dead, (2)
Oh, father may do the best he can, so many things he don't understan',
Motherless children has a hard time when mother is dead.

2. Motherless children has a hard time when mother is dead,
sometimes pleasures and sometimes fun,
Sometimes food an' sometimes none,
Motherless children has a hard time when mother is dead.

3. Yes, mother told child, "Some day I'll meet you after we're dead."
Mother told child, "Some day I'll meet you after we are dead, oh Lord.

4. Come an' shake my hand goodby,
Some days you will laugh an' some days you will cry,"
You know a motherless child has a hard —————————,
When mother is dead.

5. Yes, motherless ——————— when mother is dead,
Motherless children has a hard time when mother is ————— oh Lord,
Sometime' pleasure an' sometime'——————————,
Sometime' none when mother is dead.

6. You know ——————————————————, oh Lord,
You ——————————— has ——————————— when mother is dead,
Father will do the best he can,
So many things he don't understan',
You know a motherless child has a ———————————
When mother is ———————————.

Herman E. Johnson, vocal and guitar; Baton Rouge, May 10, 1961.

58B. *Motherless Children Have a Hard Time* (II)

1. Lord, a motherless child has a hard time when mother is dead.
When your mother is dead in her (grave),
Lord, and (you) ease around from door to door,
A motherless child has a hard (time) when your mother is dead.
Your mother is dead.

2. Yes, a motherless child has a hard time when your mother
    is dead.
When your mother is dead an' in her grave,
An' (you) ease aroun' from door to door,
A motherless child has a hard time when your mother is dead.
Your mother is dead, your mother is dead.

3. Your kindly voice I can't hear no more in the mornin' soon,
Your kindly voice I can't hear no more in the mornin' soon,
A motherless child has a hard time when your mother is dead,
Yes, a motherless child has a hard time when your mother is dead.
Your mother is dead.

4. When your mother is dead and in her grave,
When your mother is dead and in her grave,
And you ease around from door to door.
Lord, a motherless child has a hard time when your mother is
    dead.

5. Yes, a motherless child has a hard (time) when your mother
    is (dead).
Yes, a motherless child has a hard time in this world alone,
When your mother is dead and in her grave,
And you ease around from door to door.
Lord, a motherless child has a hard time when your mother
    is dead.
Oh, your mother is dead, oh Lord.

6. Yeah, you call on sister, but still and all
That ain't like that dear ole mother of mine,
A motherless child has a hard time when his mother is (dead),

When your mother is dead and in her grave an' (you) ease
  around from door to door.
A motherless child has a hard time when your mother is dead,
Mother is dead.

7. Oh, Lord, oh, Lord, my mother is dead;
Oh, Lord, oh, Lord, my mother is dead;
Oh, Lord, oh, Lord, my mother is dead and gone.
You know that left me sad,
Oh, Lord, my mother is (dead).
8. A motherless child has a hard time in this world alone,
Yes, a motherless child has a hard time in this world alone,
When your mother is dead and in her grave,
And (you) ease around from door to door.

Robert Pete Williams, vocal and guitar; Angola, March 21, 1951.

These are both variants of Blind Willie Johnson, "Mother's Children Have a Hard Time," Co 14343, Vo 03021, Anch 380, Fkwy FG 3585, Dallas, Dec. 3, 1927. Both Herman and Robert Pete carry on the traditional practice of Blind Willie of leaving out words and letting the guitar speak for the singer. Herman uses an open tuning and slides a knife blade on the strings to stop them, with frequent *glissandi* from note to note and much tremolo, the same general technique of Blind Willie. Robert Pete uses the standard guitar tuning and he obtains a somewhat similar wailing crying sound from the instrument by pushing the strings across the fingerboard, thus raising the tension briefly, usually sharping the fourth of the scale about a quarter tone. Both Herman and Robert Pete sing in their natural voices unlike Blind Willie, who in his recording used a rough false bass voice to heighten the anguish and intensity of his performance.

For a recording of Williams' performance, see *Angola Prisoners' Blues*, LFS A-3, 1958.

59. *Ordinary Blues* (I)

Well, it's just ole blues number. I made that one up myself, just ordinary blues, you know.

—*Leon Strickland*

1. Some ole day, some ole lonesome day,
Yes, some ole day, some ole lonesome day,
Lord, I won't be 'round here, treated thisaway.

2. Lord, ever since my mother been dead,
Eeh, ever since my mother been dead,
Lord, the rocks been my pillow, Lord, the cold groun' been my bed.

3. Lord, how can I stay here, all I got is gone,
Eeh, Lord, how can I stay here, all I got is gone,
Lord, you went away an' left me, ooh, Lord in this world alone.

4. Now, Rocks of Ages, come down an' pray for me,
Eeh, Lord, Rocks of Ages, Rocks of Ages, please,
Lord, I'm in a world o' trouble, ooh, Lord, bad luck all I see.

Leon Strickland, vocal and guitar; Lucius Bridges, washboard; Killona, Nov. 27, 1959.

60. *Don't You See What a Shape I'm In*

1. Lord, looka here, darlin', don't you see what a shape I'm in,
Don't you see here, woman, don't you see what a shape I'm in?
Lord, I was sittin' here worryin' all night long.

2. When a man is in trouble, it seem like he lose all his friends,
    (2)
My friends all forsaken me, Lord, since I been down.

3. My mind is weary, darlin', an' I just can't be satisfie',
Darlin', my mind is weary, Lord, I just can' be satisfie'.

4. My pore mother lay down an' died, an' I knowed that I
    was down, (2)
I had nobody to be my friend, like my mother did.

5. Don't the sun look lonesome goin' down, I ain't got no where
    to lay my worried head, (2)
When my pore mother were livin', always had some place to go.

6. Peoples, I'm goin' away to leave you,
Sad, all well bowed down.

*Robert Pete Williams, vocal and guitar; Angola, March 21,
1959.*

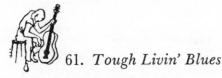

61. *Tough Livin' Blues*

Somethin' kinda hard too, eatin' pepper grass, pepper grass
that run kinda along the watermelon rind. At the white
man's house I saw he had a lot o' 'taters piled up there.
I walked in his yard there. I asked, "Boss, what you gonna
do with all them taters?"

"You can have 'em if you want 'em," he says. "I don't think
they're no good." I says, "Please give 'em to me." I say, "Ain't
got no food in my house," almost cryin', water runnin' outa
my eyes. He say, "You can have every one of 'em."

I load up a sack o' these 'taters, an' I had about three mile
to tote 'em, but I packed 'em until I packed every one with
me, so that's pretty well all I ate, 'taters an' little bread, didn't
have grease to cook it with.

So things have come from a long ways now, but that's the fact
truth. I guess you ever saw pepper grass, you heard what they
say, you know what pepper grass is, don't you? That's pepper
grass, somethin' like a mustard, it'll grow up, you can eat it
whiles it's tender, but when it gets old, it'll run, the vines'll
get long, well we have to cook that part, an' cook it with
tallow, couldn't get lard, didn't have no money, an' I always
did that pepper grass just like a cow would do the cud, you
know how a cow do her cud? She chew and she swallow it,
but we spit it out—just that tough, you know, chewed the juice
outa it, drank the juice off the pepper grass, you know, bit
the bread, we had that, we made it, but that was one struggle;
we was gettin' 10¢ a carro', but at that we didn't make no
money. . . .

Got a job for 50¢ a day, an' payin' rent outa that too, $3 a
month, wife workin' in the white folk's yard; . . . whenever
she cook, ya see, what was left from the table, she get that an'
bring it home. Well, it wasn't too much, but we could eat it, an'
call it a meal, you see. Thank the Lord for that. I fell down
on my bended knees many nights an' prayed.

Ask a man, for he's a-walkin' along, he's a big shot, an' I
say, "Say, boss, gimme that short (cigarette butt) there."

He say, "The groun' done beat ya to the short."

I say, "Looka here what this man tol' me." I say, "Bad as
I want a smoke." An' I walk just about a block an' picked up
15¢. So you could get a whole lot for 15¢ then. I went on an'

bought me a pack o' tobacco, then some cake with the wrapper, you know I had a full stomach then. I bought one of these what-you-call-it, daddy-wallers, that's a gingerbread. I eat that, drink water, an' couldn't nobody tell me I hadn't had a big ole steak dinner then. Pat on my stomach, was I full, hah, Lord! I was tanked up then an' could smoke too, so I'm gonna tell you all now, things have come a long way.

Some people wish for that time to come back, my ole lady waitin' for it to come in, but I don't have to see that time no mo' 'cause thing now is so high now that if you go to the store with 20 or 25 dollars to get yo' grocery, what you get with that, you could put in yo' pocket an' turn it back, an' you still ain't had nothin'. An' you better not have no large family, like what I got. I got a large family, huh, an' you know that puts me up to it, ya know. So, but I'm still here, long as breath be in this ole body, well an' God 'able me to get one feet ahead every year, an' I'm gonna try an' make it; I'm gonna try, thank God for it.

—*Robert Pete Williams*

The events he describes occurred in 1936.

1. *Spoken:* Lord, have mercy on poor me.
Seem like I have such a hard time in this world.
Oh, I know I work hard every day of my life,
Tryin' to do the best I can,
Oh, Lord, I know I work hard every day,
Tryin' to do the best I can.
Oh, you know I'm tryin' to keep this woman' feet outa frost an' snow,
Oh, Lord, oh, Lord, but you just won't treat me right.

2. *Sung:* Oh, Lord, I'm out here, workin, Lord, I ain't got no shoes on my feet,
Oh, oh, looka here, buddy, Lord, can ya see what a shape I'm in?
Lord, I'm out here workin', oh, Lord, I ain't got no shoes on my feet.
Lord, I believe I'm goin' back to the farm an' start in to raisin' cotton an' corn,
Oh, looka here, baby, I'm gonna move on the far, baby, I'm gonna start in raisin' cotton an' corn again.

3. Oh, workin' for a dollar an' half a day, everytime I make a payday,
God knows every time I make a payday, that woman went in an' draw out everythin' I made,
Oh, I turn aroun', frowns all in my face, just as mad as a man could be.

4. *Spoken:* Boys, you know I believe I gonna quit this woman, just won't treat me right,
I believe she see somebody out there she want,
I'm out here on this man's farm, tryin' to do the best I can.

5. Oh, looka here, I'm half-way starvin', oh, Lord, I'm eatin' once a day;
Oh, Lord, I ain't gettin' my correct meal.

6. Children runnin' aroun' here cryin' for bread,
With bare feet, I ain't got shoes on my feet,
Oh, Lord, I fell down on my knees, I believe I sendin' up a prayer,
Oh, ask the Lord to help me please, Lord, help me, please, Lord, help poor me.

Robert Pete Williams, vocal and guitar; Baton Rouge, July 31, 1961.

62. *Starvation*

1. Can't go wrong, everything I had is gone, starvation,
Since me an' my pork chops ain't together,
Keep me starvin' all the time.

2. That's no fair, there's a misery everywhere, starvation,
Since me an' my meat an' bread ain't together,
Keep me hongry all the time.

3. I can't go wrong, everything I had is gone, stormy weather,
Since me an' my girl ain't together,
Keep me starvin' all the time.

4. There's no stir, there's no meat that I can fry, starvation,
Since me an' my cornbread ain't together,
Keep hongry all the time, keep hongry all the time.

Guitar (Robert) Welch, vocal and guitar; Angola, March 21, 1959.

Sung to the tune of "Stormy Weather," of which it is a parody.

63. *Esso Refinery Blues*

1. When I was workin' at the Esso, I worked five days each
week, (2)
When I was workin' at the Esso, then I worked five days each
week,
I had plenty of clothes an' shoes, an' plenty of food to eat.

2. On the fifth day of March in 1959,
It was on the fifth day of March in 1959,
That's when that man came along an' took that job o' mine.

3. Now I am workin' Civil Service, an' it's good I don't have
a wife, (2)
Because this is the sorriest job that I've worked in my life.

4. I don't have decent clothes, neither decent shoes on my feet,
(2)
Some nights when I goes to bed, I don't hardly have food to eat.

5. Help me, please, Mr. Oster, help me, you see I can't help
myself, (2)
An' if you'll get me this job, I won't work for no one else.

*Herman E. Johnson, vocal and guitar; Baton Rouge, March
27, 1961.*

After working for fifteen years as a laborer for the big Esso
refinery in Baton Rouge, an exalted job for a Negro in the
deep south, Herman Johnson was suddenly fired. Hunting
desperately for a job, he experienced the difficulties he described
in "Depression Blues"; he finally got a Civil Service position
as a janitor at Southern University, a Negro school in Scotlandville. Although he likes working indoors out of the weather
(for a glimpse of the kind of work he did in his younger years,
see the second epigraph in Chapter III), Herman finds it im-
possible to get along on the $30 a week he has left after payroll
deductions have been made.

64. *Depression Blues*

1. I'm lookin' for a depression in 19 and 61,
And what grieves me so bad, I can't have no more fun.

2. I been drivin', I been walkin', until my hands and feet is tired,
An' I been goin' here an' yonder, but I can't find no job.

3. A man called me, down in the alley,
An' I went down there by myself,
That man had a little job,
An' he give it to someone else.

4. Then I went out, on the railroad,
My friend told me to go,
He had all the men he wanted,
An' he wasn't gonna hire no mo'.

5. Now, I'll admit, the times is hard,
An' that everywhere I go,
An' that all I do for my little woman,
She just don't be pleased no mo'.

6. I walked all night long,
My poor feet is soakin' wet,
I was lookin' for that little woman,
But I haven't found her yet.

7. I don't take the daily paper,
I don't have time to hear the news,
I'm just a-rollin', rollin', rollin',
With these depression blues.

8. I'm gonna take you for my friend,
Whoever you might be,
But if you hears of a job,
Will you break it down to me.

9. I'm feelin' sad an' lonesome,
But, man, I been sad all day,
I had a little woman,
But, well, I been tryin' to throw her away.

10. Well, it seem mighty hard,
But I brought it all on myself,
Well, she was so kind to me,
But I was lovin' someone else.

Herman E. Johnson, vocal and guitar; Baton Rouge, April 5, 1961.

65. *Hard Time Blues*

1. Well, now I say, you people, oh, you know times is hard,
Well, you know now, people, woh, times is hard,
Well, now while the depressions is on, look like me an' my
baby want to part.

2. Work done got scarce, I'm tryin' to make a livin', peoples, I
know,
Mm, work done got scarce, tryin' to make a livin', I know,
Seem like my baby, she want to put me out, she want to drive
me from her do'.

3. I ain't just all alone, there is others too,
I'm not all alone, there is others too,
I see both white and black walkin' the road, tryin' to find
somethin' to do.

4. Well, we don't know, we don't know how everything is goin'
to be, (2)
I say the way this segregation goin' on,
All I can say, Lord, have mercy on me.

*Smoky Babe (Robert Brown), vocal and guitar; Scotlandville,
March 10, 1961.*

The last line of the third stanza implies that unemployment
for Negroes is normal, but when whites are unemployed too,
there is a serious depression.

Smoky's attitude toward integration is typical of some folk
Negroes in the South; they fear such a drastic change, and
rather than face trouble, they would prefer that segregation
continue. (In the last stanza "segregation" is his term for
agitation against segregation.)

66A. *Nobody Knows You*

1. Once I lived the life of a millionaire,
Spendin' my good cash, didn't seem to care,
Takin' out all my friends for a good time,
Buyin' the best o' whiskey, champagne an' wine,
But when I got down, boys, I got down so low,
I didn't even have no place to go,
It seems mighty strange, without a doubt,
Nobody know you when you're down an' out.

2. *Spoken:* You know when I was doin' all right,
I used to throw them big parties,
Just for the thrill, givin' those big old highball,
An' cocktail parties, just for a thrill,
Well, a lot o' those guys stepped in an' finally they left,
I don't even know which way they went,
Now I'm down, I don't have any place to go,
I just can't even muscle up a dime to get a drink o' gin.

3. *Sung:* 'Cause nobody know you, when you down an' out,
They all may say, "He's been a big time ole scout,
But the jinx got him an' he got tapped out,"
But when you get back up on yo' feet,
All yo' friends you boun' to meet,
Well, it seems mighty strange without a doubt,
nobody know you when you's down an' out.
If I ever get my hand on a dollar again,
I'm gonna hold it till the eagle grin,
'Cause it seems mighty strange without a doubt,
'Cause nobody knows you when you're down an' out.

   Lemon Nash, vocal and ukelele; New Orleans, Oct. 15, 1959.

66B. *Greenback Dollar Blues*

1. An' when I had money, I had friends all over town, (2)
Well, all my money's gone, my friends have left me lone,

Well, but if I should be lucky, get my hands on a greenback
dollar bill again,
Yeah, if I should be lucky, baby, get my hand on a dollar bill
again,
I'm gonna hold that dollar bill, baby, well, Lord, till that eagle
grin.

2. Yes, an' when I had money, I had friends for miles an' miles
aroun',
Yes, when I had money, I had friends for miles an' mile aroun',
Now I have done got broke, baby, done taken down sick,
My friends done even quit comin' aroun', scared I'd ask 'em for
a favor.

3. When I had money, baby, I had friends for miles an' miles
aroun',
But if I should get lucky, get my hands on a dollar again,
Spoken: Yeah, you know I'm gonna keep it, man, till that eagle
grin.
Yeah, sho' 'nough now. Well, all right. That eagle ain't never
gonna grin.

4. *Sung:* Baby, that's just how long I'm gonna squeeze a green-
back dollar bill,
If I ever get a dollar bill in my hand again.
Yes, if I should get lucky, get my hands on a dollar bill again,
I'm gonna squeeze that greenback bill, till that eagle begin to
cry.

*Roosevelt Charles, vocal; Otis Webster, guitar; Angola, Nov.
19, 1960.*

"Nobody Knows You" and "Greenback Dollar Blues" are
folk variants of "Nobody Knows You When You're Down and
Out," composed in 1923 by James Cox, and first recorded by
Bessie Smith, New York, May 15, 1929. Although Lemon
Nash's variant is fairly close to the original song, the whole
spoken middle section and the second and third lines of the
last stanza are not in the Cox original. The song Roosevelt
Charles sings has a different tune and only a tenuous connection
with the original in terms of the general theme and specific
references to the turncoat friends and holding a dollar bill
until the eagle grins.

The theme of "Nobody Knows You When You're Down and Out" has occurred fairly frequently in recorded blues, as for example, William "Jazz" Gillum, "My Big Money Blues," Bb 34-0707, Chicago, July 30, 1942.

For a recording of Charles's performance, see *Blues, Prayer, Work and Trouble Songs,* VRS 9136, 1964.

The copyright information is "Nobody Knows You When You're Down and Out," words and music by Jimmie Cox, © Copyright MCMXXII, MCMXXIX by MCA Music, a division of MCA Inc., New York, N.Y. © Copyright renewed MCML, MCMLVI and assigned to MCA Music, a division of MCA Inc., New York, N.Y. Used by permission, all rights reserved.

67. *Bobbie's Blues*

1. *Spoken:* I want you to feel good an' take the blues like me.
Sung: Oh, if you got a good woman, you better treat her nice
   an' kin', (2)
Oh, I want to tell you, these days good woman is hard to fin'.

2. I, I thought that I had a good one, she put me out on the
   road,
Oh, I thought that I had a good one, but she put me out on
   the road,
Oh, now here, people, runnin' from do' to do'.

3. Oh, black night fallin', fallin' all roun' me, (2)
Now, here I am, baby, tryin' to feel my way along.

4. Oh, my life's gone down on me, baby, here I am feelin' lone,
Oh, my life's gone down on me, here I am feelin' my way,
Oh, that woman tole me that she love' me, but she tole me a lie.

5. Oh, the pore boy down, Lord, as I ever been,
Oh, oh, pore boy down, Lord, as I ever been.

6. Oh, listen here, baby, baby, what I got to say to you,
Oh, oh, listen here, darlin', what I got to say to you,
Oh, the Good Book tell me, you got to reap what you sow.

   *Robert Pete Williams, vocal and guitar; Baton Rouge, March
31, 1961.*

68. *Sundown Blues (I)*

1. Seems like everybody, baby, done turn their back on me,
Yes, everybody, baby, done turn their back on me,
You know bad luck in my family, little girl, an' it all done fell
on me.

2. Everybody cryin' trouble, Lord, but they don't know what
trouble mean,
Yes, everybody cryin' trouble, Lord, but they don't know what
trouble mean,
Well, if it means anythin', oh baby, please have mercy on pore
me.

3. I went to the graveyard, an' I fell down on my knee,
Yes, I went to the graveyard, fell down on my knee, boys,
I want you to give my baby everythin', Lord that her desire
ever need.

4. Save her, Lordy, please don't let her die,
Yes, save her, Lordy, please don't let her die,
I want you to pray to the good Lord to save you, baby, oh, mama,
please don't cry.

5. Graveyard ain't nothin', mama, Lord, but a great long lonesome place,
Graveyard ain't nothin', Lord, but a great big lonesome place,
You can lay flat on your back, little woman, an' let the sun
shine on your face.

6. It was late, mama, just about 9 o'clock,
Late last night, Lord, just about 9 o'clock,
Well, if I'da been lovin', Lord, just she had to leave this town.

7. I'm gonna tell you this time, mama, Lord, an' ain't gonna
tell you no mo', oh Lordy,
Yes, I'm gonna tell you this time, oh baby, an' ain't gonna
tell you no mo', baby
You know if my min' don't change, little woman, Lord, I won't
knock on your back do'.

*Guitar (Robert) Welch, vocal and guitar; Angola, March 21,
1959.*

Essentially parallel to Welch's "T.B. Blues," but no specific sickness is mentioned though the identical stanza about the graveyard occurs in both. The last two stanzas are inconsistent with the earlier ones; evidently, as he was singing Welch felt the need of extending the song and sang stanzas that rose into consciousness.

69. *Bad Luck an' Trouble*

1. I been havin' bad luck an' trouble, baby, bad luck an' trouble
everywhere I go,
I been havin' bad luck an' trouble, bad luck an' trouble everywhere I go,
Say, my cousin Sonny Boy got shot down, just as he was walkin'
out the do'.

2. He said to him, "Please, mister, please don't shoot me no
mo', (2)
'Cause my breaths are gettin' awful short, an' my heart beatin'
awful slow.

3. I'm gonna leave my mother an' father.
Spoken: Play it one time.
Sung: 'Fraid to leave my mother an' father stay,
Hate to go an' leave my mother an' father,
Hate to go an' leave my mother an' father stay,
Lord, I hope they come to see me on that Resurrection Day."

*Smoky Babe (Robert Brown), vocal and guitar; Scotlandville,
Feb. 27, 1960.*

Drawn from Sonny Boy Williamson, "Bad Luck Blues," Bb
8265, July 21, 1939, a blues about a cousin of his.

70. *Happy Days*

1. I been havin' trouble, ever since I was two feet high, (2)
Look like blues an' trouble gonna follow me till I die.

2. Lay down last night laughin', an' I woke up hollerin' an' cryin',
Lay down last night laughin', but I woke up hollerin' an cryin',
She's a brownskin woman, but she's always on my min'.

3. Well, I used to be a drunkard, an' I staggered everywhere I'd go,
But if I ever gets out this (trouble) o' mine, then I won't be bad no mo'.

4. Well, the girl I love she must be outa town,
You know the girl I love she must be outa town,
She left this mornin', her face this terrible frown.

5. I say, "Look, fair brown, what's the matter now?
Well now, look, fair brown, what's the matter now?
You tryin' yo' best to quit (me), but honey, you don't know how."

Herman E. Johnson, vocal and guitar; Baton Rouge, April 5, 1961.

71. *Matchbox Blues*

1. I was sittin' here wonderin', will a matchbox hold my clothes, (2)
Lord, I ain't got so many, but I got so far to go.

2. Baby, I sit down an' think about you at night, honey,
Oh, Lord, why's you treat me like you do?
Yes, I sit down an' think about you at night, baby, little woman,
   why's you treat me like you do?
Girl, you know I love you, an' I can't get along with you.

3. Oh, someday, someday, baby, your trouble gonna be like mine,
Oh, someday, baby, your trouble gonna be like mine,
Lord, my baby done left me, an' no one won't pay me no min'.
Spoken: You know how that is man.

4. *Sung:* I don't drink whiskey, I don't drink wine,
You oughta come back, little woman, try me one more time.

5. Got a real good job,
Get paid every day,
If you take me back, little girl,
I declare I won't mistreat you no mo',
Oh, come back, honey, Lord, have mercy on poor me.

   Otis Webster, vocal and guitar; Angola, Nov. 5, 1960.

The opening stanza, one of the most poetic in blues, first occurred on records in Blind Lemon Jefferson, "Matchbox Blues," Para 12474, 1927. Since then it has become a favorite image in folk blues.

72. *Highway Blues*

1. I was sittin' here wonderin', will a matchbox hold my clothes,

Oh, I was sittin' here wonderin', baby, will a matchbox hold my clothes,

I ain't got very many matches, but I got so many miles to go.

2. I'll stand out on the highway, I'm gonna catch the first thing I see,

I'll stand out on the highway, baby, I'm gonna catch the first thing I see,

I'm a pore boy here, I'm a long way from home.

3. I'm standin' here on the highway, I'm tryin' to thumb me a ride, baby,

Seem like to me, darlin', everybody tryin' to pass me by.

4. That's all right, that's all right, darlin',

I'm gonna have to walk, I'm goin', darlin', if I have to walk.

Robert Pete Williams, vocal and guitar; Denham Springs, Oct. 5, 1960.

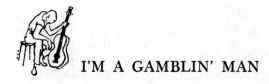 I'M A GAMBLIN' MAN

73. *I'm a Gamblin' Man*

1. I'm a gamblin' man, an' I gamble all over the South, (2)
Dollar, five, I shoot, when it's a nickel I pass.

2. I've been gamblin' all night, baby, I declare you won't treat
   me right,
You know gamblin' is my pleasure, I'm a gamblin' man, baby,
   an' I been gamblin' all my life,
Now you run aroun' town, you wearin' the best o' clothes,
I win them on the dice, from seven, eleven, you know I win,
I catch four, baby, I make money,
I'm a gamblin' man.

3. Why don't you shoot the dice, man?
I swear I'm bettin' it all fas'.
Just keep on bettin', an' the dice won't pass,
I'm gonna send you home on yo' yass, yass, yass.

4. I'm a gamblin' man, baby, an' I gamble the whole South
   roun',
I woke up early this mornin', I had a pair, six, ace, flats,
I had a pair of four', elevens;
I declare I just don't win, I don't see the reason why.

5. 'Cause I'm a gamblin' man, baby, an' I gamble all the time.
Spoken: Play a bit o' this 25 and a nickel, 50 more an' a nickel,
   I pass.

6. You got my bet covered over there?
I'm lettin' these dice roll, let 'em roll, man.
Look at 'em gallopin', goin' 'cross that board.
The houseman says eleven, you know by that I had to win.

7. I went early this mornin', I knocked on the door,
I heard my baby say, "Who is there?"
"You know this ole gamblin' chile, baby, I been gamblin' all
   night long."
She says, "Don't come in here, daddy, less'n you got some
   money."

8. "Baby, I got all my pockets full o' money,
An' my shoes too, I can't hardly walk,
For the twenty dollar bills, they hurt my foot."
I'm a gamblin' man, an' I gamble all over the South.

Roosevelt Charles, vocal; Otis Webster, guitar; Angola, Nov. 19, 1960.

When a player rolls the two dice, the total he gets becomes his "point," if it is not 7 or 11, which wins at once, or 2, 3, 12 (craps), which lose. To win he must roll that total again before rolling a 7, which loses. If he succeeds, it is called a "pass" and he retains the dice.

For a recording of Charles's performance, see *Blues, Prayer, Work and Trouble Songs*, VRS 9136, 1964.

74. *Georgia Skin*

1. Yes, this is the game they call Georgia Skin,
Get yo' deck an' yo' skin box,
We gonna throw 'em out the box a while;
Man, I got a stack o' dollars jus' won't wait.
Spoken: But you keep turnin' out the deck,
Stack o' dollars leaves.

2. *Sung:* I been skinnin', baby, for years, Lord, I been skinnin'
for many days,
You know sometime' I'm lucky, sometime' bad luck overtake me,
Yes, that's why they call it Georgia Skin, baby; it do make you
rob an' steal.

3. Now I have pawned my shoe', I even down an' pawn the
suit off my back,
I woulda pawn my sock', but they got holes in 'em;
That's what skin'll do for you if you follow long enough.

4. "Yes, turn it, Mr. Dealer, I bet my car, people, on your – – –.
Yes, turn it, Mr. Dealer, would you bet twenty more."
He told me no, for I missed the nine.
I told him, "Leave my card back, buddy, I catch yours."
That's what you call Georgia Skin, baby.

5. I been skinnin' all night long, you know my money rise
an' fall,
Because I'm bettin' on every deal;
I don't see the reason what that you just wanta break poor me;
How in the world can I win, when my woman don't want me to
gamble?
She said, "Looka here, daddy, why don't you leave Georgia Skin
alone?"
I told her, "Baby, that's my life, let me live it like I please."

6. Oh, Georgia Skin, baby, 'll make you turn yo' mother down,
Oh, Georgia Skin, woman, cause me to lose my baby (in) town,
I pawn my home, bran' new automobile,
Just to play another game o' Georgia Skin;
I gamble all night long, baby, till just the break o' day.

Roosevelt Charles, vocal; Otis Webster, guitar; Angola, Nov. 19, 1960.

Georgia Skin is perhaps the favorite Negro game for gambling with cards, one in which a skillfull crooked player can cheat readily.

Two players act as "principals" and take it in turns to deal, alternating when one or the other loses—or "falls"—on a card. Each "piker," as the player is called, is dealt a card and as a player "falls" a further deal is made. After the deal, the players sing, "Let the deal go down" as the principal flips the cards from the top of the deck. Bets are placed on the cards as they drop but a player may "scoop one in the rough" by selecting any card from the deck on payment of an additional sum to the principal. (Oliver, p. 155).

Odum and Johnson, *The Negro and His Songs*, p. 230, quote a gambling song, "Baby, Let the Deal Go Down," collected c. 1906, typical of the folk tradition drawn on by Roosevelt Charles in "I'm a Gamblin' Man" and "Georgia Skin."

1. Baby, let the deal go down,
Baby, let the deal go down,
Baby, let the deal go down,

2. I gamble all over Kentucky,
Part of Georgia too.
Everywhere I hang my hat
Is home, sweet home to me.

3. I lose my watch an' lose my chain,
Lose ev'ything but my diamon' ring.
Come here, all you Birmingham scouts!
Set down yo' money on number six.

Among numerous recorded blues dealing with Georgia Skin perhaps the most memorable is Peg Leg Howell, "Skin Game Blues," Co 14320D, Atlanta, April 20, 1928.

75. *Your Dice Won't Pass*

1. Just keep on bettin', an' your dice won't pass, (2)

Chorus: But someday, baby, you won't worry my mind any more.

2. That's all right, baby, s'all right for you,
Just change your way, the way you do,

Chorus:

3. Well, you keep on bettin', an' your dice won't pass, (2)

Chorus:

Spoken: All right.

4. *Sung:* Well, goodby, baby, if you gone an' gone,
You're a sweet little girl, but you won't last long,

Chorus:

5. Goodby, my little boy, goodby, my little boy,
All your dice won't pass,

Chorus:

Smoky Babe (Robert Brown), vocal and guitar; Sally Dotson, vocal; Hillary Blunt, guitar; April 14, 1960.

The tune and chorus sung here resemble those in Big Maceo, "Worried Life Blues," Bb 8827, June, 1941; and Lightnin' Hopkins, "You're Not Going to Worry My Life Anymore," Ald 3117, c. 1946.

SHE DONE CAUGHT THAT MEAN
OLD TRAIN AN' GONE

76. *Heart-Achin' Blues*

1. Oh, the freight train comin', red an' green light behin', (2)
An' the reason I've a worried min', oh————————, oh, oh,
oh—————.

2. Oh, goin' down to the river, gonna get me a rockin' chair,
Well, I'm goin' down to the river, settin' in a rockin' chair,
If the blues overtake me, I'm gonna rock on 'way from here.

3. I'm got a airplane now, baby, gonna get me a submarine, (2)
So when I get the one I'm lovin', I'm gonna be seldom seen.

4. Oh, I went to the depot, babe, an' I looked up on the
boa'd, (2)
I said my home ain't here, it was further on down the road.

5. Eat my breakfas' in Memphis, get my supper in New
Orleans, (2)
I'm gonna get me a brownskin woman like I've never seen.

6. I asked the ticket agent how long the train been gone,
Oh baby, well I asked the ticket agent how long the train been
gone;
He said, "Yon the train your fair brown is on."

7. I couldn't buy me no ticket, baby, I walked through the
do', (2)
My baby lef' town, an' she ain't comin' back no mo'.

8. Well, I woke up this mornin' with my sho' 'nough on my
min', (2)
I had to raise a conversation, I went to laughin' jus' to keep
from cryin'.

9. Oh, I woke up this mornin', I was ramblin' for my shoes,
Well, I woke up this mornin', I was ramblin' for my shoes,
Well, my little woman she done left me with the worried blues.

10. Well, if I had wings like a jaybird in the air, (2)
I'd fly to my baby, well, if she's in this world somewhere.

11. I'm gonna lay my head, baby, on some lonesome railroad
line,

I'm gonna lay my head on some ole lonesome railroad line,
'Cause the ole freight train comin', satisfy my worried min'.

12. She long an' tall, she six feet from the groun', oh darlin',
Yes, she long an' tall, six feet from the groun',
She's stric'ly tailormade, an' she ain't no hand-me-down.

Butch (James) Cage, vocal and fiddle; Willie B. Thomas, vocal and guitar; Zachary, Feb. 10, 1961.

This blues consists of a series of standard blues stanzas strung together as they popped into the heads of the two singers. The first line, for example, appears in Black Ivory King, "The Flying Crow," De 7307, Feb. 15, 1937, and also in Leroy Ervin, "Rock Island," Gold Star 628, c. 1947; the second stanza and the second to last resemble stanzas in "Trouble in Mind." There is an example of the fourth stanza in Odum, *Negro Workaday Songs*, p. 217; the seventh stanza occurs in Blind Lemon Jefferson, "Dry Southern Blues," Para 12347, Feb. 1926. Some of these stanzas are likely to crop up in any improvised blues Butch and Willie sing during a jam session.

77. *Easy Rider*

What is an "easy rider?" It'd be a hoss or anythin', an' in this he's talkin' about the ole lady right there, to tell you frank about it. She save in the house, he had a nice-lookin' woman there; she save in the house when he brought her there; he went along easy while he had her. . . . When she left from there, when she caught the Cannonball an' left, why from there an' then that was kinda rough. An' he wants some one to tell him where his easy rider gone. He had a hard time, couldn't take care o' the children, save the money an' take care o' the house as she was doin'; he didn't know how to cook.

You see, after the mother had left, daddy was wonderin' where easy rider had gone, lookin' an' askin' everybody, went to the station an' everythin'. That ole train didn't burn any coal, come to be a oil burner. Little girl say, "Don't worry about mamma, comin' a time when a woman won't need no man." Little brother say, "You better hush yo' mouth before daddy gonna hear that kinda stuff."

—*Willie B. Thomas*

1. Oh, easy rider, died on the road. (3)

Chorus: Will you tell me where my easy rider gone,
           Tell me where my easy rider gone,
           'Cause that train carry my baby so far from home.

2. Comin' the time you gonna hear the howlin' win', (2)
Say, my shoes ain't got no bottom, my pants gettin' mighty thin.

3. Say, comin' the time a woman won't need no man, (2)
Sis, hush your mouth, 'fore your daddy hear the same.

Chorus: Oh, tell me, etc.

4. That train I ride on don't burn no coal at all, (2)
She's gonna shoot way off, she's call' the Cannonball.

Chorus: Oh, tell me, etc.

5. It's comin' the time, gonna hear the howlin' win',
Comin' the time, gonna hear the howlin' win',
Say, my shoes ain't got no bottom, my pants gettin' mighty thin.

6. Comin' the time, woman won't need no man, (2)
Says, "Hush your mouth before your daddy hear you sayin' the
    same."

7. Well, train I ride don't burn no coal at all, (2)
She's gonna shoot way off, she's call the Cannonball.

Chorus: Please tell me where, etc.

*Willie B. Thomas, vocal and guitar; Butch (James) Cage,
fiddle; Zachary, Feb. 10, 1961.*

In addition to the meanings of "easy rider" suggested by
Willie—a horse that is comfortable to ride, a woman who is
pleasant to make love to, who manages the household smoothly
and economically—the term also sometimes means someone
who rides without paying, a pimp who lives in. (Handy, *Blues:
An Anthology,* p. 13.)

78. *Train Blues*

1. Yeah, when 'a Santa Feel lef' this mornin', woman, I was
   layin' down in my bed, (2)
Yeah, my baby done lef' me, yeah, there was no word she said.

2. *Spoken:* Yeah, well, I tell all you men folks,
Don't ever let one woman worry yo' min',
She keep you worried an' bothered all the time.
This mornin', do you know!
My baby done packed her suitcase,
An 'er trunk was already gone.
One night she tole me, sh' said,
"Boy, you gotta wake up."
Then when I woke up I hear the Santa Feel,
Tryin'—a get away;
My baby gone an' packed her suitcase,
An' her trunk was already gone.

3. That train were late that mornin',
I wisht you c'd hear
That sucker spinnin' on the tracks that mornin',
Tryin'—a get away.
When she got away a good while,
She give that highball blow.
Me, big fool, so worried an' blue,
Don' know what to do.

4. I thought about my ole guitar, right back in a corner,
Come to playin', my babe is gone.
My baby gone————————————————.

5. Lord, I know that mornin', boy, that train run so fast,
You couldn't hear nothin' but that bell on him.
Conductor run up to the engineer, say, "We's 15 minutes late.
If we can't catch it up, what we gonna do?"

6. I wish you'd heard that train runnin' that mornin'.
But when you got t' the corner 'fth av'nue, boy!
You could hear nothin' but that bell.

7. When the got there jus' 15 minutes late,
I wish you could've hear them conductors,
Meetin' one another with their watches in their hand,
I wish I had them watches 't was tickin' that mornin'!

*Leon Strickland, vocal and guitar; Lucius Bridges, washboard;
Killona, Nov. 27, 1959.*

The general pattern and theme are similar to Bukka White,
"Special Stream Line," Vo 05526, March, 1940, which is also
in a talking blues form, but Leon's text is more or less original.

As the train speeds up, so does his accompaniment until
finally it is rolling along at a furious pace. The washboard
imitates the clatter of the wheels on the tracks.

Although the focus of the song during the first half is the
singer's disturbance at the departure of his sweetheart, he gets
so fascinated by the sound of the bell, by the sight of the conductors anxiously viewing their watches, the dazzling speed of
the train, that he forgets about his woman.

79. *Been Out West, Headed East*

1. I've been out west, I'm headed east,
I want my baby, back home with me,

Chorus: But she done caught that mean old train an' gone.

2. I love the little woman, love her for myself,
I wouldn't mistreat her for no one else.

Chorus: For she, etc.

3. I got somethin' to tell you, you oughta know,
Leave you this time, ain't comin' back no mo'.

Chorus: For she, etc.

4. I been out west, I'm headed east,
I want you send my baby home to me.

Chorus: For she, etc.

5. Now, ain't no monkey, don't climb no tree,
No woman don't make no fool outa me.

Chorus: For she, etc.

6. I'm gonna tell you, I ain't gonna tell you no mo',
I'm in love with you, gonna let you go.

Chorus: 'Cause you done, etc.

Spoken: Yes, you can go, baby.

Otis Webster, vocal and guitar; Angola, Oct. 20, 1959.

80. *Leavin' Blues (I)*

1. I wanted to leave here this evenin', but I will stay here all
   night long, (2)
Because the girl that I love, she caught that westbound train
   an' gone.

2. An' the road is so foggy, God knows I can't see the road,
This road is so foggy, God knows until I can't see the road,
It'll take me so long to make it, because I have to drive so slow.

3. I'll eat my breakfast here, eat my supper in Mexico, (2)
So goodby, Miss Corinna, 'cause I won't see you no mo'.

   *Herman E. Johnson, vocal and guitar; Baton Rouge, May 12,
1961.*

81. *No Special Rider*

1. Now Lord, ain't got no special rider here, (2)
I'm gonna leave now, baby, 'cause I don't feel welcome here.

2. Well, my mama she done tole me, an' my papa tole me too,
Well, my mama she tole me, an' my papa tole me too,
I ain't got no, I ain't got no friend with you.

3. Now Lord, ain't got no special rider here, (2)
If you wanta bring your friend, she ain't no friend to you.

4. Well, I was standin' at the station, watchin' the Southern
whistle blow,
Lord, I was standin' at the station, watchin' that Southern
whistle blow,
My baby gone an' left me, say she won't be back no mo'.

5. Lord, I ain't got no special rider here,
Now Lord, ain't got no special rider here,
I'm gone leave now baby, 'cause I sure have my share.

*Smoky Babe (Robert Brown), vocal and guitar; Scotlandville,
Jan. 6, 1961.*

82. *No Letter Blues*

1. Oh, mailman runnin', baby, I declare he don't leave no mail,
Say, mailman runnin', I declare he don't leave no mail,
I believe that my baby, that my babe must be dead an' gone.

2. Well, I wrote a letter this mornin', tryin' to find out what's
goin' on wrong,
Well, if I don't get no answer, I believe some other man has
taken my place.

3. I believe I telephone, 'cause a letter is most too slow,
I believe I telephone, baby, because a telegram might get lost.
Spoken: Now call her one time, boy.
"Hello, Central, gimme Dickens 4-2093, please."

4. *Sung:* I hear my telephone ringin', I declare my baby ain't
home, (2)
I believe she have packed her suitcase, an' done caught that
evenin' train.

5. Goin' down to the station, goin' check on the last train south,
Goin' down to the station, checkin' on the last train south,
If my baby didn't go south, she must be around in this town
somewhere.
Spoken: By, by, baby.

*Roosevelt Charles, vocal; Hogman (Matthew) Maxey, guitar;
Angola, Oct. 20, 1959.*

The telephone number belongs to his girl friend in Baton
Rouge, Cora Mae. The central theme occurs frequently in
prison blues.

83. *Mean Ole Frisco*

1. Well, that mean ole, ole Frisco, an' that lowdown Santa Feel,
Lord, that mean ole Frisco, an' that lowdown Santa Feel,
Taken my babe away, Lord, an' blow black air on me.

2. Lord, I wonder, do she ever think of me, (2)
My babe, Lord, I wonder, I wonder, do she ever think of me.

3. Lord, ain't go no special rider here, (2)
Well, I b'lieve I go, I don't feel welcome here.

4. Lord, I wonder, what's the matter now, (2)
My baby gone, an' I don't care nohow.

5. One of these ole mornings, won't be long,
Gonna look for me, baby, an' I'll be gone,
Yeah, I'm worried inside, for you know I stayed too long.

Otis Webster, vocal and guitar; Angola, Nov. 5, 1961.

Based on the popular Arthur "Big Boy" Crudup, "Mean Old Frisco Blues," Bb 34-0704, Vic 20-2659, April 15, 1942. The last line of the Crudup first stanza is, "Done took my babe away, Lord, and blowed back at me." Webster has made the thought more effective by making the picture more concrete and by suggesting a meaner personal malice on the part of the train. Most of Webster's variant follows the idea of the original but with a considerably different text.

Webster's blues is a folk variant of "Mean Old Frisco Blues," Words and music by Arthur Crudup, © Copyright MCM-XLVII, MCMLXIII by Duchess Music Corporation, New York, N. Y. Used by permission. All rights reserved.

84. *Oh, Lord, the Sun Is Shinin'*

1. Woh, Lord, it's rainin' an' the sun is shinin' bright,
Woh, Lord, the sun is shinin', woh, Lord, both night an' day,
Woh, Lord, it hurt me so bad when my baby walked away.

2. Operator, operator, what time your next train leave goin'
west? (2)
Woh, I got to leave here, baby, 'cause the Hogman can't see
no rest.

3. Woh, can't you 'member, mama, you drove me from your do',
You had the nerve to tell me, that you can't love me no mo',
Can't you remember, mama, when I knocked upon your do',
Woh, Lord, I can hear you, baby, I'm gonna have to let you go.

4. Oh, fast life woman, you can't get very far, (2)
Oh, she always got a gang of men followin' after her.

*Hogman (Matthew) Maxey, vocal and guitar; Angola, March
21, 1959.*

85. *Great Northern Blues*

1. Oh, if I miss that Great Northern, Lord, I should catch the
    Santa P,
Oh, if I miss the Great Northern, Lord, I should catch the
    Santa P,
Lord, if I don't keep on ridin', my baby come back to me.

2. Operator, what time your next train leave goin' west?
Operator, operator, what time your train goin' west?
If I wanta stay with you, God know I done my best.

3. Woh, I love you, but can't stay here in your town, (2)
Well, I got my suitcase packed, baby, an' won't leave till the
    sun go down.
Well, that Great Northern, this mornin' take my baby away,
Woh, I'm prayin' to the good Lord, she will return one day.

4. Woh, Lord, I missed her, woh, I couldn't say a word,
Woh, I missed my baby, oh, couldn't say a word,
Woh, wasn't nothin' I done, baby, woh, just somethin' my baby
    heard.

*Hogman (Matthew) Maxey, vocal and guitar; Angola, Feb.
27, 1959.*

86. *Standin' at that Greyhound Bus Station*

1. I was standin' at that Greyhound bus station, when my baby got on board, (2)
I was standin' up, beggin', baby, please don't go.

2. When the Greyhound bus was leavin', with my baby all inside, (2)
I couldn't do nothin', Lord, hang my head an' cry.

3. Why should I cry, there's a bus goin' that same old way?
Why should I stand here cryin', there's a bus goin' that same old way,
Lord, maybe I find my baby, find my baby some day.

4. Mm, Lord, have mercy, (2)
What more, baby, can I do?
No matter where I go, woman, I can't get along with you.

Otis Webster, vocal and guitar; Angola, Nov. 19, 1960.

For a recording of this performance, see *Southern Prison Blues*, ISD SLP 125, 1962.

I TAKEN A FREIGHT TRAIN
FOR MY FRIEND

87. *Freight Train Blues*

1. I'm just an old hobo, baby, tryin' to hobble my way through this worl',
Well, I'm down on a railroad, baby, waitin' for the train to come my way,
Lord, I can't hear no whistle blow,
Deep down in my heart, I can hear that lonesome freight train bell playin'.'

2. Lord, I been just sittin' here waitin', waitin' for that ole train to come by my way,
Well, you know I don't have a nickel, baby, I don't even have a lousy dime;
Well, when I first start to hoboin', Lord, I taken the freight train for my frien', (2)
Well, every time a freight train whistle blow, ooh, well Lord, it trouble my min'.

3. Well, I hear my train a-comin', baby, you know, you know that I can't be late.
Spoken: Now you know that I can't be late.
Go on an' blow that whistle, man.
Listen to it whippin' that rail.
All along the rail, she ballin' the jack too.

4. *Sung:* Mm, by, by, baby, I got to make that freight train, find me another land,
Because you know my train is runnin', baby, an' I just can't be left here no mo'.

Roosevelt Charles, vocal; Otis Webster, guitar; Angola, Nov. 19, 1960.

This expression of wanderlust to some extent draws on Lightnin' Hopkins, "Freight Train Blues," SIW 658, Houston, c. 1948, or a similar song. After a few spoken remarks, the Hopkins song begins with:

When I first start to hoboin', 'boin', 'boin', I taken a freight train to be my frien'.

For a recording of Charles's performance, see *Blues, Prayer, Work and Trouble Songs,* VRS 9136, 1964.

88. *Rollin' Stone*

1. My papa tole mama, before I was born,
You got a boy chile comin' be a rollin' stone,
Got a boy chile comin', be a rollin' stone. (2)

2. I was standin' in my window, lookin' down the railroad track,
Standin' in my window, lookin' down that lonesome railroad,
Here come a train along, a train comin' along, puffin' along,
I'm gonna ask trainman, see would he take me along.

3. Out on the highway, gonna thumb me a ride,
Out on the highway, out on the highway, try to thumb me
— — — — —,
Seem like everybody tryin' to pass me by.

4. Let me tell you, mama, the reason why I lef' home, (2)
My daddy (went) from the South, oh Lord, before I was born.

5. I'm goin', goin', mama, perhaps oh for half the worl'.

Robert Pete Williams, vocal and guitar; Baton Rouge, Nov. 11, 1960.

The opening stanza resembles the beginning lines of Muddy Waters, "Rollin' Stone," Chess, c. 1948.

For a recording of Williams' performance, see *Free Again*, PrB 1026, 1960.

89. *Long about Midnight*

1. Well, long about midnight, baby, you rollin' along from town to town,
Lord, you haven't got a friend, you just rollin' long from town to town.
When I was makin' lot's o' money, I had friends from miles and miles aroun',
But now all my hard-earned money is gone,
I haven't got a friend to be foun',
I made up my mind, baby, if you want somebody else,
Go on, may God bless you, an' have fun.

2. Oh, I'm lonesome, baby, you'll see what a fool you been.
Lord, when my poor ole mother were livin', I could take this world at ease,
Oh, when my poor ole mother were livin', I could this world at ease,
But now she is dead an' gone, freight train are my only home. (2)

Roosevelt Charles, vocal; Otis Webster, guitar; Angola, Nov. 19, 1961.

"Long about Midnight" combines several basic blues themes, the self-pity of the wanderer because of his loneliness, his friends desertion of him when his money is gone, the special isolation of not having a mother to turn to, and less common, resigned acceptance of his woman's preferring someone else.

90. *Hobo Worried Blues*

1. I got all my frien's sittin' roun' me, watchin' me play these
   lonesome blues, (2)
   If you know just how sorry I was in my heart, darlin', they
   sure would try to give me some ease.

2. Lord, I'm sittin' here an' moanin', I don't know what in the
   world to do sometime', (2)
   Sometime' I feel like packin' my suitcase, woman, an' leavin'
   this ole lonesome place.

3. I fell down on my knees, sent the good Lord up a prayer,
   I fell down on my knees, darlin' sent the good Lord up a prayer,
   I feel so worried sometime', darlin', I believe that he'll answer
   my prayer.

4. Me an' my frien's all sittin' aroun', they can't help me an'
   I can't help them, (2)
   We all broken down, like a hobo out on the road.

*Robert Pete Williams, vocal and guitar; Baton Rouge, Sept.
30, 1960.*

For a recording of Williams' performance, see *Free Again*,
PrB 1026, 1960.

91. *Long Way from Home*

Spoken: Well, I'm jus' a pore boy here,
Long ways from home,
I got mother 'n sisters 'n brothers,
I been away too long.
I believe I go back,
See how they all get along;
I got a mistreatin' woman here,
Boy, she always doin' me wrong.
That's all right, people,
I ain't gonna worry no mo'.
I got a mother, an' I got a father;
However, if I don't see my people,
If I don't get back no mo',
Yeah, I sit here wonderin',
Wonderin' all to myself,
How that woman mistreat me, woman,
An' she got somebody else.
Back down in the town,
The times sho' is hard,
Sittin' aroun' with nothin' to do,
I'm thinkin' about my people,
Lord, I don't know what to do.
I'm goin' home, won't be lonesome no mo',
Wanta see my mother, father, sisters, brothers,
That's the place I wanta go.

Smoky Babe (Robert Brown), vocal and guitar; Scotlandville, Feb. 10, 1959.

Although this is an original talking blues, it falls into a well established tradition of the wanderer's song of self-pity, about which Odum and Johnson (*The Negro and His Songs*, pp. 168-169) have written:

Perhaps no person is sung more among the Negroes than the homeless and friendless wanderer, with his disappointments in love and adventure. In no phases of Negro life do self-feeling and self-pity manifest themselves more than in the plaintive appeals of the wanderer. With his characteristic manner, he appeals to both whites and blacks for sympathy and assistance. He especially appeals to his women friends, and thus moves them to pity him. His pleas for their sympathy are usually effective; and the Negro thus gets shelter, food, and attention.

While such songs are now sung much less frequently than in 1925 when Odum and Johnson made these remarks, the tradition is still active.

For a recording of Smoky Babe's performance, see *Hottest Brand Goin'* PrB 1063, 1961.

92. *I'm Goin' Back to Mississippi*

1. Well, I'm goin' back to Mississippi, baby, I ain't doin' no
   good here,
I'm goin' back to Mississippi, baby, I ain't doin' no good here,
Well, I don't feel lucky, because my home ain't here.

2. Sometime' I's treated right, an' others I'm treated wrong,
I'm in Louisiana, but Mississippi is my home,
Well, I'm goin' to go back to Mississippi, well, that's where
   I want to be.

3. Well, I'm goin' back there, baby, don't you wanta see,
Well, I'm down in Mississippi, doin' as I please,
I either work, or don't, I have to leave,
Goin' back to Mississippi, Louisiana not my home;
Well, I'm goin' back there, goin' back to my only home.

4. Well, my boss not mean, my baby's not deaf,
Looka here, peoples, but I'm here, I'm goin' back to Mississippi,
   that's where I want to be,
Well now, jus' my home, jus' where I wants to be.

5. Well now, work ain't hard, boss not mean,
Looka here, baby, you one I never seen,
Oh hey, goin' back home, Mississippi that's my home,
Spoken: Play it one time, Robert Brown.

   *Smoky Babe (Robert Brown), vocal and guitar; Scotlandville,
Feb. 10, 1959.*

   Although Smoky sings frequently of his home in Mississippi,
he seldom returns and then only for brief visits.
   For a recording of this performance, see *Hottest Brand Goin'*,
PrB 1063, 1961.

93. *S. P. Train*

Say, I'm about sick o' this plantation, an' I'm gonna leave way from here, 'cause Mr. Charles promise me that he gonna give me a dollar a day an' dinner, an' on Saturday I be off, an' now he's tryin' to change it; he's workin' me on a Saturday evenin' an' then sometime' on Sunday. 'Cause I be high sometime' on Sunday mornin', I don't feel like gettin' up, an' I know what I gonna do, 'cause he got a bull dog an' a cowhide, so best thing for me to do is catch the S.P. when she comes along.

—Willie B. Thomas

1. Don't you see that train comin' down the railroad track, (2)
An' the smoke is rollin', rollin' down from that ole smoke stack.

2. *Spoken:* I think I hear her comin' now.
I say I can't hear the bell ringin',
But I can tell that train from the Saint James,
From that steamboat, when she comes round the curve,
I can see her smoke stack, an' I know, now she blow that whistle,
I know the sound of her whistle.

3. *Sung:* If I had listen' to my gal Liza Jane,
If I had listen' to my black gal, Liza Jane,
I wouldn't a-been in Angola with a ball an' chain.

4. I hate to see that evenin' sun go down, (2)
But it make me believe that I'm on my last go roun'.

Willie B. Thomas, vocal and 5-string banjo; Baton Rouge, July 15, 1961.

The 5-string banjo has been obsolete in folk Negro circles in the South for a couple of generations, although Willie used to play the 4-string banjo. The instrument he played in this song is one I gave him as a gift. So far he uses the same frailing technique as he does on the guitar.

The incident he described in the introduction and in the song did not happen to him, but was typical of the experience of people he knew. The same kind of complaint about working more than the promised five and a half days occurs in Otis Webster's "I Want to Tell You, Bossman," No. 28.

94. *The Bachelor's Blues*

See, I lives alone, an' I'm quite experienced in the bachelor's life, but the on'iest way he can make it, is to make it like a romantic man. He got to hold up his head.

—*Herman E. Johnson*

1. I'm not gonna marry, neither settle down,
Just ride from town to town, from town to town,
I believe I will ride from town to town. (2)

2. I got a woman in Tennessee, don't seem to care for me,
She don't care for me,
I'm talkin' about that chick in Tennessee,
But that old fool just won't care for me.

3. Prettiest woman that I have ever seen,
Was in the city of New Orlean',
She's in New Orlean', an' she said her name was Josephine,
And she lived in the city of — — — — — —.

4. I love to see the young folks run,
See them dance an' have their fun,
Now come on young folks, you can have your fun. (2)

5. See that chick with those dark shades on?
She can dance just as sure as you're born,
Just as sure as you're born.
I'm talkin' about the chick with those dark shades on,
An' she's tailor-made, just as sure as you're born,
An' she's tailor-made, just as sure as — — — — — — — —.

6. Says she like the way I sing,
An' the way I picks that thing,
Way I picks that thing,
Come on, Mr. Johnson, an' pick that thing,
Come on, Mr. Johnson, an' — — — — — — — — — — — — — — — —.

7. Don't drive me away from here,
Until I drinks this beer, (2)
Just as soon as I finish,
I'll be movin' on;
Just as soon as I finish,
I'll be movin' on.

8. Go ahead, go ahead, go ahead, go ahead, (2)
Now go, an' go ahead, go ahead, go ahead,
Now go ahead, go ahead.

9. Let's go, that's for sho'.
When I leave you this time, I won't be back no mo',
Because you mistreated me, an' you drove me from your do'.

10. Now, go ahead, go ahead, go ahead. (2)

Herman E. Johnson, vocal and guitar; Baton Rouge, May 10, 1961.

Herman got the idea for the framework of this song while watching students dancing to a jukebox in the Union lounge at Southern University in Scotlandville, where he works as a janitor. He says:

At Southern in the Union living room, those children dance. An' I notice Ray Charles got a piece. I copied the tone after Ray, course I made the words. The kids never stop; they just dance an' dance in that hit, "Tell 'em What I Say."

95. *Bugle Call Blues*

1. Got a min' to ramble, got a min' to head for town,
Got a min' to ramble, I won't settle down.

2. Oh, 'scuse me for knockin' on yo' do',
Now, 'scuse me for knockin' on yo' do',
If my min' don't change, I won't knock there no mo'.

3. Now when you left Felicia, there's somethin' goin' on
   wrong, (2)
Now, baby, I believe you ain't gonna be along.

4. Oh, brown, wonder what's the matter now, (2)
You always tryin' to leave me, an' you don't know how.

5. I woke up this mornin', 'tween night an' day, (2)
Put my hand on the pillow, where the brownie used to lay.

6. Well, I'm goin' to the river, gonna take me a rope an' a rock,
If the blues overtake me, gonna jump right over the top.

7. Oh, 'scuse me for knockin' on yo' do', (2)
If my min' don't change, I'll never knock there no mo'.

Butch (James) Cage, vocal and fiddle; Willie B. Thomas, vocal and guitar; Zachary, Oct. 4, 1960.

The fiddle in its breaks imitates a bugle call. The stanzas are all standard, more or less spontaneously strung together during the singing.

96. *Rock Island Blues*

1. Oh, Rock Island, oh, Rock Island train, (2)
Got a gal in town, but I'm scared to call her name.

2. When you see me comin', put your man outdoor', (2)
When you see me comin', baby, put your man outdoor'.

3. Hey, Rock Island, oh, Rock Island train, (2)
Got a gal in town, but I'm scared to call her name.

4. I had a little girl, used to treat me nice an' kin',
Oh, I had a little girl, used to treat me nice an' kin',
But now thata woman keep me worried all the time.

5. I ain't gonna tell you what the Dago tol' the Jew, (2)
Don't like me, baby, be sure don't like you.

Charles Henderson, vocal and guitar; Butch (James) Cage, fiddle; Zachary, Feb. 5, 1961.

The same basic tune occurs in Leroy Ervin, "Rock Island Blues," Gold Star 628, c. 1947. The opening lines dealing with the Rock Island constitute the only similarity in text. The same thought as in Henderson's last stanza occurs in Little Brother Montgomery, "Chinese Man Blues," Bb 6658, New Orleans, Oct. 16, 1936, with the difference that the remark is about "Chinese man," rather than about a "Dago." In Huddie Ledbetter, "Honey, I'm All Out and Down," Mlt 13326, New York City, Jan. 23, 1935, there are lines which pair a "Dago" and a "Jew" as Henderson does.

97. *Hobo Blues*

Spoken: Hey, Mr. Conductor, hol' that train, let me get on board.

1. *Sung:* I hear the train whistle blowin', baby, Lord, she comin' on down the line,
I hear a train whistle blowin', an' she comin' on down the line,
Baby, an' I feel mistreated, baby, an' I'm sure gonna ride the blin'.

2. I'm goin' to the station, I'm gonna look up on the sign,
You know I'm goin' to the depot, an' I'm gonna look up on the sign,
You know I'm got to special deliver, an' I'm sure gonna leave yo' town.

3. It wasn't but one thing, baby, that worried my troublin' min',
Yes, wasn't but one thing, that worried my troublin' min', mama, Lord,
You know the woman all was crazy 'bout me, baby, Lord, but the men didn't want me 'roun'.

4. I say my heart struck sorrow, baby, Lord, tears rollin' down,
(2)
Well, I never miss my companion, Lord, until she said goodby.

5. Now, she's little an' low, weighs only ninety-four poun's,
Yes, she's little an' low, weighs only ninety-four poun's,
Boy, you know she tailor-made, an' she right down on the groun'.

6. I ain't no race horse, an' baby, I ain't built for speed,
Ain't no race horse, an' baby, I ain't built for speed,
Well, I'm just a common ole guy, baby, got everything I need.

Guitar (Robert) Welch, vocal and guitar; Angola, March 27, 1959.

A stanza like the fifth one occurs in Jimmy Rushing, "Evil Blues," De 2922, BrE 02894, New York, Feb. 2, 1939:

> She's little an' low, she's built up from the ground,
> She's little an' low, an' built up from the ground,
> But that's my baby, she makes my love come down.

SETTIN' OUT ON THE HIGHWAY
ATLANTA, GEORGIA, TO THE GULF OF MEXICO

98. *Thumbin' a Ride*

1. Settin' out on the highway, tryin' to thumb myself a ride,
Settin' out on the highway, babe, tryin' to thumb myself a ride,
An' it seem like to me, darlin', everybody try to pass me by.

2. I'm gonna buy myself a automobile,
I'm gonna buy myself a automobile, darlin',
I'm gonna stop walkin', woman, everywhere that I go.

3. What I got on my min', is to buy me a Fairlane,
What I got on my min', babe, is to buy me a bran' new Fairlane,
I'm gonna let you be my chauffeur, baby, ain't gonna pick
    nobody up on the highway.

4. I gotta plenty money to do anythin' that I want to do,
I gotta plenty money, darlin' to do anythin' that I want to do,
I sit here now, wishin' an' worried, wishin' for everythin.'

5. Make yo' bed up, rider, an' turn yo' lamp way low,
Make yo' bed up, baby, an turn yo' lamp way low,
I'm gonna satisfy you, mama, Lord, if it's all night long.

Robert Pete Williams, vocal and guitar; Baton Rouge, Oct. 16, 1960.

It is significant to note the logic of free association which links the verses of "Thumbing a Ride." He begins with the depression of a hitch-hiker, discouraged because everyone races by. This idea leads to a wish that he had a car of his own, followed by daydreaming of having a chauffeur, plenty of money, and finally a woman to sleep with. The line "I'm gonna let you be my chauffeur" and the Ford car are probably echoes of Memphis Minnie, "Me and My Chauffeur Blues," OK 06288, Chicago, May, 1941, in which driving is used as a *double entendre* for fornication. Robert Pete's final lines continue the sexual theme with an assertion of virility.

For a recording of Williams' performance, see *Free Again,* PrB 1026, 1960.

99. *Car Trouble Blues*

1. *Spoken:* Well now, look here, people, me an' my boss was together,
We's leavin' our Louisiana town, headin' for Mississippi;
Well, we hit this ole road, they call the Highway 61,
Come from out Vicksburg,
You know, Vicksburg on a high hill, Louisiana down below;
Well, we was tryin' to make it on to Mississippi,
Travellin' that road all alone, just me an' him,
An' so I was glad I was there along with him.

2. *Sung:* I was glad I was with him, trouble we had on the way,
Well, his automobile got broke, we had to find some place to stay.

3. *Spoken:* Well, we jumped out at a place called Itta Bena, Itta Bena, Mississippi,
Got a crossroad headin' back to here, I mean, you know what I'm talkin' about,
Goin' on to Clarksdale, an' all of them towns through here.

4. We could hardly find the parts, we finally got 'em,
Got everything fixed, but I'm tellin' you we was in a trix,
Special order wasn't no word.

5. Then we started travellin',
Sung: Highway 82, we was Chicago boun',
Highway 82, we was headed for Clarksdale boun',
Well, a good thing about it, we was in this ole Mississippi town.

6. There was one thing about it, we come on to my mother's house,
An' I'm right here now, an' I'm feelin' all right, feelin' fine,
I'm not all alone, thanks the Lord that she here,
Sittin' here, lookin' at her, talkin' with her, jus' enjoyin' myself,
Me an' my boss, my bossman, Lord, have mercy, done made everythin' all right.

Smoky Babe (Robert Brown), vocal and guitar; Vance, Mississippi, August 11, 1961.

In the summer of 1961 I decided to drive North, and since Smoky Babe was out of work at the time, I offered to pay him to come along with me as far as his mother's place in Vance, Mississippi, about forty miles from Clarksdale, some four hundred miles north of Baton Rouge, my home base. He had told me many times about what an excellent guitar player his mother was, better, he said, than he was himself—a description which sharply whetted my appetite to hear and record her since Smoky is such an exciting performer.

He was delighted at the suggestion so off we went in my 1955 De Soto, zooming at eighty miles an hour on the narrow but fast two lane highways. We stopped over in Vicksburg. In later making up the song, Smoky naturally thought of the most familiar blues about the city, and as a result, the fifth line comes from Little Brother (Eurreal Montgomery), "Vicksburg Blues," Para 13006, Cen 4011, JC L-44, Grafton, Wisc., Sept. 1930.

The fuel line sprang a leak near, by a curious coincidence, Itta Bena, the town where Smoky was born. I stayed with the car while he hitched a ride to Clarksdale with a Negro preacher and his family. Within a couple of hours he was back with a new fuel line; he got it installed in a matter of minutes. When there was difficulty getting the gas flowing into the carburetor he resorted to a "shade-tree" mechanic's trick; he sucked some gas through the fuel line into his mouth and spit it into the carburetor. The system worked beautifully.

Another twenty miles further the generator belt broke and we had to drive about eighty miles off the route to find the right size.

At any rate at nightfall we reached the country shack of Annie Brown. Though her place is fundamentally a typical rickety unpainted little building with sheets from Sunday rotogravure newspaper magazines stuck on the walls for decoration and for protection against the elements, she had beautiful vines growing profusely over the cottage and a garden rich with flowers and vegetables surrounding it.

Smoky's mother is relatively genteel and polished compared to her son. She speaks with clear diction, whereas Smoky has the blurred mumbling speech of the more illiterate country Negroes. She grew up in a white household of people of British descent, working for them as a maid and playing with their children. Her favorite songs are ones she learned from the young ladies of the household—southern mountain and Anglo-Saxon songs like "Billie Boy" and "A Paper of Pins." Significantly, she lacks the feeling for rhythm which most Negro women of her age have in the South. I suspect that growing up in a white environment during her formative years, she never absorbed the musical sensitivity and feeling for syncopated phrasing such as her son has. (Another possible explanation is of course that she inherited little musical talent.) Unfortunately, I never did get the opportunity to evaluate her guitar playing since, crippled with arthritis, she had stopped playing a couple of years before.

The "Car Trouble Blues" Smoky improvised for the crowd of friends and relatives lacks the concreteness and colorfulness of imagery the better Negro folk creations have, but the vigor of his performance and his brilliant guitar playing made up for the limitations of the text.

100. *Back Home Again*

1. Well, I'm so glad t'be back with my frien's again, (2)
Well, I'm crazy about it, gonna see all my frien's.

2. I'm in Vance, Mississippi, you knows about that stuff,
In Vance, Mississippi, in my mother' home, an' you knows about
    that stuff,
I'm with my other frien's, an' you know that's good enough.

3. I wants to give 'em one nice time, 'cause I been gone a
    day too long,
Wanta give 'em one nice time, baby, 'cause you know,
Well, they's my frien's, I'm glad they walk on in, they walked
    on in my home.
Spoken: Play it one time now, Robert Brown.

4. *Sung:* They is my frien's, I know they mines too,
Well, they is my frien's, I know they my frien's too,
I just think about them things we use' to do.

5. Oh yeah, oh yeah, oh yeah, oh yeah, I know they my frien's,
An' I wants them to know that they's my frien's too.

*Smoky Babe (Robert Brown), vocal and guitar; Vance, Mis-
sissippi, August 11, 1961.*

When the word got around the shacks in the farm country
where Smoky's mother lives that he was back in town, a crowd
of old friends and relatives assembled inside, his older sister,
Mary Sassafras, who had taken care of the children while their
mother was working, a couple of nieces, various people he had
knocked around with. Smoky sang them this song of welcome.

101. *Friends, Goodby*

1. I say, I met my frien's, gonna tell 'em all goodby,
I met my frien's, gonna tell 'em now all goodby;
Robert Brown been here an' gone away.

2. Won't be back now for, now for a while,
I hope now, baby, don't be now too long,
Well, I hope, I hope now, baby, that you don't be too long,
I'm goin' back to Louisiana, but Mississippi, Mississippi, Mississippi is my home, home, home.

3. Well, you know my people, this is my home state,
This is my home, I go down to Louisiana to play,
Say now, frien's goodby, yes I got to go,
I say, me an' my bossman gonna hit that same ole lonesome road.

4. Well, by by, by by, by by, yes, by, people, know well I'm not just gonna stay,
It ain't gonna be no long time, I soon, soon be back in some ole day.

Smoky Babe (Robert Brown), vocal and guitar; Vance, Mississippi, August 11, 1961.

Late in the evening after delighting his friends with his swingy guitar playing, he made his farewells appropriately in an improvised blues.

102. *61 Highway*

1. Yes, 61 Highway, longes' road I know,
61 Highway, longes' road I know,
I say it run from Atlanta, Georgia to the Gulf o' Mexico.

2. Hey, when you see me comin', put yo' black dress on,
Lord, when you see me comin', put yo' black dress on,
I swear the graveyard gonna be yo' restin' place, an' hell gonna
be yo' home.

3. I ain't never love' but four womens in my life,
I swear I ain't never love' but four womens in my life,
That was my mother an' sister, Lord, my sweetheart, an' my
wife.

*Charles Henderson, vocal and guitar; Butch (James) Cage,
fiddle; Zachary, March 15, 1961.*

The first stanza Henderson sings occurs toward the end of
Will Batts, "Highway No. 61 Blues," Vo 02531, Aug. 3, 1933.

103. *I Went Down 61 Highway*

1. I went down 61 Highway, I went down in my V-8 Ford, (2)
Lord, it rainin' an' stormin', I couldn't hardly see the road.

2. It was rainin' an' stormin', an' the cloud was dark at night,
   (2)
I could hardly control my Ford, I couldn't make things just
right.

3. That 61 Highway, man, I rode it all up an' down,
Say now, 61 Highway, yes, I rode it all up an' down,
Say, I was lookin' for my baby, oh, but she have put me down.

*Smoky Babe (Robert Brown), vocal and guitar; Scotlandville,
April 18, 1961.*

104. *Key to the Highway*

1. My mama, key to the highway, Lord, baby, I'm got to go,
I'm gonna leave her runnin', walkin' too slow.

2. Give me one kiss, oh mama, woman just before I go,
I'm gotta key to the highway, woman, now feel I got to go.

3. I'm gotta key to the highway, woman, Lord, well, I'm got to
go,
I'm gonna leave here runnin', walkin' mos' too slow.

4. When the moons jumps on the mountain, Lord, I'm gonna
be on my way,
I'm gonna be on this ole highway, until ole dollar a day.

5. I'm gonna leave here now runnin', woman walkin' mos' too
slow,
But I've got the key to the highway, an' I feel I got to go.

Leon Strickland, vocal and guitar; Killona, Nov. 27, 1961.

Big Bill Broonzy made up "Key to the Highway," but it was
first recorded by William "Jazz" Gillum, Bb 8529, 1940, recorded by the author, OK 06242, Cq 9929, May 2, 1941. Leon's
performance makes use of one stanza from the original, which he
repeats several times. The fourth stanza is a much more imaginative folk variant of the original lines:

When the moon creeps over the mountain, honey, I'll be on
my way, (2)
Honey, I'm gonna walk this highway until the break of day.

Leon Strickland's song is a folk variant of "Key to the Highway," words and music by Big Bill Broonzy and Chas. Segar,
© Copyright MCMXLI, MCMLXII by Duchess Music Corporation, New York, N. Y. Used by permission. All rights reserved.

105. *California Blues*

1. I was standin' in my back do', lookin' way over in the east,
Lord, I was standin' in my back do', lookin' way over in the east,
Lord, my min' was in California, an' I was standin' here on the beach.

2. Lord, if I was just where my min', Lord, I wonder would things be any better with me,
Oh Lord, if I just was where my min', baby, I wonder would things be any better with me;
Oh Lord, one day, baby, I be right where my min' was today,
Oh Lord, oh Lord, I be where my min' was one day.

3. Lord, I got a little ole woman, right where my min' was today,
Well, I got a little ole woman, right where my min' was today,
One day, one day, darlin', I be right by yo' side.

4. Oh Lord, tell me, baby, why don't you want me some time,
Oh, tell me, baby, why don't you want me some time,
Well, you know I get lonesome, darlin', oh Lord, by bein' all alone.

5. Well, I'm down an' worried, by worryin' with this time, (2)
But one day, darlin', I won't have time to worry 'bout.

6. Goodby, baby, be a good gal whiles that I'm gone,
Goodby, baby, I want you to be a good gal while poor Bob is gone,
Well, I'm goin' away to leave you, darlin', an' I won't be gone to stay alway'.

7. This is my telephone number, you can call whiles that I'm gone,
Mm, mm, mm———————————————.

Robert Pete Williams, vocal and guitar; Baton Rouge, June 30, 1962.

During World War II defense industry in California drew a large influx of Negroes from the South. Brooding over his "time," that is that he has seven years of parole left, during which he cannot leave the state of Louisiana, Robert Pete wonders whether his lot would be any better in California.

106. *New Orleans Blues*

1. Been aroun' the world, there's lots of things I've seen, (2)
Purtiest gal, down in New Orleans.

2. Well, you ever was down on St. Peter Street,
You ever was down on St. Peter Street?
Got the purtiest little gal that I have ever seen.

3. I met a purty gal, asked what might be her name, (2)
She was really purty, an' they call her Susie Ann.

4. An she asked me what might be my name, (2)
Tole her call me Papa Lemon, that's a famous name.

5. I been roun' the world, lots of things I seen,
I been roun' the world, there's lots of things I seen,
But the purtiest little gal was down in New Orleans.

Lemon Nash, vocal and ukelele; New Orleans, Oct. 15, 1959.

An original song.

107. *Chicagobound*

1. Yes, I know I been talked about, peoples everybody knowed
   it in town,
I know I have been talked about, everybody knowed it in town,
Said my home in Mississippi, but you know I'm Chicagoboun'.

2. Well, I'm goin' to see my baby, people she done moved all
   up there, (2)
I say I'm gonna work hard, I'm gonna try to get my fare.

3. I'm gonna leave town, everybody know it all aroun', (2)
I say I just wanta fin' my woman, I'm gonna be Chicagoboun'.

4. *Spoken:* Yeah, I got to leave, my baby gone,
What do I wanta hang aroun' here about?

5. Now you know I been talked about, yeah, everybody know
   it in town,
No sooner do I get my fare, you know I sho' Chicagoboun'.

*Smoky Babe (Robert Brown), vocal and guitar; Scotlandville,
Feb. 10, 1961.*

108A. *Baby, Don't You Want to Go*

1. You can steal my hen, sho' can't make her lay,
You can steal my good woman, sho' can't make her stay,
Come on, baby, don't you want to go,
Back to my ole city, sweet home, Chicago.

2. Well, I love you, you know, pretty baby, you have done me
   wrong,
Looka here now, little girl, want you to come back home,
Cryin', oh, come on baby, don't you want to go,
Back to my ole city, sweet home, Chicago.

3. Well, I know one 'n' one is one,
Two an' two is three,
Looka here now, pretty mama, change now,
Cryin' hey honey, don't you want to go,
Back to the ole city, mama, sweet home.
Spoken (to the guitar): Tell the truth.

4. *Sung:* Well, I'm goin' away to leave you, ain't gonna say
   goodby,
Won't be long, I'm goin', don't hang yo' head an' cry,
Cryin', oh baby, don't you want to go,
Back to that ole porch you left, sweet mama, sweet home.

   *Smoky Babe (Robert Brown), vocal and guitar; Scotlandville,
Feb. 10, 1960.*

108B. *Sweet Home Chicago*

1. Come on, baby, don't you wanta go, (2)
To the same ole place, sweet home, Chicago.

2. One an' one is two, two an' two is fou',
Come on, baby, baby, don't you want to go,
One an' one is two, two an' two is fou',
Come on, baby, baby, don't you want to go,
To the same ole place, sweet home, Chicago.

3. My baby tole me, "Where you goin'?"
I say, "People, goin' about my business."
Come on, baby, don't you want to go,
To the same ole place, home, Chicago.

4. No, I tole her, "I ain't goin' nowhere wi' you,
You can go by yourself."

Clyde Causey, vocal and harmonica; Scotlandville, March 15, 1961.

Both "Baby, Don't You Want to Go?" and "Sweet Home Chicago" are ultimately derived from Robert Johnson, "Sweet Home Chicago," Vo 03601, San Antonio, Nov. 23, 1936.

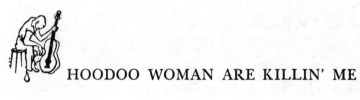# HOODOO WOMAN ARE KILLIN' ME

109. *Black Cat Bone*

1. I'm gonna buy me a Black Cat Bone, (2)
Remember 'bout me, woman they tell me this all right.

2. Well, I had, well, I had me a black cat one time,
Let me tell what I had, I had me a black cat one time,
Well, I taught that cat, an' I found him in bed in my – – – –.

3. People always taught me about a black cat,
You can go play safe an' leave those cats.

4. Well, I go any place I want, any place I want to, darlin',
You know that I can disappear,
I can walk in places people can't see me move.

5. I wanta tell you, I wanta tell you, baby, what yo' black cat
foun', oh Lord,
Don't you want no runnin' water at all,
Yo' black cat guess that?

Robert Pete Williams, vocal and guitar; Butch (James) Cage, fiddle; Zachary, June 12, 1961.

The Black Cat Bone is prized as a powerful talisman for control of wayward lovers. Its rarity and value are enhanced by the elaborate ritual of preparation. Zora Neale Hurston, who attended such a ceremony, had to fast first for twenty-four hours with only a glass of wine at four-hour intervals for refreshment.

A black cat was captured in the dark after a heavy fall of rain—not an easy task in itself—and hastily taken deep into the woods where in a ring protected by nine horseshoes a new vessel on which the sun had not been permitted to shine was filled with water and brought to a boil. Into the water was thrown the cat, three times cursed as it screamed in agony. At midnight the remains of the cat was drawn from the boiling water and its bones passed through the mouth until one was found which tasted bitter—the Black Cat's Bone. The ceremony was attended by a state of tension and terror that she found almost indescribable, but in the morning she returned with the precious bone in her hand. (Oliver, p. 140.)

This charm is believed to have the power to bring back a love who ran off or to win the love of someone the holder desires, as for example in Blind Lemon Jefferson, "Broke and Hungry Blues," Para 12443, 1926:

> I believe my good gal has found my Black Cat's Bone, (2)
> I can leave Sunday mornin', Monday mornin' I'm sittin' back
> home.

In addition to power over women, Robert Pete Williams believes that a Bone can give the ability to make oneself invisible. Contact with running water, however, destroys such magic powers.

110. *Goin' Back to New Orleans*

1. Goin' back to New Orleans, get me a mojo hand, (2)
Well, I'll show all you women, how to treat your man.

2. Well, I'm gonna tell all you men, ain't gonna tell you nothin' else,
I'm gonna tell all you men, ain't gonna tell you nothin' else,
Well, you's a fool if you think you get her by yourself.

3. I don't eat me nothin', I don't drink no tea,
I don't eat me nothin', baby, I don't drink no tea,
Well, you know, little woman, you can't poison me.

4. Mam tole me, an' papa tole me too,
Mam tole me, papa tole me too,
Well, you better be careful, she's gonna kill you.

5. Well, my mojo played out, goin' back an try it again, (2)
Well, I don't want you, woman, you got too many men.

Otis Webster, vocal and guitar; Angola, Nov. 5, 1960.

An early blues with some similar stanzas is Little Hat Jones, "Two String Blues," OK 8712, San Antonio, June 15, 1929, which ends with the lines:

> Lord, I'm goin' to Louisiana, I'll get me a mojo hand,
> I say I'm goin' down to Louisiana, I'll get me a hoodoo hand,
> I'm gonna stop my woman, an' fix her so she can't have another man.

The traditional center of voodoo in the South is New Orleans, the logical place to buy a mojo hand, a magic talisman with African and Haitian antecedents. A mojo hand is assembled of personal fragments and bits of natural objects.

> Hair from the armpits or pubic region, finger-nail parings, pieces of skin are considered especially effective in love charms as too are fragments of underclothing, or menstrual cloth and other closely personal effects. Combined with parts of night creatures, bats or toads, and with ashes and feathers from sources selected for a symbolic significance relative to the pur-

pose for which they have been selected, they are tied into small "conjure-bags," or put into an innocuous-looking receptacle and either carried to exert their power upon the victim when contact is made with him, or buried beneath his doorstep, or hidden in his bed or hearth.   (Oliver, p. 140.)

111. *Black Cat Blues*

1. My mama, babe, an' my daddy too,
Oh, my mamma, Lord, my daddy too,
You got so many women, Lord, what's gonna come o' you.

2. I woke up this mornin' with the blues all roun' my do',
Woke up this mornin', blues all roun' my do',
My baby left me, she don't want me no mo'.

3. Lord, trouble, trouble, follow me all my day,
Oh Lord, it's trouble follow me all my day,
Lord, it seem like trouble gonna kill me dead.

4. Lord, my mama don't want me, my daddy even th'owed me
away, (2)
Oh, that's all right, you gonna need my help one day.

5. Lord, it must have been a black cat, sure done crossed my
trail, (2)
Lord, the reason I say it, I seen where he drug his tail.

*Hogman (Matthew) Maxey, vocal and guitar; Angola, March
21, 1959.*

112. *The Midnight Rambler*

1. Lord, I been mistreated so long, I don't know how to act
sometime',
I been mistreated so long, I don't know how to act sometime',
You midnight women don't know how to treat no man.

2. You been dealin' with the devil, you better leave that man
alone, (2)
You gonna wake up some mornin', you gonna find yo'self outdoor'.

3. Mama, mama, mama, please talk to yo' daughter fo' me,
Oh mama, mama, please talk to yo' daughter one time fo' me,
You don't love that woman, no, she don't pay pore Bob no min'.

4. I'm goin' to the hoodoo, I'm gonna put you under my feet,
(2)
I'm gonna have you, baby, do anythin' in the worl' I want you
to do.

*Robert Pete Williams, vocal and guitar; Scotlandville, Feb.
10, 1961.*

113. *Hoodoo Blues*

1. Oh, listen here, woman, know you can tell me no lie, (2)
Oh, darlin', the way you smell, darlin', I know you been with
the hoodoo, an' you can't see a — — — — —.

2. Now looka here, woman, I want you to tell the truth,
Darlin', tell me where you been,
You been outside in the alley, down in that hoodoo man's house.

3. Now, tell me, baby, if that what you done,
If I'd a-knowed it, I'd a-let you go;
I don't want no hoodoo woman foolin' roun' with me,
Oh, Lord knows I don't.

4. That's the reason you walkin' roun' here, smellin' so sweet,
I been askin' you what you had on yo' head,
You tole me you had Banberry (from) Walgreen drug store,
You had been to that hoodoo, oh woman, don't lie,
I know a hoodoo man fooled with you.

5. I want you to know, in the mornin' soon.
Pack yo' trunk, I want you to leave,
Don't stay long, I don't want no hoodoo woman, oh Lordy,
Oh, you know this hoodoo woman are killin' me.

6. Lord, I'm gonna give you why, don't fool with the hoodoo,
Already a gal is spotty not too far away,
Now I know she ain't leave, darlin', God knows she gone
walkin'.

*Robert Pete Williams, vocal and guitar; Butch (James) Cage,
fiddle; Zachary, June 12, 1961.*

DARK CLOUD RISIN'

114. *Lightnin' Blues*

Oh, thun-der an' light-nin', ba-by, oh, the wind
be-gin to blow, oh, thun-der light-
nin', ba-by oh, the wind be-gin
to blow,
Lord, I be-gin to won — der once in my life,
won-der would I have to go.

1. Oh, thunder an' lightnin', baby, oh, the wind begin to blow, (2)
Lord, I begin to wonder once in my life, wonder would I have to go.

2. Woke up this mornin', Lord, the wind howlin' roun' my do',
Lord, I didn't have no way, baby, didn't have nowhere to go.

3. Lord, it's somethin', somethin' on my min',
Somethin', oh Lord, is on my min',
Lord, I said here come a blue streak from the west, baby, an' mowed that pore boy down.

4. Oh, it must have been lightnin', don't nothin' else travel that fast,
Oh, Lord, it must have been lightnin', don't nothin' else travel that fast,
Oh, I thought every minute, oh Lord, it was gonna be my last.

5. Oh Lord, in the west thunderin' an' lightnin' every day, (2)
I, Lord, I done 'cide tomorrow to change my wicked way.

Hogman (Matthew) Maxey, vocal and guitar; Angola, Oct. 10, 1959.

When Hogman mentioned to me that he had been struck by lightning three weeks before and had somehow survived, I congratulated him on his toughness. "Can you sing a song about being hit by lightning?"

"Sho' can!" He grinned and immediately began to sing "Lightnin' Blues," improvising it as he went along.

When he had finished, Hogman and Roosevelt Charles started kidding about the incident. With Hogman strumming the guitar casually, their speech fell naturally into the semi-rhythmic pattern of a talking blues:

Charles: Say, man, what happen' to you Friday mornin'
When a dark cloud rose from the west?
Hogman: Well, man, I don't know, I'm just telling the truth.
Well, it felt more like a shock from a 'lectric wire than anythin'
    I ever got hold of.
Well, I tell you somethin' else that happen' to me the other day,
You know my buddy out there, some of us call him Shorty,
    you know,
He love to smoke a pipe, you know.

An' he had his cigarette lighter loaded up with gasolene,
An' had my back to him. It was dark in the place.
He haul off an' rip that thing, an' the fire flew out,
Knock down nine dogs before I could think straight to see what
   he done.
Thought it was another streak o' lightnin.'

115. *Where Were You When the Archeta River Went Down?*

That happened back in the year of 1937, during the high water. There was an ole boy, was standin' on the levee when the water was beginnin' to rise, an' the back water begin to run away. He had woman, she was down in the bottom, an' he was wonderin' whichaway did she go; did she go to a high hill, or was she down in the bottom below. Which he knowed, if she was in the bottom, the poor girl had to be drowned. But if she was up on the high hill, the little girl had to be saved, so the little boy begin to sing the blues, he got blue as a man can be, he begin to holler, an' he hollered out loud—

1. Well, tell me, baby. Woh, little girl, where were you when that old Archeta River went down?
Please tell me, baby, please tell me, little girl, where were you when that ol' Archeta River went down?
Was you up on that high hill, baby? Or was you in the valley below?

2. Now backwater has been dreadful, wonder where that little girl o' mine,
Backwater has been dreadful, wonder where that little girl o' mine,
Did the poor girl get drowned, or did the poor girl get saved?

3. I been aroun' the town, been all out through the hill,
I can't find my little woman, no matter where I go,
I ain't heard nobody tell me they seen any little girl call' Irene.
An' I wonder, did she get drowned, or did the poor girl get saved?

4. I been all aroun' in Texas, all down in Tennessee,
I been roun' in Texas, baby, been aroun' in Tennessee,
I can't find my baby, no matter where I go.

5. I'm gonna ring up St. Peter, man, gonna ring up old St. Paul,
If my baby ain't in heaven, she must be on this earth somewhere.

Roosevelt Charles, unaccompanied vocal; Baton Rouge, May 10, 1959.

116. *Mississippi Heavy Water Blues*

1. I was walkin' down the levee with my head hangin' low,
Live by my sweet mama, but she ain't here no mo',
Chorus: That's why I'm cryin', Mississippi heavy water blues.

2. I'm so blue, my house am washed away,
I'm cryin', "How long before another pay day?"
Chorus:

3. Lord, Lord, Lord, thought I heard a voice,
Say, little boy, put it to her an' run.
Chorus:

4. I'm so blue, house am washed away,
An' I'm cryin', "How long before another pay day?"

5. My gal in Mississippi, all in this mud an' water,
An' my gal in Louisiana with the high water blues.
Chorus:

6. Says I'm down low as a man can be,
I ain't got no body to feed 'n' care for me.
Chorus:

7. Says I'm worried as a man can be,
Feel just like I'm 'bout to lose my mind.
Chorus:

Robert Pete Williams, vocal and guitar; Guitar (Robert) Welch, guitar; Angola, March 21, 1959.

Derived from Barbecue Bob (Robert Hicks), "Mississippi Heavy Water Blues," Co 14222D, June 15, 1927. The third, sixth, and seventh stanzas of Robert Pete's variant are not in the original. In the fifth, Robert Hicks' line "with mud in my shoes" has become "all in this mud an' water."

Between April and June in 1927 the worst flood disaster on record along the Mississippi engulfed whole townships and drove people for shelter for the hills at Helena and Vicksburg. The homes of 750,000 people were flooded. (Oliver, pp. 235-237.)

117. *Hurricane Audrey Blues*

1. *Spoken:* People, this is mighty sad news, an' sad in min',
It might be sad roun' the town, mothers, sons, daughters,
When ole Cameron went down in a storm;
You know it was a dark cloud rose in Texas, an' a storm rose
   up from the Gulf,
An' the cloud rolled across the sky, an' the wind begin to blow.

2. *Sung:* You know it was a dark cloud risin', baby, risin' in the
west,
You know the storm rose up from the Gulf, baby, Lordy, rolled
   out 'cross the world.
Spoken: Lord, have mercy.

3. *Sung:* I was standin' in my cell. Ole cell begin to roll and
rock.

The wind was howlin' for miles around.
Lord, I wonder why do that storm rise thisdaway.
Spoken: Bad, man! It's bad!

4. *Sung:* You know it fell over Cameron, washed that poor
town away,
You know it was mothers, sons and daughters, Lord, didn't have
no place to stay,
You know that mothers, sons, and daughters, fathers, all outside.
Spoken (to guitar player): Come on, whip it out, boy.

5. *Sung:* Woh, the wind was howlin', man, yes the lightnin'
begin to flash,
Lord, the wind was howlin', man, yes, the lightnin' begin to flash,
Lord, the wind was howlin', yes, the lightnin' begin to flash,
Well, I fell down on my knees, I cried, "God help poor me."

*Roosevelt Charles, vocal; Otis Webster, guitar; Angola, Nov.
19, 1960.*

On June 27, 1957, Hurricane Audrey struck Cameron Parish,
an area on the Southwest coast of Louisiana extending from the
town of Cameron to Little Pecan Island. Most of the homes
were completely destroyed by nine to ten foot tidal waves and
gales up to 110 miles per hour; dead or missing were more
than five hundred inhabitants of southwest Louisiana.

Charles's blues is in a well established tradition of Negro
folksongs inspired by natural disasters, for example, Elzadie
Robinson's "St. Louis Cyclone Blues," Para 12573, Chicago, c.
Nov., 1927, describes such an event in similar terms.

BLACK, BROWN, AND YELLOW

118. *I Don't Want No Black Woman*

1. Woh, I don't want no black woman, babe, to bake no bread
   for me,
Lord, I don't want no black woman, yeah, to bake no bread for
   me,
Because black is evil, Lord, I'm 'fraid that she might poison me.

2. You walk in in the mornin', call that black gal by her name,
You hear her answer you, man, like she pullin' off a .45,
That's why I don't want no black woman, Lord, to bake no bread
   for me.

3. You catch a yellow gal, wake up smilin' in the mornin',
Call you sweet names at midnight,
Yellow woman she gonna call you daddy all day long,
But a black woman so evil,
She'll call you baby now, after a while she'll want to cut yo'
   throat.

4. She'll lay down with a butcher knife in her right hand, a
   razor in her left,
If you move in the bed, she be ready just to cut yo' throat,
That's why I don't want no black woman, hey, to bake no
   bread for me.

5. *Spoken:* Now looka here, my mother she tole me,
My father he tole me too,
Say, "Looka here, son,
Don't eat no black hen's eggs,
An' please don't drink no black cow's milk,
Because a black cow might eat some bitter weed,
That'll make her milk bitter,
An' a black hen, she may eat some strychnine,
That'll poison her egg',
That's to let you know, son.

5. *Sung:* That a black woman is so evil, Lord, to bake no bread
   for me.
Yellow woman is so nice an' kind."
Woh, I'm gonna love my yellow woman until the day I die.

Roosevelt Charles, vocal; Otis Webster, guitar; Angola, Nov. 19, 1960.

In April, 1956, when I paid a visit to Melrose Plantation, built in 1834, near Natchitoches, Louisiana, Francois Mignon (a native of France), the manager, showed me a little chapel he had fixed up for the few black Negroes in the area. The mulattoes, who form a unified community, he explained, refused to let the darker Negroes worship in the same church. To make the black Negroes more at home he had set up in the chapel an imposing statue of a black saint. He confided, "They would be shocked to learn that their saint had a white father."

Big Bill Broonzy has described a similar point of view within his own family in his grandmother's time. His grandmother's family "throwed her out when she married my grandfather, because he was real black. I remember when I was big enough I had to walk my grandmother to church and sit outside the gate and wait until the church meeting was over and take her home. The reason I had to sit outside was because they didn't allow black Negroes in their churches and schools." (Broonzy, p. 5.)

One of the earliest reflections in song of mulatto prejudice against blacks is quoted by Talley, pp. 10-11; the verses are at least one hundred years old:

Stand Back, Black Man

Oh!

> Stan' back, black man,
> You cain't shine;
> Yo' lips is too thick,
> An' you hain't my kin'.

Aw!

> Git away, black man,
> Git away, black man,
> You jes' hain't fine,
> I's done quit foolin'
> Wid de nappy-headed kin'.

Say?

> Stan' back, black man!
> Can't you see
> Dat a kinky-headed chap
> Hain't nothin' side o' me.

About these lines Talley wrote, "In a few places in the South, just following the Civil War, the Mulattoes organized themselves into a little guild known as "The Blue Vein Circle," from which those who were black were excluded. This is one of their rhymes." (Talley, p. 11.)

White quotes a number of songs collected before 1920 which express prejudice of Negroes against their race, p. 378, I; p. 379, 2; 3A, B; p. 381, 7. For a significant discussion of color distinctions in blues, the attitudes toward different shades of color, see Oliver, pp. 76-83. Broonzy, p. 111, quotes a stanza which is identical to the one sung by Charles on this subject.

An interesting example of self-hatred, a sociological phenomenon typical of many minority groups, occurs in Mary Johnson, "Black Gal Blues," De 7014, 1934, in which the singer thinks of getting a bull dog to protect her from the evil impulses she feels because she is black. See also, among numerous blues recordings expressing prejudice against those who are black, Texas Alexander, "Evil Woman Blues," OK 8688, New York City, June 17, 1927 (attacking brown and black, praising yellow); Barbecue Bob, "Chocolate to the Bone," Co 14331-D, April 13, 1928 (attacking black and yellow, praising brown).

In this collection a stanza like Charles's first occurs also in Otis Webster, "Woman Done Me In," No. 137, and in Leon Strickland, "How Long, Blues," No. 132.

119. *Please Give Me Black an' Brown*

1. Don't your kitchen feel lonesome when your biscuit-brown
   is not around', (2)
It makes you feel like leavin', leavin' this town.

2. 'Cause some crave for yellow, please give me black an' brown,
Some say some crave for yellow, please give me black an' brown,
Your black gal be wit' you, when your yellow gal turn you
   down.

3. Well, I knew she didn't love me when I first met her,
Well, I knew she didn't love me when I first knew her name,
She broke my heart, just for another man.

4. Now, I'm goin' away, I'm not comin' here no mo', (2)
'Cause the way she treat me, I'm boun' to lose my min'.

5. Come here, baby, give me your right hand,
I said come here, baby, give me your right hand,
I've got a bran' new woman, won't you please get you another
   man.

Lemon Nash, vocal and ukelele; New Orleans, Jan. 15, 1959.

The key stanza, the second, differs little from one in Trixie
Smith, "Trixie's Blues," Vo S217, BS 2039, Para 12161, New
York, 1921. See also Peetie Wheatstraw, "Give Me Black or
Brown," De 7391, Chicago, March 30, 1937. "Biscuit-brown"
has three meanings: cook, brownskin woman, and sexual partner.

WHEN I SAY "BOOGIE,"
EVERYBODY BOOGIE

120A. *Pine Top*

1. *Spoken:* Looka here, I want all you women to know this is
a Pine Top boogie woogie,
When I say, "Hold yourself," I want you to hold it, don't move
a pace,
Now boogie woogie. When I say, "Stop," you just stop.

2. Now when Leon says, "Jook," it means jook,
When I say "Boogie," I mean — — — —,
When I say, "Stop," I mean stop.
Don't zip or zat, that's what I'm talkin' about.
All right, boogie woogie now. Hold it, everybody.
Now boot that thing.

Leon Strickland, vocal and guitar; Killona, Nov. 27, 1959.

Almost every blues performer I have met knows a boogie
woogie based on "Pinetop's Boogie Woogie," the blues from
which boogie woogie takes its name. Pinetop was Clarence
Smith, a Negro from the South "who worked in the Black Belt
of Chicago. . . . In Pinetop's recording of his 'Boogie Woogie'
he gives a spoken commentary as he plays, 'Now listen here all
of you! This is my Pinetop Strut. I want everybody to dance
just like I tell you.' Then follow instructions to 'Hold y'self!'
'Git it!' 'Mess around!' " (Lang, p. 66), reminiscent of the
dance which went with the music of Benny French in Memphis.
The routine was already well established when French and
Pinetop took it over. Duke Ellington was present at such a
dance in 1913 in Washington at a rent party, then called a
hop or a *shout*. (Lang, p. 66.)

120B. *Boogie*

1. *Spoken:* Now looka here, boys, what I'm gonna say,
This ole guitar boogie,
An' when I say, "Boogie," I mean everybody boogie,

An' when I say, "Stop," I want everybody to stop.
Now listen, "Stop," now, "Boogie."

2. *Sung:* Looka here, sweet mama, what you done done,
Made me love you, baby, now your man done come,
Gonna leave, pretty mama, goin' on back to my home,
Takes a woman I'm love to ease my trouble' min'.

3. Nickel is a nickel, dime is a dime,
A man get tired o' one woman all the time,
Gonna leave, pretty mama, goin' back to New Orleans,
Takes a woman I'm lovin' to pacify my worried soul.

Guitar (Robert) Welch, vocal and guitar; Angola, March 21, 1959.

These two boogies are folk variants of 'Pinetop's Blues,' words and music by Pinetop Smith, © Copyright MCMXXIX by MCA Music, a division of MCA Inc., New York, © Copyright renewed MCMLVI and assigned to MCA Music, a division of MCA Inc., New York, N. Y. Used by permission, all rights reserved.

121. *Boogie*

1. Yeah, I got the blues, baby, feel like boogyin' all the time,
   (2)
I got a good-lookin' gal, but she don't pay me no min'.

2. Keep me worried, bothered all the time,
Keep me worried, worried, bothered all the time,
Baby, now she done gone evil, she don't pay me no min.'

3. Yes, I wonder, I wonder all to myself,
Yeah, I wonder, yes, I wonder all to myself,
I wish she was with me, when she's with somebody else.

4. I got the boogie blues, got 'em all in my shoes, (3)
Say but I'm blue, baby, it's you I hate to lose.

Smoky Babe (Robert Brown), vocal and guitar; Scotlandville, March 6, 1960.

In the early days of jook joints, the least pretentious Negro dives used one to three guitars for a dance.

> One guitar was enough for a dance. . . . To have two was considered excellent. Where two were playing, one man played the lead and the other seconded him. The first player was "picking" and the second was "framming," that is playing chords while the lead carried the melody by dexterous finger-work. Sometimes a third player was added, and he played a tom-tom effect on the low strings. (Zora Neale Hurston, quoted in Lang, pp. 63-64.)

Eventually in jook joints the piano supplanted the guitar, but the musical approach was taken from the guitar.

122. *Goin' Downtown Boogie*

1. *Spoken:* Yes, I talk to my baby last night,
Told her, "Let's go out a while,
'Stead of us settin' down here in most awful jive";
She says, "Look here, daddy,
I ain't dressed just right."
I says, "Look here, baby, put on what you got;
We gonna make everythin' all right.

'Cause I'll get my-self a drink,   have my-self a time,

Gon-na get my-self a drink   have my-self a time.

Just'n you 'n' I,   We gon-na have a good time,   We gon-na

be a while,   How you talk - in' to me, ba-by.   Oth-er night,

laid in my bed,   I tell   her,   "Lis-ten here,   Good thing

you have said.   You my   loved   one,   no   one   else but you."

"What cha mean, ho-ney?"   I don't mean no-bo-dy,   No-

bo-dy else but you."

2. *Sung:* 'Cause I'll get myself a drink, have myself a time,
Gonna get myself a drink have myself a time.

3. *Spoken:* Just'n you 'n' I,
We gonna have a good time,
We gonna be a while,
How you talkin' to me, baby."

4. Other night, laid in my bed,
I tell her, "Listen here,
Good thing you have said.
You my loved one,
No one else but you."
"Whatcha mean, honey?"
"I don't mean nobody,
Nobody else but you;
Go ahead on an' play it a while an' see."

5. "Look out, daddy, you also got the blues."
"No, honey, I ain't thinkin' of no one,
No one else, nobody but you.

6. Spent all my money, t'buy you nice fine clothes, (2)
Say, I don't want no other woman,
But you that I never know."

6. "That's all right, you don't want nobody but me,
Just have a nice time,
Settle down an' be ourself.
Yeah, yes, cool it, daddy,
All down an' burden'."

   *Smoky Babe (Robert Brown), vocal and guitar; Scotlandville,
Nov. 3, 1960.*

   For a recording of this performance, see *Country Negro Jam
Sessions* FL 111, 1960.

123. *Dirty Dozens*

1. Oh, you sister' fall in line, shake yo' shimmy like I shake mine,
Shake yo shimmy, shake it fas',
Can't shake yo' shimmy, shake yo' yass, yass, yass.

2. Dirty mistreater, robber an' a cheater,
Sister an' yo' dozens, mama an' yo' cousins,
Dozens an' dozens, Lawdy, mama,
Doin' the Lawdy Lawd.

3. Mama killed a rooster, thought it was a duck,
Brought him in the house with his legs stickin' up,
Sister come a-runnin', a-runnin' up fas',
Gonna get a nickel for my yass, yass, yass.

4. God made the elephant big an' stout,
He wasn't satisfied 'till he made him a snout,
Made him a snout, wasn't satisfied until he made him too high,
Made too high, overlook the grass, satisfied my yass, yass, yass.
Made him sick, an' made him well,
Ever since then been catchin' hell,

5. Repeat 1.

6. Take a walk, all you ladies bes' take a walk,
I'm gonna start my dirty talk,
I hate yo' mama an' yo' papa too,
You foun' out that yo' papa won't do,
I got yo' sister an' I took her quite a ways,
Got a movement like a Cadillac eight.

7. Repeat 1.

Butch (James) Cage, vocal and fiddle; Willie B. Thomas, vocal and guitar; Zachary, May 15, 1962.

of America, ©) Copyright MCMLXII by Music Corporation of America, 322 West 48th Street, New York, N. Y. 10036, used by permission, all rights reserved.

In the late nineteenth century the folk game of "Putting in the Dozens" or the "Dozens" developed. The name comes from "the dice throw of twelve, the worst in crap-shooting." (Oliver, p. 130.) A group of Negroes would get together and compete in how obscenely insulting they could get, trying to goad each other into a fury by references to bastardy, prostitution, incest, and homosexuality.

> If a particular person is the subject of enmity in a Negro folk community the offended man would 'put his foot up'— in other words jam the door of his cabin with his foot and sing a blues that 'put in the Dozens' at the expense of his enemy, 'calling him out of his name.' This was the 'Dozens' with a vengeful intent but often youths would 'play the Dozens' to work off their excesses of spirits in harmless and cheerfully pornographic blues singing competition. (Oliver, p. 28.)

Roger D. Abrahams, who has collected Negro folklore intensively in Philadelphia, reports that "Playing the Dozens" is most common among lower class Negro adolescents, for whom the game serves complex psychological functions. For many such youths, often raised only by a mother (casual alliances are common in lower class Negro groups), the process of assuming manhood and casting off the mother's control takes on special complications. The adolescent boy, writes Abrahams,

> must in some way exorcize her influence. He therefore creates a playground which enables him to attack some other person's mother, in full knowledge that that person must come back and insult his own. Thus someone else is doing the job for him, and between them they are castigating all that is feminine, frail, unmanly. (This is why the implications of homosexuality are also invoked.) But by such a ritualizing of the exorcism procedure, the combatants are also beginning to build their own image of sexual superiority, for these rhymes and taunts not only free otherwise repressed aggression against feminine values, but they also affirm their own masculine abilities. . . .
> But the dozens functions as more than simply a mutual exorcism society. It also serves to develop one of the devices by which the nascent man will have to defend himself—the verbal contest. Such a battle in reality is much more important

to the psychical growth of the Negro than the actual physical battle. In fact, almost all communication among his group is basically agonistic, from the fictive experience of the narratives to the ploying of the proverbs. Though the children have maneuvers which involve a kind of verbal strategy, it is the contest of the dozens which provides the Negro youth with his first opportunity to wave verbal battle. ("Playing the Dozens," *JAF*, LXV (1962), 214-215.)

Verses similar to those about the elephant in the Cage-Thomas variant are reported by White, p. 136, collected 1915-16, and by Perrow, p. 160, collected in 1913. The elephant stanza is an offshoot of the "Creation Song," found in most of the minstrel books from 1846 to 1861.

Some of the recorded variants are Speckled Red (Rufus Perryman), "The Dirty Dozens," Br 7116, Memphis, Sept. 14, 1929, which was so successful commercially that a host of imitations followed; Speckled Red, "Dirty Dozens No. 2," Br 7151, Chicago, April 8, 1930; Frankie "Half-Pint" Jaxon, "The Dirty Dozens," Vo 1478, Memphis, c. Jan. 1930, De 7304, Chicago, March 12, 1937; and a more sophisticated form, Sweet Pease Spivey, "The Double Dozens," De 7204 A, c. 1936.

ME AN' MY BUDDY
GOT A LIFETIME HERE

124. Joe Turner Blues

1. Joe Turner in this town,
Tell me Joe Turner in this town,
They tell me Joe Turner in this town.

2. Yes, they tell me Joe Turner in this town,
They tell me Joe Turner in this town. (2)

3. Tell all you women, turn all your dampers down, (2)
Because they tell me Joe Turner in this town.

4. I heard Joe Turner in this town,
They tell me Joe Turner in this town. (2)

5. We don't want no weak men hangin' roun', (2)
'Cause they tell me Joe Turner in this town.

6. They tell me Joe Turner in town,
Well, they tell me Joe Turner in this town. (2)

Willie B. Thomas, vocal and guitar; Butch (James) Cage, fiddle; Scotlandville, Oct. 4, 1960.

Willie says that this "is the oldest blues," an opinion which W. C. Handy shared: "The tune was widely known all over the South, was so known before there was a wide-spread singing of the folk-blues." He has also hypothesized that all early blues "may have been 'Joe Turner' sung to the best of the individual's memory (which might be bad) and to such words as came to his mind." According to Handy, Joe Turner was Joe Turney, the prison official who had the job from around 1892 to 1896 of taking Negro prisoners from Memphis to the penitentiary in Nashville and to "farms" along the Mississippi. The song developed out of a woman's lament, "Joe Turner got my man and gone." (Handy, *Blues: An Anthology*, pp. 40-41.)

Big Bill Broonzy sang a "Joe Turner Blues" in a talking blues form, which he first recorded as "Blues in 1890," VgF LDO 30, VgE V2074, Paris, Sept. 21, 1951, and later for Folkways, FA 2326, in *Big Bill Broonzy Sings Country Blues*, and for Verve, MG V 3000, *The Big Bill Broonzy Story*, July, 1957.

According to him, the tune was already being played by his uncle and a friend in 1890. In 1892 there was a terrible flood along the Mississippi delta, followed by a drought in 1893. The Negro farmers were left without food or clothing. A kindly white man who preferred to keep his generosity unknown, entrusted Joe, an old Negro employee, with the task of secretly leaving in the cabins of those who were destitute such basic necessities as flour, meat, molasses, coffee, sugar, oil for the lamps, clothing, shoes, and even beds. When the Negroes returned home from hunting and found these gifts, they would ask old Joe who their benefactor was, but he would evade them, "Oh well, it's Joe Turner who left it there." And he would start to humming this tune, *Tell Me Joe Turner Been Here and Gone*. And they would all sing it with him." This went on for about twenty years and only then, when the benevolent white man had died, did they learn who Joe Turner was. (Broonzy, pp. 27-33.)

Some of the texts of the other Joe Turner blues occur in Handy, *Blues: An Anthology*, p. 41, pp. 79-82; Odum and Johnson, *The Negro and His Songs*, p. 206; Scarborough, p. 265; Sandburg, p. 241.

The earliest recording of the tune was Wilbur Sweatman and His Jazz Band, "Joe Turner Blues," PA 20167, New York, c. April, 1917.

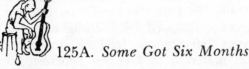

125A. *Some Got Six Months*

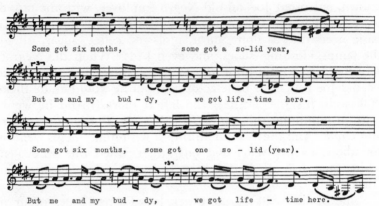

Some got six months, some got a so-lid year,

But me and my bud - dy, we got life - time here.

Some got six months, some got one so - lid (year).

But me and my bud - dy, we got life - time here.

1. Some got six months, some got a solid year,
But me and my buddy, we got lifetime here.
Some got six months, some got one solid (year).
But me and my buddy, we got lifetime here.

2. Six months, oh baby, let me go to bed,
I've drunk white lightnin',
Gone to my head, it gone to my head.

3. I've got so much time, darlin',
It worryin' me, oh babe,
You know this time killin',
But I just can't help it, darlin', I just got to roll.

4. You know that ole judge must been mad,
Yeah, that ole judge must been mad, darlin'.
When he gave me my sentence, he throwed the book at (me.)

5. First time in trouble, I done get no fair trial at all, oh Lord,
Seem like to me, baby, they locked the poor boy in jail.

*Robert Pete Williams, vocal and guitar; Angola, Feb. 12,
1959.*

125B. *Some Got Six Months*

1. Some got six months, some got a solid, some got a solid year,
Some got six months, some got a solid year,
Now me an' my buddy, we got a lifetime here.

2. The judge wrote it, as he wrote it, yeah he wrote it,
Judge he wrote it, judge he wrote it down,
Judge he wrote it, must be judgment boun'.

3. Make my supper in the evenin' early, let me go to bed, Lord,
Fix me supper, let me go to bed,
I've been drinkin' white lightnin', done gone to my head, Yeah.

Spoken: Yay now! Yeah!

4. *Sung:* Oh rider, judge as he wrote it down,
Oh rider, judge as he wrote it, as he wrote it down,
Oh that sinner, must be prisoner boun'.

5. He say, "I sent for you yesterday, but here you come today,
You got yo' mouth wide open, an' you ain't got a word to say."

Jimmy Cage, vocal and guitar; Butch (James) Cage, vocal and fiddle; Zachary, Oct. 4, 1960.

Odum and Johnson, *The Negro and His Songs*, p. 232 in "I Got Mine" include lines which resemble the opening of these two blues:

Some o' them got six months,
Some o' them paid their fine.
With balls and chains all 'round their legs, I got mine.

The same tune and two stanzas roughly similar to the first and second stanzas in the variant sung by Butch and Jimmy (Butch's nephew), occur in Gus Cannon, "Viola Lee Blues," Vic V-3852, Bb 5389, Memphis, Sept. 20, 1928. Jesse James, "Lonesome Day Blues," De 7213, VoE V1037, June 3, 1936, is similar only in that its last stanza is like the first in the two variants in this collection. The James recording has a chorus and it differs also in tune and style. A verse about drinking white lightning occurs in Bukka White, "Shake 'Em on Down," Vo 03711, 1937.

126. Penitentiary Blues

1. "You oughta been listenin'," I answer, "Ma'am."
I know no one to tell you, oh, down in Birmingham,"
I begin to think of you, baby, you know,
I begin to walk off, now, my baby, go.

2. My mama call me, I answer, "Ma'am,
I 'gin to move out, out in Birmingham."

3. She often tol' me, "Oh, baby, you know that woman,
No good, child, will be.

4. You oughta heard that big bell ring, (2)
You gonna call 'm now in a ball an' chain.

5. Six months ain't no sentence, two years ain't no time, (2)
I got a friend in prison here, doin' ninety-nine.

Otis Webster, vocal and guitar; Angola, Nov. 5, 1960.

127. *Pore Red*

1. Pore Red, what's you gonna do? (2)
I'm sick an' tired, foolin' roun' with you.

2. Oh Red, what you gonna say? (2)
I'm sick an' tired, foolin' roun' with you.

3. Now, oh Red, Red in jail.
Pore Red, Red in jail,
Ain't got nobody to go ole Red's bail.

4. Pore Red, what's you gonna do?
I'm sick an' tired, foolin' roun' with you.

5. Oh Red, wish you was dead,
Wish you was dead,
Ain't got nobody to raise ole Red's head.

6. Now, ole Red, what you gonna say?
Ole Red, what you gonna say?
I'm tired o' foolin' roun' this way.

7. Now, oh Red, Red is in jail,
Pore Red, Red is in jail,
Ain't got nobody to pay ole Red's bail.

Leon Strickland, vocal and guitar; Killona, Nov. 27, 1961.

"Pore Red" closely resembles Blind Boy Fuller, "New Oh Red," Mlt 7-05-56, Vo 03276, Cq 8778, Co 37778, 30080, Feb. 10, 1937.

128. *Those Prison Blues*

1. Well, it's early in the mornin', sun jus' begin to rise, yeah, yeah,
Oh well, it's early in the mornin', the sun jus' begin to rise, yeah, yeah,
Oh well, I know what I've to do if they're gonna try an' skin me alive.

2. Those prison blues finally got the best o' me, yeah, yeah, (2)
Those prison blues finally got the best o' me, yeah.

3. Well, I had an interview, talked to the warden, today, yeah, yeah,
Well, I had an interview, talked to the warden today, yeah,
I only had a few lines an' this is what I had to say, yeah.

4. Well, warden you know I'm mighty sick an' tired o' this job, (2)
Well, I said that last July, I know I was only riskin' my life, yeah, look out.

5. But the warden got mad, "Throw this man in a cell,"
But the warden got mad an' said, "Throw this man in a cell.
He must be crazy, but only the doctor can tell."

6. Well, he took me to an asylum, throwed me 'cross a beat up bed, (2)
Well, while they was doin' it, somebody hit me 'cross the head.

7. These old prison blues, finally got the best o' me. (3)

Cyprien Houston, vocal with Cool Cats (rock-and-roll band); Junior Jones, drums; Robert C. Milton, piano; Arthur Williams, tenor sax; Edward Davenport, alto sax; Philip Armour, lead guitar; Fred Hollingsworth, rhythm guitar; Angola, May 10, 1959.

Although blues among young Negro singers tend to lack the fresh creativity and spontaneity of utterance of their elders who are more folk and closer to the old-time tradition, this blues by twenty-two year old Cyprien Houston is deft in its irony and the wryly comic tone of his singing is solidly in the main-stream of laughing just to keep from crying.

At Angola, as part of a program to keep the convicts pro-ductively engaged, the authorities provide facilities, instruments, and rehearsal time for two colored Rock-and-Roll bands, a white rockabilly (combination of Rock-and-Roll and hill-billy) band, a Negro progressive jazz band of usually about ten musicians, and a white progressive jazz ensemble of three or four. These groups give regular performances all over the prison.

129. *My Baby Blues*

1. Soon in the mornin', be just before the break o' day,
Baby, just before the break o' day,
Well I go marchin' down the road,
See my baby, deep down in a dream.

2. I been worried in min',
I been troubled the whole day long,
I can't hear nobody, I been talkin',
I be talkin' all to myself.

3. I have a mule named Karen,
I giv'n one mule, "Say, Dot, 'n get away."
Lord, I just can't hardly make a day.
Spoken: You know them animals done got wild, man.

4. *Sung:* I don't know what done got wrong with me,
Each an' every day, even though it's the same doggone thing,
I be walkin' 'long the road.

5. *Spoken:* I hear somebody say, "You ain't doin' a thing!"
Sung: Lord, I be movin' so fas', man, I can hardly see my way.
Spoken: Boy, you know things have got rough when them mules
  get mad.

6. *Sung:* I begin to cry deep down in my min',
I declare I ain't gonna do wrong no mo',
Please help me, somebody, please help me to wag my way along;
I can't see nothin', man,
But the other end of just all on my min'.

7. I want you to hurry good time,
Oh, let me go back away from here.
Well, be up early in the mornin',
Lord, all late in the evenin'.

8. I hear somebody say, "Where in the world you workin' at?
You know, way across over yonder.
Spoken: "Way across over where?"

9. *Sung:* Way on the other island on the other side,
Sounds like I can hear my baby callin' me,

God, I look all around me, little girl,
God knows I can't see nothin',
Well, I cry deep down inside, baby,
Why don't you please come home?

10. *Spoken:* She ain't gone no where,
I'm the man that's gone somewhere.
I swear it hurt me to go.
They got me shanked, they got handcuffs on my hands.

11. An' I swear I just can't go nowhere,
I wonder why they treat a poor man thisaway,
Sure is a mean disposition, a lowdown way,
But I just can't see the reason why,
That early in the mornin',
Just before the sunrise.
Let me call my baby,
Just one more time before I go.

12. *Sung:* Baby, baby, you know the sun is risin', (2)
Lord, I woke up this mornin', God knows I was all alone.

13. *Spoken:* I looked in my cell, boys, there was sixty-one more;
I don't mean days, an' I don't mean years,
But there was sixty-one men, just like me,
Just like a dream, baby, Lord, but that poor girl couldn't see
    me.

14. *Sung:* Baby, baby, baby, please come on home.

*Roosevelt Charles, vocal; Hogman (Matthew) Maxey, guitar;
Angola, Oct. 10, 1959.*

"You know them animals got wild" is a reference to the accident he described in "Cultivator Blues." "I want you to
hurry, good time" is his imaginative way of longing for time
off his sentence for good behavior. The picture of himself
manacled, which is effective dramatically, is figurative rather
than realistic.

130. *My Baby Sure Gonna Jump an' Shout*

1. Oh, I know my baby sure gonna jump an' shout,
I know my baby, sure gonna jump an' shout,
When she get that letter, done roll my long time out.

2. Oh, baby, don't quit me, I don't care what I do,
Lord, I ain't the same one made that mistake too.

3. Oh, the sun sure look good, look good goin' down,
Don't the sun look good, goin' down,
It makes me happy when your good man not aroun'.

4. Woke up this mornin', an' I sure was feelin' fine,
I had you in my arms, you restin' on my min'.

5. I'm gonna leave you, baby, cryin' won't make me stay,
Leavin' baby, cryin' won't make me stay,
Lord, the harder you cry, the further you drive me away.

6. I know my baby got her another man, (2)
Oh, it's so hard, an' she just won't understan'.

Hogman (Matthew) Maxey, vocal and guitar; Angola, March 21, 1959.

In this song Maxey expresses a typical series of thoughts, connected by a logic of association—first wish fulfillment, then a plea to his woman not to abandon him, a promise not to get into trouble again, next a reminiscence of the past—how welcome the coming of night was when her husband (or regular lover) was not around; then a mention of a dream of having her in his arms, then a statement that he is going to leave her despite her crying for him to stay—just bravado on his part, a desire to save face, for his real conviction is expressed in the last stanza; he is sure she has gotten another man.

A line like the opening one occurs in Big Maceo, "County Jail Blues," Bb B8798, June 24, 1941. The fifth stanza has appeared in Muddy Waters, "Rollin' Stone," Chess, c. 1948.

131. *The Government Street Blues* (II)

1. I was standin' on the corner, 13 an' Government Street,
I had my flask, baby, I had my flask in my han',
Said a roller roll up, he said, "Jump in, Bud,
Be a long time 'fore you get another drink again."

2. Take me to the parish jail, yes, an' he locked me in,
Yeah, the judge found me guilty, an' the D.A. wrote it down,
Said, "Thirty days in jail" with my back turned to the wall.

3. I ain't got no money, an' my friends have turned me down,
So long, baby, with my back turned to the wall.

4. You know, when I was out on the streets, I had frien's all
over town,
Spoken: "Say, come on, boy, let's get another drink."
Sung: But now I'm locked down in jail, my frien's done quit
comin' roun'.

5. Yes, when I get up on my feet, ain't gonna pay my frien's
no min',
My baby put me down when the D.A. wrote my charge down,
Boy, the jurymens found me guilty, an' the judge he passed
the sentence on me.

6. I was knocked out an' loaded too, I didn't have a word to
say,
Said, "Now looka here, little R.C., what do you have to say?"
I raised my head, "I ain't got a thing to say today."

7. "I'm gonna lock you back in jail just thirty more long days."
Mean ole judge, boy, an' a lowdown D.A.,
Say the judge passed my sentence, man, an' the D.A. wrote it
down.

8. Now you know my baby call me up this mornin' on the
telephone,
These are the words I heard her say,
Said, "Now you know, baby, times is hard,
I don't have no money today,

I was down to see yo' lawyer, but he was not in,
I would bring you some money, baby, Lord, but I don't know
  when."

*Roosevelt Charles, vocal; Otis Webster, guitar; Angola, Nov.
5, 1960.*

A "roller" is a police car.

Although this is an original song, many of the lines and
phrases are traditional in blues presenting arrest, trial, and
conviction, for example, "the judge found me guilty, an' the
D.A.   wrote it down," "with my back turned to the wall,"
"Mean ole judge, boy, an' a lowdown D.A."

132. *How Long Blues*

1. Been down on Angola,
Oh, God, I've been down in a pen,
I done killed my little ole woman,
Gotta serve that time again.

2. Lord, the judge have found, found, found me guilty,
An' the clerk she wrote it down,
"Son, I ha—hate to tell you, you got fourteen to ninety-nine."

3. Lord, please write an' tel—tell my mother,
Oh, woman, please don't wait on me,
Tell 'er, I'm got a lifetime sentence now, never will go free.

4. If you ever been down, down, down, down,
Oh, woman, you know just how'r I feel,
Lord, I ain't got me no connection, just to feel my care for me.

5. Lord, I'r ain't, ain't, ain't gonna be your lowdown dog no mo',
'Fore I do, woman, I pack my clothes an' go.

6. Now, I're motherless, fatherless, sister (less) an' brother (less)
   too,
Lord, I ain't got nobody, just to take my troubles to.

7. How long, baby, how long, is I got to wait?
You gonna fool 'round here, woman, until I hesitate.

8. Eh, comin' to your house tomorrow,
Ask me where your man gone be,
If he won't be in your kitchen,
I want you to kiss poor me.

9. Eh, six months ain't no sentence,
Woh, twelve months ain't no time,
Lord, they give me an' my buddy,
Fourteen to ninety-nine.

10. *Spoken:* That's the truth, boy.

Sung: How long, woman, how long,
Is I'm got to wait?
You gonna fool 'round here, woman,
Will I hesitate.

11. I don't want no jet black woman,
Oh, to fry no meat fo' me,
Lord, black is evil,
She like to kill poor me.

Spoken: Hear it, I'm talkin' 'bout.

12. *Sung:* Oh, 'fore day this mornin',
Lord, my luck come tumblin' down,
I was lookin' for my baby,
An' I swear she couldn't be foun',
Heyah, heyah comes that woman,
Oh Lord, she's so bad drunk again,
Lord, her pocket full o' money,
An' her belly full o' gin.

Leon Strickland, vocal and guitar; Killona, Nov. 27, 1959.

Typical of many blues in its rambling organization, this song moves back and forth among several themes—the sadness of going to prison for killing his woman; refusal to be treated like a lowdown dog by his woman, who is mean, alcoholic, and unfaithful; the conviction that black women are evil and murderous; the loneliness of one without family, friends, or sweethearts; and an affair with another man's woman, who hesitates about giving in to him.

133. *Dark Alley Blues*

1. Take her down in the alley, please don't murder her here,
Take her down in the alley, please don't kill her here,
You know the girl has to wait a — — — — — — — — — — — — — — —.

2. I'm gonna write you a letter, baby, I'm gonna send it to you
   by air, (2)
Oh Lord, have mercy, baby, if you have me to spare.

3. I picked up the receiver, called my baby over the telephone,
Oh, oo, baby, over the telephone,
You can tell by that, pretty mama, baby, baby, I ain't gonna be
   here long.

4. I want you to tell me, little girl, who can your lover be,
Oh, tell me, baby, who can your lover be,
Oh, the reason I asked you baby, it might be a change for me.

5. May be the last time, you can hear your baby say,
May be the last time, baby, you can hear your baby say,
It's your time, little woman, but it's gonna be mine some day.

   *Guitar (Robert) Welch, vocal and guitar; Angola, March 21,
1959.*

134. *Lorraine Blues*

1. *Spoken:* But since I been down here in Angola, it look like she done foun' her another man.

2. *Sung:* Would you believe that I cried all night long?
Woh, oh, would you believe that I cried all night long?
Said, I miss you, little girl, from the time I let you in my house.

3. Well, I'm gonna buy us a Cadillac, baby, this time I'm comin' home in class.
I'm gonna buy us a Cadillac, baby, this time I'm comin' home in class;
Say, we gonna talk about the future, ah, forget about the pas'.

4. *Spoken:* Play it on out for me a little bit, yeah.
You better hold it up; they gonna call the dogs this time.

5. *Sung:* She got a jook joint aroun' the corner, all night long they play the blues,
Well, she got a jook joint aroun' the corner, all night long they play the blues;
Say, we used to have lots o' fun, ridin' home on ole grandpa mule.

6. Oh, baby, look what you done done to me,
Woh, baby, look what you done done to me,
You done made me love, an' I'm jus' as lonely as Andy can be.

7. Oh, I'm gonna cry all night this time, little girl, an' I won't cry no mo',
I said, I'm gonna cry all night this time, little girl, an' I won't cry no mo',
Because if I make parole on this September, woh, I'm goin' on from do' to do'.

Andy Mosely, vocal and guitar; Angola, March 21, 1959.

In thinking about the happy day when he will be released, Andy first engages in a flight of wish-fulfillment about coming home in style in a Cadillac, but in the last stanza, he presents a realistic and humble picture of himself as a free man, someone knocking around from door to door.

The line about calling out the dogs is an amusing and clever variation on the usual invocations to the guitar or another musician. Andy, addressing Hogman Maxey, was humorously suggesting that his playing was so exciting that the authorities were apt to get alarmed and take action against a prison break.

The second to last stanza affords a significant example of how a blues singer often takes a standard verse and alters it slightly to fit his own personal situation. A traditional combination is:

> Oh, baby, look what you done done,
> You made me love you, now your man done come,

lines which wander freely from blues to blues, appearing most frequently in "C. C. Rider."

135. *Mean Trouble Blues*

1. Lord, I see trouble, man, that's all in the world I see,
My woman have got me down in trouble, now she tryin' to put
 me down,
She won't write me no letter, won't even telephone.
Just give me this woman, Lord, sweetest that I ever seen.

2. Well, my woman have gone an' left me, I just can't help
 myself,
You know the warden won't give me release, an' the governor
 won't sign my discharge,
Mean trouble, that is all in the world I see.

3. But if I live an' just don't die, I gonna let my baby take me,
Take me by the hand, baby, an' lead me on,
Just mean trouble, yeah, all right now.

4. If my trouble ever end, Lord, I will be easy,
I'm gonna catch my baby, an' we gonna be at ease,
Just me an' trouble, that will be the end of me.

   *Roosevelt Charles, vocal; Otis Webster, guitar; Angola, Nov.
19, 1960.*

   For a recording of this performance, see *Blues, Prayer, Work
and Trouble Songs*, VRS 9136, 1964.

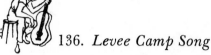 136. *Levee Camp Song*

1. Oh, buddy, I'm goin' on down the road,
Well, every friend I had, mama, done sure have been gone.

2. I wake up in the mornin', partner, with the risin' sun,
I wake up in the mornin', with the risin' sun,
Well, captain call me, I say, "Sorry, baby, gone."

3. In the mornin', 'fore the sun go down,
Well, in the mornin', 'fore the sun go down,
I'm gonna be in Montana with them long-eared houn's.

Robert (Guitar) Welch, vocal and guitar; Angola, March 21, 1959.

137. *Woman Done Me In*

1. You take a no good woman, don't mean no good,
She'll put you in a place, man, in your neighborhood,
I wouldn'ta been here, baby, it hadn'ta been for you,
I thought you loved me, honey, you wasn't even true.

2. I ran home an' got my shotgun, an' one or two shells,
If I don't get some competition here, it gonna be trouble here;
Little woman looked at me, she begin to run,
The police walked up an' tol' me,
"Man, don't you shoot that gun!"
I cried, "Oh Lord, what gonna become o' me."

3. You know the third day o' May,
They handcuff my han',
They tol' me I had to go down to Angola,
An' cultivate some lan'.
I stood before the judge,
He cried out, "Now I'm gonna give you some time, man."
I don't care no how.

4. You know my little woman run up to me,
Made like she was so sad,
I found out later on that the little girl was glad.
She got her a divorce, an' there was, I understan',
'Bout the reason why she quit to writin' me,
She had another man.

5. I don't drink no black cow's milk,
I don't eat nothin' no black woman cook for me,
You might get evil, an' she might poison me.

6. She ran in the kitchen, began to make up dough,
I said, "Looka here now, little girl, you don't cook for me no
    mo',
She turn aroun' an' looked at me, like she didn't understan',
I know she had been talkin' with her other man.
So evil, evil as a man can be,
Yes, I'm a hoochie coochie man,
Don't nobody mess with me.

5. I look at the little woman, she could hardly see,
You talk about a man I'm supposed to be,
I mess up your ears,
I mess up your face,
I leave you with both your legs outa place,
So evil, evil as a man can be,
I'm a hoochie coochie man,
Don't nobody mess with me.

Otis Webster, vocal and guitar; Angola, Nov. 5, 1960.

Here Webster tells the story of how he got into prison for attempted murder. Similar lines attacking black women occur in this collection in Charles's "I Don't Want No Black Woman," No. 118, and Strickland's "How Long Blues," No. 132.

138. *Cane Chopping Song*

1. *Spoken:* Lord, I was walkin' down the headland this mornin',
Thought about my baby, boys, it's hard,
She way there, an' I'm way here,
Man, I couldn' help but for to sing the blues,
'Cause they was all 'cross my min', farmin';
They was hollerin' 'bout get out the way,
An' I swear, I didn't have gettin' out the way on my min',
I was thinkin' about my little angel chil'.

2. He say, "Why don't you go ahead on somewhere, Roosevelt,
'Cause you don't need to be here."
I tol' him, I say, "Well, if I go somewhere,
There'll be a whole lot of yonder over yonder talk about it,
An' I couldn't res' in peace nohow."
He said, "Well, what you gonna do about?"
I say, "Well, I'm gonna mosey along just to keep lookin' busy
　all the time,
But I swear I got my baby on my min'."

3. He say, "Well, why don't you do somethin' about it?"
"There ain't but one thing I can do about it."
I say, "As I go down there 'bout middle way the field,
I'm gonna try this ole cane knife
An' see what it'll do for me;
If it don't sing the right tune,
I'm gonna sing it myself."
Whip it out on that cane knife, over there, boy,
I swear that don't sound exactly right to me,
I believe I call her myself.

4. *Sung:* Lucille, Lucille, baby, why don't you write me just a
　few lines?
Woh, oh Lucille, baby, why don't you write me just a few lines?
You lotta consolation, baby, oh, oughta make everythin' all
　right."

5. You know my coffee's cold, you know my tea is done got
　warm,

Woh, I can't get to the headland, my dear child won't cut me
   loose,
I got to go early in the mornin',
When I feel like I wanta know,
I hear the ding dong ringin',
Lord, I believe, I believe I got to go,
I just can't hold on workin', the way they treated me.

   *Roosevelt Charles, vocal; Otis Webster, guitar; Angola, Nov.
5, 1960.*

   For a recording of Charles's performance see *Blues, Prayer,
Work and Trouble Songs,* VRS 9136, 1964.

139. *Love Trouble Blues*

1. I love my baby, boys, I tell the world I do,
Yes, I love my baby, boys, I tell the world that I do,
She's the sweetest little ole woman in this ole roun' world to me.

2. Tell me, baby, what make you love me so?
Please tell me, darlin', what make you love me so?
You call me your baby boy, God know I call you my baby girl.

3. So far distant, so far distant away,
You know I can't see your face, little girl,
Lookin' at your picture all in a frame.

4. So many years, baby, hangin' over my head,
So many years, baby, hangin' all over my head,
But if life do last me, baby, God knows your love will be home
    some day.

5. Lord, if I live, just to pay the debt I owe,
Baby, if I live, little girl, just to pay the debt I owe,
I will hold you deep in my arm', call you my little baby girl.

6. Woh, Cora, oh—oo, woh, baby, please come on home,
Say, that'll be the day, little woman;
We gonna lock the door, throw away the key,
That'll be the day, baby, that I'll prove my love to you,
That'll be when I'll pay, baby, I'll pay the debt I owe.

7. That mean ole judge, he parted me from my love,
That mean ole D.A., he found a bill against me,
Left my baby standin', leave her in the courthouse cryin'.

8. That mean ole judge, "Please don't send him to the electric
    chair,
Get a pore boy sinner, someday that he might return."

*Roosevelt Charles, vocal; Hogman (Matthew) Maxey, guitar;
Angola, Oct. 10, 1959.*

140. *Wasn't I Lucky When I Got My Time?*

1. Wasn't I lucky, Lord, when I got my time?
Oh, wasn't I lucky, man, when I got my time?
You know my partner got a hundred, I got ninety-nine.

2. Well, I was just sittin' in the jail house, man, I been lookin'
out through the bars,
Yes, I was just sittin' in the jailhouse, man, I been lookin' out
through the bars,
Yes, I was thinkin' about tomorrow, baby, gonna be my tryin'
day.

3. Well, I was sittin here wonderin' what that mean ole judge
was gonna say,
Yes, I was just sittin' here wonderin' what that mean ole judge
was gonna say,
Lord, when I walked in, this is what I heard that mean judge
say:

4. *Spoken:* "Now looka here, boy, you been mighty good in yo'
country,
All yo' ole folks, they is good folks;
Here you are comin' up here, an' you gotta commit wrong."
I say, "Judge, would you please spare my life?
I'm a good man that understan'."
He said, "No, son, I don't believe that you understan' nothin',
Had you, wouldn'ta did what you had to do."
He said, "Now for yo' buddy, I'm gonna give him a hundred,
An' I'm gonna give you ninety-nine."
Sung: That mean ole judge, boys, he give me ninety-nine.

5. *Spoken:* He says, "Now looka here, son, when you do them
ninety-nine years,
An' come back, you be a good boy."
I say, "Judge, how in the world can I do ninety-nine years?
If I don't be a dead boy, I be a ole boy,
Because they is natchal born rollin' down on that river line."

6. *Sung:* Lord, wasn't I lucky, Lord, when I got my time,
Yes, wasn't I lucky, man, Lord, when I got my time,
Well, my ole partner, yay, an' I got ninety-nine.

Roosevelt Charles, vocal; Otis Webster, guitar; Angola, Nov. 15, 1960.

The opening stanza occurs frequently in prison worksongs. In the clever and vivid scene with the judge Roosevelt gives himself the kind of brash retort he would not dare to make in a courtroom.

For a recording of Charles's performance, see *Blues, Prayer, Work and Trouble Songs*, VRS 9136, 1964.

141. *Electric Chair Blues*

1. *Spoken:* "Say there, ole pardner, how about let's goin' down
the road a-piece an' havin' a ball."
"O.K., Bob, I don't care if I do."

2. *Sung:* I'm gonna shake hands with my pardner, I'm gonna
ask him how come he here, (2)
You know I had a wreck in my family, they're gonna send me to
the ole electric chair.

3. Wonder why they electrocute a man at the one o'clock hour
at night? (2)
The current much stronger, people turn out all the light.

4. Oh well, I guess I'll have to go back home,
Oo—oo—oo—oo, baby, I'll have to go back home;
Seem like my trouble, baby, it ain't gonna last me long.

5. I believe, I believe, baby, I believe I'll go back home,
I believe, oh baby, Lord, I believe I'll go back home;
This old life I'm livin', baby, Lord, it ain't gonna last me long.

6. Goodby, little girl, fare you well, goodby, goodby,
Goodby, little girl, goodby, farewell, goodby,
I'm got a special deliver', pretty mama, baby, an' I'm gotta
leave your town.

7. I heard a rumblin' this mornin', baby, was deep down in the
groun',
Rumblin' this mornin', Lawdy, was deep down in the groun',
Oh, that must have been that old devil, tryin' to chain my baby
down.

*Guitar (Robert) Welch, vocal and guitar; Angola, Jan. 27,
1959.*

This grimly yet whimsically ironic blues is derived from
Blind Lemon Jefferson, " 'Lectric Chair Blues," Para 12608,
Chicago, c. Feb., 1928. The last stanza occurs in William
"Jazz" Gillum, "The Devil Blues," Vic 20-3118, Chicago, Nov.
10, 1947.

For a recording of Welch's performance, see *Angola Prisoners' Blues*, LFS A-3, 1958.

142. *Up an' Down Blues*

1. You know a lotta time', I wisht, baby, that, I wisht that I
was dead an' gone,
You know a lotta time', baby, hey, I wish that I was dead an'
gone,
I'll tell you the reason why I wish that, baby, you know a crim-
inal ain't no more'n a dog.

2. When I do this time, you know I'm gonna put Louisiana
down,
When I do this time, hey, you know I'm gonna put Louisiana
down;
Says I'm goin' so far, darlin', I'm goin' where the water tastes
like cherry wine.

3. You know when a man is down, it ain't long 'fo'e his folks
forget all about where he is,
You know when a pore man is down, hey, it don't be long 'fo'e
the folk get him off thei' min'.
Sometime' I sit an' wonder why they treat me thisaway.

4. Sometime' that I sit down, I have to write to my own self
sometime',
Sometime' that I sit down, baby, hey, I have to write my own
self sometime',
I have to fool these yother inmate' like I'm receivin' mail from
home.

5. I was sittin' here wonderin', baby, hey, why pore Bob have
so many ups an' downs.
I was sittin' here wonderin' why I have so many ups an' downs.

6. You know I prayed every day, baby, but I don't know what
else I could do;
You told me that you loved me, baby, but you just only told
pore Bob a lie;
After I fell in trouble, you showed me how you made behind.

*Robert Pete Williams, vocal and guitar; Angola, March 21,
1959.*

He expresses a frequent complaint of prisoners; since he has been in jail his family and his woman have abandoned him.

The line "I'm goin' where the water tastes like cherry wine" has its counterpart in Jelly Roll Morton, "Michigan Water Blues," Cir 58, Washington, D. C., May or July, 1938:

> Michigan water taste like cherry wine,
> Mississippi water taste like turpentine.

Similar lines are sung by Southern whites, as for example in "I'm Goin' down that Road Feelin' Bad."

143. *Pick 'em up Higher*

Spoken: Pick 'em up! Drop 'em down!

1. *Sung:* Oh, you pick 'em up a-higher, let 'em drop on down,
Jus' pick 'em up higher, let 'em drop on down,
Do you want t'know the diff'rence 'fore the sun go down?

Chorus: Oh, pick 'em up higher, let 'em drop on down,
Jus' pick 'em up higher, let 'em drop on down. (2)

2. Well, you want t'know the diff'rence, oh when the sun go
down,
Jus' looka yonder, boy, what's the matter,
Oh, with Number 2, there's Number 1, man.

Chorus: It's pickin' up higher, let 'em drop on down, down,
down,
Well, pick 'em up higher, let 'em drop on down.

3. Oh, Number 1's gone, man, and Number 2 fallen,
Number 3 got to get out the way, boy,
Number 4 is flyin'.

Chorus: Let 'em drop on down,
Well, you want t'drop 'em on down, let 'em drop on
down.

4. Well, this ole hoe, man is mos' too heavy for a lightweight
man, (2)
Well, it's been roun' the 'gola, woh, two, three time', boys,
an' it's goin' down.

Chorus: I'm a headlanded man, an' I can't be late,
Jus' pick 'em up higher, an' drop 'em on down.

5. Oh, you want t'know the diff'rence, boys, when the sun go
down, hi, yoe,
Oh, drop on down, boys, drop on down,
'bout the middle o' the fiel', boys,
An' we gonna break, man, for the other end.

*Roosevelt Charles, vocal; Otis Webster, guitar; Angola,
November 19, 1960.*

A blues fashioned from a prison worksong used for hoeing, "Pick 'em up Higher" performed several functions as sung by field gangs—it supplied a basic rhythm to make group work go more easily, it served as a vehicle for expressing the prisoners' complaints and resentments, and it permitted them to fantasize about escape.

For a recording of Charles's performance, see *Blues, Prayer, Work and Trouble Songs,* VRS 9136, 1964.

144. *Pardon Renied Again*

1. Lord, I carr'd myself on the Pardon Board,
You know I got renied (denied) again.
Been on the board three times,
Each time I was renied,
But I hopes in the good Lord,
Lord, have mercy on me.

2. They tell me the governor's on the board,
All aroun' the board lookin' at them people's case,
Lord, they must have passed mine roun' in – – – –,
Because they renied me again.
Lord, have mercy on me. (2)

3. I been tryin', I been tryin',
Lord, every day of my life,
Please, Lord, have mercy on me.

4. Says I work, that I work hard,
They won't give me some kinda – – – –,
Please, please, Lord, give me heart,
Some people, write 'em to the Pardon Board,
Lord, that I feel sorry, too.

5. Lord, have mercy on po' me,
Mm– – – – – – – – – – – – – – – – – –,
I fell down on my knee,
I prayed, I prayed both night an' day,
Hopin' the people would help me along,
Lord, have mercy on my dyin' soul,
Oh Lord, on me.

6. Well, I know my case isn't any too bad,
I just can't see, I just can't see,
Why they treat me thisaway;
Lord, have mercy on my dyin' soul.

7. I got, I got a big family on my han',
They's out there in that free worl',
Waitin' for me to reappear.
Oh Lord, may I return again, back to my home.

8. Oh Lord, have mercy on me, I got a man
Tole me that he would write now a letter to the Governor for
   me,
An' I hope he would help me 'long,
Grant to the Lord he hear my prayer,
I wish that Governor would take sides with me,
Lord have mercy on me.
This is all I got to say to you today,
Please help me 'long, in the name of God.

Robert Pete Williams, vocal and guitar; Angola, June 10, 1960.

Robert Pete's poignant statement of his sadness at the rejection of his third plea for a pardon. The line about the letter to the Governor refers to me.

For a recording of Williams' performance, see *Those Prison Blues,* FL 109, 1959.

145. *Freeman Blues*

1. *Spoken:* Yes, I'm so glad that I met you again,
I met a friend o 'mine;
He came to see me today,
How glad I was to see him,
I shook his hand.
He did a whole lot for me,
Helped get me outa prison.
I have him a lotta thanks too.
He was a mighty help to me,
When I was up there,
He'p me in the cigarette'.

2. You know I worried a whole lot,
When I was down behin' the bars,
Many day', I wrung my hand',
But now I don't believe I haveta cry no mo',
'Cause I'm free now,
I made parole, Lord, I'm doin' good,
I don't believe I go back.
I'm with some good people,
Give my anythin' that a pore man need.

Robert Pete Williams, vocal and guitar; Scotlandville, Feb. 21, 1960.

Convinced that Robert Pete was a great blues singer and that given another chance he would stay out of trouble, I wrote letters on his behalf to Governor Earl Long and the Pardon Board in New Orleans, enclosing record albums which I had produced featuring him, *Angola Prisoners' Blues*, LFS A-3, which was issued in April, 1958, and *Those Prison Blues*, FL 109, issued in November, 1959. He was released on parole in December, 1959, after having served only three-and-a-half years of his life sentence for murder. Robert Pete had sung his way out of prison—a well established tradition in the South. Leadbelly sang his way out of both the Texas Central Prison Farm and Angola; Lightnin' Hopkins, out of an East Texas road gang. Texas Alexander is reputed to have won release from a prison in the same way. In fact, there is such a story about many blues singers. Mance Lipscomb describes a revealing incident of this type as background to his performance of the murder ballad, "Frankie."

That fella was really in Marlin (County) jail and he sung his way out. Way it come up, you know we have a jailer feed you every morning, and went down to the jail to feed this fella and when he got to the jail, the fella was on the inside with his guitar playing and he heard it and he just stood there with the breakfast and listened at him, and it struck his attention so he went back to town and didn't give him anything to eat. Went on back and told the sheriff from that fella's request on the guitar, his song and the way he rimed it out and made it up, 'I don't think you should find anything agin him.' So the sheriff he went back down there and this fella was still playing "Freddie"—and they both stood on the outside and listened at him. Then they went in there and unlocked the door and told him he could go. He just declared himself with a song. (*Mance Lipscomb, Texas Sharecropper and Songster,* Arhoolie F1001, p. 3 of notes by Mack McCormick.)

"Freeman Blues" was recorded at a jam session in the home of Robert Pete's sister, Mable Lee, a tall slender, shy woman, the one he referred to in "Prisoner's Talking Blues," who was like a mother to him and remained loyal throughout his difficulties with the law.

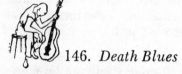

146. *Death Blues*

1. *Spoken:* You know I walk along sometime' an' talk to myself,
I wonder is everybody have the same idea that I got;
Sometime' I have the min' to leave this place,
I tell my people that sometime',
But they say, "You know you doin' time
But I thinks about my brothers then,
All them is way off, an' I the one's hangin' aroun' here,
I take the blues bad sometime'.

2. I got somethin' to tell you, baby,
But I hate to tell you this;
You may not want to hear it;
Sometime' I be walkin' along,
Feel like to me I'm gonna fall dead.
She ask me what's wrong with me,
I don't know, maybe my nerves bad,
'Cause I don't drink that much.
But I think the most of it, just 'bout work' down,
But you know the way I work out here, baby,
I have some min' to go back to Angola.

3. You know they do allow a man a break up there,
But I ain't had none out here since I been out, work every day.

4. *Sung:* But I don't blame nobody but myself,
I don't blame nobody, darlin' but myself,
Lord, what I did, darlin', brought it all on myself.

5. You better buy me an insurance, darlin',
So you can have somebody to depend on,
'Cause I'm liable to haul up an' die, baby,
An' there ain't a thing you can get out o' my death.

   Robert Pete Williams, vocal and guitar; Baton Rouge, October 18, 1960.

"Death Blues" expresses despair at several elements in Robert Pete's life on the farm near Denham Springs to which he had been paroled—his being forced to stay in a job and in a place he is eager to leave, the crushing effects of the eighty or ninety hours of work every week (much more oppressive than the work at Angola, which at present is not particularly burdensome), and the destitution his family would suffer if he suddenly dropped dead. The thought that his wife should go get some insurance is ironic since a wage of $75 a month and board are not enough to cover the most basic essentials of supporting a family.

For a recording of Williams' performance, see *Free Again*, PrB 1026, 1960.

147. *Farm Blues (II)*

1. *Spoken:* You know it's too early for me to be gettin' up like
   this,
'Specially every day, seven days a week,
Just to milk one or two cow',
Make fire sometime'.
Sometime', it'll be cold, no fire,
But I go ahead an' make it.
I say, "Man, what you want a fire this time mornin'?"
"Just do what I tell you do."
"All right then." "You done fed yo' horses?"
"Not yet." "All right, I want you to go with me."

2. Man work me so hard, I don't know what to do.
Sometime I ask him, sometime',
"Man, do you ever get tired?"
He tell me, "No."
"I know why you don't get tired,
You watchin' me do it."
He have to laugh to himself sometime'.

3. Well, one day I be free.
Ah, he tole me, "Oh, I'm gonna tell you what I'm gonna do;
I'm gonna bring on the Pardon Board."
"Man, I shore would appreciate that."
He say, "I want to tell you this much,
I won't compel you,
Don't stay with me if you don't wanta."
"Sho' 'nough, man," I laughed,
You ain't jokin' is you?"
He say, "No."
He say, "I'm gonna tell you somethin'.
You gonna be cut loose on this March board."
Oh Lord, didn't I get happy, almost high.

*Robert Pete Williams, vocal and guitar; Baton Rouge, April
15, 1961.*

148. *Free Again*

1. *Spoken:* You know I got my frien's with me here today,
I want to make 'em all happy,
Two frien's is what I meant to say, an' my son,
We's out on a spree today.
Boy, I tol' 'em all the drinks is on me today,
I got ballin' on my min'.

2. *Sung:* I'm gonna ball, baby, till the sun go down,
I'm gonna ball, baby, till the evenin' sun go down,
I lef' home this mornin', with ballin' on my min'.

3. Well, I tol' my wife, don't look for me back home soon.
When I get there ballin' an' swingin' out with some little ole
    teenage gal,
I'm gonna have myself a ball.

4. I'm a ballin', man, an' I don't care what you women say,
I'm a ballin', man, Lord, an' I don't care what you women say,
I'm a ballin', man, Lord, an' I don't care what you good gals say.

5. Well, I don't feel welcome, woman, no where to lay my
    worried head,
Well, I don't feel welcome, baby, no where to lay my worried
    head,
Feel worried, though, everywhere that I go.

6. Well, I'm worried, but I won't be worried long,
I'm worried, baby, Lord, I won't be worried long,
I'm gonna leave here, woman, if I have to walk an' crawl.

Robert Pete Williams, vocal and guitar; Baton Rouge, Nov. 10, 1960.

"Free Again" describes the temporary sense of freedom he
has in going off on one of his infrequent sprees. Although he
starts off the song in an exuberant frame of mind, his mood
shifts as he is singing with the result that the last two stanzas
express his underlying worries and his intense yearning to
escape from the oppressive job on the farm near Denham
Springs to which he was paroled.

For a recording of Williams' performance, see *Free Again*, PrB 1026, 1960.

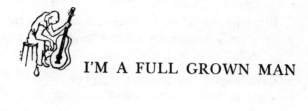

I'M A FULL GROWN MAN

149. *Army Blues*

1. You know I left home, when I was in my teens,
I left home, when I was in my teens,
Oh, I wished I had listened at what my mother said,
I wished I had listened at what my mother said.

2. I did wrong when I broke my mother's rule,
That what, I did wrong when I broke my mother's rule;
Now looka here, mama, yo' son is home for good. (2)

3. Uncle Sam, Uncle Sam, done give me my furlough home,
You gonna have trouble, mama, keepin' yo' son at home. (2)

*Robert Pete Williams, vocal and guitar; Hogman (Matthew)
Maxey, guitar; Angola, Jan. 28, 1959.*

For a recording of Williams' performance, see *Those Prison
Blues,* FL 109, 1959.

150. *Walk-Up Blues*

1. You know I been walkin' along to myself sometime', makin'
   out these ole blues,
I be talkin' to myself, darlin', makin' out these ole lonesome
   blues to myself sometime',
I keep boogyin' on my min', I guess that's the reason why that
   I makes up all these ole lonesome — — — — —,
An' people just can't understan' me.

2. Well, I tol' my mother last night,
Mama, I believe that I'm a man;
I went along until now just like a man will,
An' you can't tell what to do,
I ain't gonna take any more order from you now, mama.

3. Don't you know, I'm way past that, like my daddy did;
Look on the top my lip, I got mustache too,
I workin' on a job, just like my daddy too,
An' I drawin' my pay, go out on Saturday night,
An' have a good time, come back home when I get ready,
Was nobody gone be my boss.
Mama, I want you to know that I'm growin' too like my daddy,
Now you two gettin' the switch for me,
I want you to know that too.

4. Mama, I may be yo' seventh chil',
It look like I'm the odd one,
Well, I gets treated dirty,
I wonder why you treat me so doggone col'.

*Robert Pete Williams, vocal and guitar; Baton Rouge, July
31, 1961.*

PEACHES, JELLY ROLL, GROUNDHOGS
AND MACHINES

151. *Somethin' Wrong with My Machine*

1. Woh, yeah, somethin' wrong with, Lord, with my little
machine, (2)
Well, my baby she got standard carburetor, man, put in bad
gasolene.

2. Well, I'm gonna get in my airplane, baby, I'm goin' sailin'
all aroun',
I'm gonna get in my airplane, baby, I'll be sailin' all aroun',
Well, my baby she put in bad gasolene, I don't like this ole way
nohow.

3. Well, I come home, see my baby, she was layin' 'cross her
bed, (2)
She was drinkin' ole bad whiskey, talkin' all out her head.

4. Woh, yeah, somethin' wrong with my little machine, (2)
Well, my baby she got a standard carburetor, man, she put in
bad gasolene.

*Smoky Babe (Robert Brown), vocal and guitar; Scotlandville,
Feb. 10, 1961.*

This blues is in the same general tradition as Sonny Boy
Williamson, "My Little Machine," Bb 8674, June 1941—an
extended metaphor comparing a woman to an automobile. The
following song, "Terraplane Blues," which is full of sexual
double entendres, is more typical of the idiom.

152. *Terraplane Blues*

1. Well, I feel so lonesome, want you to hear me when I moan, (2)
Well, I been hearin' an earful 'bout you since I been gone.

2. I flash the light, mama, hoo, yo' horn even blows, (2)
Well, I got a good connection from way down below.

3. Come out here, little baby, you know I'm boun' to check yo' oil,
I'm gonna have to look, baby, you know I'm boun' to check yo' oil,
Well, I was livin' way down in Arkansas.

4. I'm gonna mount yo' hood, baby, you know I'm boun' to check yo' oil,
I'm gonna mount yo' hood, mama, you know I have to check yo' oil,
Well, when I was livin', hoo Lord, way down in Arkansas.

5. Baby, I'm a highway man, hollerin' hoo baby, don't block the road,
Baby, I'm a highway man, hollerin' hoo, don't block the road,
Well, I'm lickin' cool one hundred now, baby, hoo Lord, I'm lookin' to go.

Smoky Babe, vocal and guitar; Vance, Mississippi, August 11, 1961.

"Terraplane Blues" is most directly derived from Robert Johnson, "Terraplane Blues," Vo 03416, Nov. 23, 1936; the accompaniments and several of the stanzas are similar. It is also in the same general tradition as a host of blues, such as Little Bill Gaither, "Old Model A Blues," De 7563, June 23, 1938; Lightnin' Hopkins, "T-Model Blues," GS 662, c. 1947; Brownie McGee, "Auto Mechanic Blues," Nixa NJE 1060, 1958.

153. *Jelly Roll*

1. Oh, jelly roll, jelly roll, roll in the can,
Lookin' for a woman ain't got no man.

Chorus: Wild about jelly, crazy 'bout sweet jelly roll.
If you taste good jelly, satisfy yo' weary soul.

2. Up she slipped, down she fell,
Opened her mouth like a mussel shell.

Chorus:

3. Ain't been to hell, but I been tol'
Women in hell got sweet jelly roll.

Chorus:

4. Reason why grandpa like grandma so,
Same sweet jelly she had a hundred years ago.

Chorus:

5. Repeat 1.

Butch Cage, vocal and fiddle; Willie B. Thomas, vocal and guitar; Zachary, Oct. 21, 1960.

The instrumental combination, the tune, the chorus, and the fourth stanza all resemble those in Peg Leg Howell, "New

Jelly Blues," Co 14210, Atlanta, 1927, in which Howell sings and plays the guitar, Eddie Anthony plays the fiddle in the rough syncopated style characteristic of folk Negro fiddlers. The stanza which is similar in the Howell recording is:

> Reason why I like my best gal so,
> Same sweet jelly she had a hundred years ago.

For the Cage and Thomas performance, see *Country Negro Jam Sessions*, FL 111, 1960.

154. *Rock Me, Mama*

1. Rock me, mama, rock me all night long,
Oh, I want you to rock me, like my back ain't got no bone.

2. You see me comin', run an' get a rockin' chair,
See me comin', run an' get a rockin' chair,
Oh Lord, ain't no stranger want to lay right here.

3. Roll me, mama, like you roll your dough, (2)
Oh, I want you to roll me, roll me over slow.

4. Woke up this mornin', found my baby gone, (2)
Oh, that hurt me so bad, broke up my happy home.

5. See me comin', raise your window high, (2)
When you see me leavin', hang your head an' cry.

Hogman (Matthew) Maxey, vocal and guitar; Angola, Feb. 27, 1959.

Maxey's blues resembles Ruby Glaze, "Rollin' Mama Blues," Vic 23328, Bb 5362, Feb. 22, 1932, which has the line "Roll me, mama, like a baker rolls a dough"; Arthur "Big Boy" Crudup, "Rock Me, Mama," Bb 34-0725, Vic 20-2978, Dec. 15, 1944; Lil Son Jackson, "Rockin' an' Rollin' No. 2," Im 5204, c. 1951. For a discussion of the last stanza, see the note to "She Was a Woman Didn't Mean No One Man No Good," No. 188.

For Maxey's performance, see *Southern Prison Blues,* ISD SLP 125, 1962.

155. *Biscuit Bakin' Woman*

1. Buy me a doggone wheel, you know, kill somebody with my jelly roll,
She's a biscuit bakin' woman, she's a biscuit bakin' woman,

Chorus: She's a biscuit bakin' woman o' mine.

2. Well, she bake them biscuit, bake them nice an' brown,
Say, little woman, I'm gonna leave this town,

Chorus:

3. Love you, baby, sweetheart too,
I love you, mama, don't care what you do,

Chorus: You's a biscuit bakin' woman o' mine.

4. Well, you bake those biscuit, bake 'em nice an' brown,
Love that woman, she can really go to town,

Chorus:

5. Well now I can tell the way she roll her dough,
She can bake them biscuits once mo',

Chorus:

6. Now looka here, baby, see you the other night,
I don't want you ever outa my sight,

Chorus:

Smoky Babe (Robert Brown), vocal and guitar; Scotlandville, Feb. 6, 1960.

A blues with a similar theme is Sonny Jones, "Dough Roller," Vo 05056, Memphis, July 13, 1939, in which the man boasts of his "rolling."

156. *Fruits on Your Tree*

Well, you've got fruits on your tree, ma-ma, an' le-mons on your shelf, I know lo-vin' well, ba-by, you can't-a squeeze them by your-self, Please let me be your le-mon squee-zer, Lord, un-til my love come down, Now let me be your le-mon squee-zer, ba-by, un-til my love come down.

1. Well, you've got fruits on your tree, mama, an' lemons on
   your shelf,
I know lovin' well, baby, you can't-a squeeze 'em by yourself,
Please let me be your lemon squeezer, Lord, until my love
   come down,
Now let me be your lemon squeezer, baby, until my love come
   down.

2. Lord, I saw the peach orchard, the fig bush too,
Don't nobody gather fruit, baby, only like I do,
I can make you a bag, honey, begin to tote out,
I know my number, baby, anywhere I go.

3. Let me be your lemon squeezer, while I'm in your lonesome
   town,
Now let me be your lemon squeezer, baby honey, until my love
   come down.

4. Yes, she spied a black panther, he wanta jump down,
He wanta cut my throat when they ain't nobody else aroun',
Lord, she spied a black panther, an' he's 49 inches long,
He ease up to my baby, Lord, one more time or two.

5. I wanta tell you, baby, an' I don't wanta tell you no lie,
The way you're doin', now, little girl, you can't get by;
I'm lookin' at you, woman, with all eye,
I want you to sit down now, baby, an' stop your jive,
Because I'm gettin' evil as a man can be,
I don't want nobody here messin' with me;
I love you baby, I don't want nobody else,
Yes, I got a black panther waitin', I don't want nobody else.

Otis Webster, vocal and guitar; Angola, Nov. 19, 1960.

Webster's "Fruits on Your Tree" draws primarily on two Sonny Boy Williamson recordings, "Until My Love Comes Down," Bb 7576, March 13, 1938, and "Black Panther Blues," Bb 340701, Chicago, Dec. 11, 1941, but members of this family of songs were an already well established tradition when Williamson came on the scene. See, for example, Blind Lemon Jefferson, "Peach Orchard Mama," Para 12801, March 1929; Bumble Bee Slim (Amos Easton), "Squalling Panther Blues," Bb 5517, 6649, March 23, 1934; Bumble Bee Slim, "Lemon Squeezing Blues," Vo 03005, July 11, 1935; Art McKay, "She Squeezed My Lemon," De 7364, c. 1936.

The earlier circulation of this song in folk tradition is suggested by a couple of lines in "Mamma's Darling" in Talley, *Negro Folk Rhymes,* p. 188:

> I has apples on de table
> An' I has peaches on de shelf.

157. *I'm a Prowlin' Ground Hog*

1. I prowl an' I prowl, baby, I prowl all night long,
I prowl an' I prowl, baby, I prowl the whole night long,
I'm gonna keep on prowlin', baby, till I find the girl I love.

2. Here you caught me rootin', pretty mama, when the grass
was very high,
I'm gonna keep on rootin', baby, until the day I die.

3. I'm a prowlin' ground hog, baby, an' I prowl the whole night
long,
Oh, I lays in my den th'ough the day, concentrate on my baby
at night,
Go out prowlin' th'ough the night, baby,
See how the grass done growed th'ough the day,
I'm a prowlin' ground hog, I prowl all night long.

4. Now looka here, little girl, you caught me rootin' when I
was young,
Told me I was the man you love,
Now come to find out you in love with someone else,
I'm a prowlin' ground hog, an' I prowl the whole night long;
I'm gonna keep on rootin', baby, until the day I die.

*Roosevelt Charles, vocal; Otis Webster, guitar; Angola, Nov.
5, 1960.*

"I'm a Prowlin' Ground Hog" has several similarities to Washboard Sam, "I'm a Prowlin' Ground Hog," Mlt 61055, June,
1936; the two have in common stanzas about prowling all night
long and rooting in the grass, and the chorus line, "I'm a
prowlin' ground hog an' I prowl the whole night long." Among
the great number of recorded blues in this vein are: Cow Cow
Davenport, "Dirty Ground Hog Blues," Vo 1227, Chicago, Oct.
25, 1928; Big Bill Broonzie, "Prowling Ground Hog," Pero
0313, Mlt 13311, Oct. 19, 1934; Big Joe Williams, Rootin'
Ground Hog Blues," Bb 7065, 1936; William "Jazz" Gillum,
"Boar Hog Blues," Bb 7563, 1936; Sonny Boy Williamson,
"Ground Hog Blues," Bb 9031. In general, the prowling
ground hog is a metaphor for the sex-seeking male. Oliver, p.

125, suggests a further significance at a deeper level—that such terms as "pigmeat," "rooting ground hog," "dirty ground hog," are a deliberate acknowledgement of the law status accorded the Negro in the past." "The Negro," he goes on to say, "prides himself on being a rooting ground hog, even a dirty ground hog in challenging self-abasement."

158. *I Wisht I Was an Ant*

1. Well, I wisht I was an ant, baby, build my nest down in the groun', (2)
Well, I was standin' here, God knows I was standin' here in yo' side,
An' I was so hid in my nest, baby, Lord, way down in the groun'.

2. Now I'm in this thing, well, I'll sting you too,
Lord, you'll be hunting my nest, baby, yes, after I'm gone;
Well, you know I'm a little crawlin' ant baby, gonna crawl up on yo' han',
Well, when I sting you baby, well, you won't let me be,
I'm gonna build a levee, baby, right above my hole,
An' you gonna be lookin' for that little ant that stung you, baby,
I'm a crawlin' ant, baby, an' I crawl all over the lan'.
Spoken: Yes, crawl on, boy, yeah, long time.

3. *Sung:* Mm, I'm a stingin' ant, baby, crawl all over Louisiana, down in Texas too,
Gonna build my nest, baby, by yo' front step,
Gonna crawl up higher, then you gonna try to get rid o' me.

4. I'm a crawlin' ant, baby, I'm gonna sting you, little girl, ain't gonna let you be,
Till you find the end o' me.

Roosevelt Charles, vocal; Otis Webster, guitar; Angola, Nov. 19, 1960.

159A. *Black Snake Blues*

1. Somebody, somebody, got me them black snake blues, (2)
Black snake blues, they sho' killin' me.

2. Black snake, black snake blues, crawlin' in my room,
Black snake blues, crawlin' in my room,
Somebody, somebody, got me with these here black snake blues.

3. Looka here, baby, look here, woman, what in the world are
   you tryin' to do,
Looka here, baby, what in the world are you tryin' to do,
You made me love you, darlin', now yo' man done come.

4. Well, I'm worried, woman, as a pore man can be,
I'm worried, baby, as a pore man can be,
You got me off, baby, an' you treat me so lowdown.

Robert Pete Williams, vocal and guitar; Butch (James) Cage, fiddle; Zachary, March 8, 1961.

159B. *Black Snake Blues*

1. I woke up this mornin', my baby was goin' walkin' 'cross the
   floor in her lovin' stockin' feet, (2)
Somebody gonna get these blacksnake blues, somebody, mm,
   mm, gonna get these blacksnake blues.

2. Blacksnake blues killin' me, mm, mm, black snake crawlin'
   in my room,
Mm, baby, black snake crawlin' in my room,
Somebody give me these blacksnake blues.

3. Oh, Lord, I ain't got no mamma now,
Mm, mm, I ain't got no mamma now,
Somebody say, "You ain't got no mamma now."

Robert Pete Williams, vocal and guitar; Baton Rouge, July 31, 1961.

Rich in connotations of slimy clandestine sin long before Genesis, the snake appears frequently in blues metaphors dealing with infidelity. Among numerous recorded blues with this image are Victoria Spivey, "Black Snake Blues," OK 8338, St. Louis, May 11, 1926; Blind Lemon Jefferson, "That Black Snake Moan," Para 12407, Chicago, c. Sept. 1926; Victoria Spivey and Lonnie Johnson, "New Black Snake Blues," OK 8626, New York, Oct. 13, 1928; Huddie Ledbetter, "New Black Snake Moan," Per 0315, Mlt M13327, Para 14017, TpoE R13, JClE L 108, Fkwy FP 24, New York City, Jan. 23, 1935.

160. *King Bee without a Queen*

1. I'm a king bee, baby, sailin' aroun' the sky,
Yes, I'm a king bee, baby, swarmin' aroun' the sky,
Lord, I don't have no hive, because I don't have no queen bee.

2. Just only lookin' for a queen bee, just to build a little hive
   with me,
Just only lookin' for a queen bee, baby, to build a little hive
   with me.
Spoken: Now I hear a whole lot o' buzzin', man,
Sound like I hear a queen bee on the road.

3. *Sung:* Yes, I hear a lot o' buzzin', man, sound like I hear a
   queen bee on the way,
Woh, queen bee, please come an' mate along with me;
I wanta build a hive, baby, just to last from this day on.

4. *Spoken (to guitar):* Please buzz me a little while, man, yeah;
Look at that queen bee, buzz, buzz a while.

5. *Sung:* Oh, just a lonely king bee, Lord, all by myself,
Yes, just a lonely king bee, Lord, all by myself,
I been lonely huntin' for a queen bee, just to come an' build a
   hive with me.

6. Lord, I been tryin' so hard, can't get no queen to join with
   me,
We will have a lonely hive, baby, yes, stop an' settle down.

   *Roosevelt Charles, vocal; Otis Webster, guitar; Angola, Nov.
5, 1960.*

   Records which make use of a similar central metaphor are
Bo Carter, "I'm an Old Bumble Bee," OK 8852, October, 1930;
Bo Carter, "Queen Bee," Bb 5489, 1934; Slim Harpo, "I'm a
King Bee," Exclo, c. 1935.

161. *Please Throw This Dog a Bone*

1. Baby, baby, please throw this old dog a bone, (2)
Well, well now, please throw this old dog a bone,
Mm, mm —————————————————.

2. When I first met you, baby, I hunted way down South,
You don't go no place, baby, but the church an' niggers' Sunday
    School;
You way up here now, you run aroun' now, baby, in every
    rotten joint in town.
You done got to the place where you don't pay me no min'.

Clarence Edwards, vocal and guitar; Cornelius Edwards, guitar; Butch (James) Cage, fiddle; Zachary, Oct. 27, 1959.

162. *Heart Beatin' Like a Hammer*

1. My heart beat like a hammer, an' my eyes are full o' tears,
You been gone for two or three years,
But it seems like a thousand years.

2. Well, I love my woman better than I do myself,
An' I love my woman better than I do myself,
I wouldn't min' it too bad, I know she's in love with somebody
   else.

3. I went down unto the river, an' I walked down 'bout the sea,
I got to thinkin' about my little woman,
Boy, somebody has to bury me!

4. Oh, I love my woman, tell the world I do,
Oh, an' I love my woman, tell the world I do,
Now, what made me love her, yeah, you can love her too.
Spoken: Yes, yes, yes, yes, yes, I hear you.

5. *Sung:* Min' all you women, I want all you men to know,
You got to min' how you treat a stranger,
You got to reap just what you sow.

6. I love my woman, an' I tell the world I do,
An' I love my woman, tell the world I do,
Now what made me love her, yes, you can love her too.

7. Now you know (I) love her, been doin' wrong yourself,
Now, doggone you, woman, sure you been doin' wrong yourself,
I wouldn't min' so bad, I know she lovin' somebody else.

*Jimmy Cage, vocal and guitar; Butch (James) Cage, fiddle;
Zachary, January 15, 1961.*

The first stanza closely resembles the opening three lines of
Sonny Boy Williamson, "Million Year Blues," Bb B-8866-B,
recorded in Chicago in 1941. Cage's highly emotional vocal
style resembles that of Walter Davis, who made about a hundred
records between 1930 and 1945.

163. *My Wife Done Joined the Club*

1. My wife done joined the club,
An' I know that she's doin' somethin' wrong,
'Cause those two days in the week,
That club work must be carried on.

2. Some say she was out last night with Mr. Jackson,
Some say she was out with Mr. Lee,
I don't care who the dog she was out with,
Just so long as she come home to me.

3. Some say she was out last night with Mr. Jackson,
Some say she was out with Mr. Lee,
I don't give a doggone who she was out with,
Just as long as you bring her home to me.

Butch (James) Cage, vocal and fiddle; Willie B. Thomas, vocal and guitar; Zachary, October 19, 1960.

Probably derived from Walter Roland, "Club Meeting Blues," Per 60157, March 14, 1935, which has a similar tune and an almost identical text. In the recording, however, Roland uses a standard three line blues stanza and there is one verse threatening the woman with "hell on her hands."

164. *Hard Time Lovin' Blues*

1. I love my baby, but my baby just don't treat me right,
Yes, I love my baby, but my baby just don't treat me right;
Now looka here, woman, let me tell you what you can do,
You can hook me to a log wagon, now I'll pull just like an ox;
You tell me, woman, what more you want me to do?
I love you, woman, baby, you just won't treat me right.

2. Now you want me, baby, to be like bad man Jesse James,
Rob some kinda train, baby, hold up that first night in the bank,
Now tell me, baby, what more can a poor man do?
Yes, you know I love you, woman, but you just won't treat me right.

3. Now you wake up early in the mornin', just about the break o' day,
You got a butcher knife in your right han', an' your left han' drawed back,
Now tell me, baby, what more can a poor man do?
You know I work hard every day, baby, an' you treat me this-away.

Roosevelt Charles, vocal; Baton Rouge, May 12, 1959.

An image which is similar to Charles's picture of the abject lover as an ox hooked to a log wagon occurs in Rabbit Brown, "James Alley Blues," Vic 20578, New Orleans, March 11, 1927:

> She tried to hitch me to a wagon
> She tried to drive me like a mule.

A similar Jesse James metaphor appears in Washboard Sam, "Jesse James Blues," Vo 03375, Chicago, July 3, 1935; William "Jazz" Gillum, "Just Like Jesse James," Bb 7615, Chicago, April 5, 1936.

165. *Wants You to Be My Chauffeur*

1. Wants you to be my chauffeur, (2)
Yes, I want you to drive me,
I want you to drive me roun' town,
Well, I drive so easy, I can't turn him down.

2. Well, I'm gone buy him, well, I'm gone buy him,
A bran' new V-8, a bran' new V-8 Ford,
I don't need no passengers, yes, I'll be yo' load.

3. I want my chauffeur, I want my chauffeur for to drive me
   roun',
Yeah, drive me roun' the worl',
I'm gonna be yo' boy, if she be my girl.

4. Well, I don't want him well I don't want him to be ridin'
   these girls,
Be ridin' these girls aroun',
I'm gonna steal me a pistol, shoot my chauffeur down.

*Charles Henderson, vocal and guitar; Butch (James) Cage,
fiddle; Zachary, Dec. 11, 1960.*

This is a blues almost all country blues singers in Louisiana
know and sing with substantially the same tune and text as the
original popular recording, Memphis Minnie, "Me and My
Chauffeur Blues," OK 06288, 1941.

166. *He's a Railroad Man*

1. That train I ride is eighteen coaches long, (2)
An' the man I love done been here an' gone.

2. I'm gone fall on my knees, pray to the Lord above, (2)
You mistreat me, daddy, you the only man I love.

3. He's a railroad man, sho' do love to ride,
He's a railroad man, an' he sho' do love to ride,
If it ain't ridin' that Santa Feel, sho' ain't satisfied.

4. Come here, baby, let me sit down on yo' daddy's knee,
Come here, baby, let me sit down on my daddy's knee,
Well, I just wanta tell you how you mistreated me.

5. When the train in the station, he sho' do fool aroun', (2)
He got a sweet-lovin' mama, sho' won't put me down.

6. He's a railroad man, sho' do love to ride,
He's a railroad man, an' he sho' do love to ride,
If he ain't on that Santa Feel, he sho' ain't satisfied.

*Annabelle Haney, vocal; Butch (James) Cage, fiddle; Willie
B. Thomas, guitar; Zachary, May 23, 1961.*

The opening line is similar to that in Little Junior Parker,
"Mystery Train," Sun 192, c. 1948:

The train I ride on is sixteen coaches long.

"Come here, baby, sit down on your daddy's knee," appears in
Joe Turner and Pete Johnson, "Cherry Red," PaE R 717,
originally recorded c. 1938. Annabelle Haney's singing style
reflects the influence of the female popular blues singers of the
twenties.

167A. *Shake, Shake, Mama*

1. Yes, shake, shake, mama, gonna buy you a beady dress, (2)
If you don't shake, mama, gonna work on you like the res'.

2. My gal tol' me somethin', but she sho' did tell a lie, (2)
Said the eagle on the dollar, he was gonna take wings an' fly.

3. When I get into heaven, ask St. Peter for his chair, (2)
I'm gonna ask St. Peter, do he sell white lightnin' there.

4. Gimme a nickel, I'll buy some wine, (2)
Gimme a nickel, an' put (it) with mine,
If you cry 'bout a nickel, you'll die 'bout a lousy dime.

5. Did you get that letter I crammed in yo' back do'?
Did you get that letter, baby, fell in yo' back do'?
High water was risin', an' I can't stay here no mo'.

6. Gimme a nickel, I'll buy some wine, (2)
If you cry 'bout a nickel, you'll die 'bout a lousy dime.

7. Got forty-nine women, baby, all I want (is) one more, (2)
If I have to lose five, I'll still have forty-four.

8. Gimme a nickel, let's buy some wine, (2)
If you cry 'bout a nickel, you die 'bout a lousy dime.

9. I'm gonna play this time, baby, ain't gonna play no mo', (2)
You's a dirty mistreater an' you drove me from yo' do'.

Charles Henderson, vocal and guitar; Butch (James) Cage, fiddle; Zachary, Nov. 27, 1960.

167B. *Shake, Shake, Mattie*

Chorus: Got a nickel, I'll buy some wine, (2)
If you cry 'bout a nickel, you'll die 'bout a lousy dime.

1. Gonna shake, shake, baby, gonna buy you a beady dress,
Gonna shake, shake, Mattie, gonna buy you a beady dress,
If you don't shake, baby, gonna th'ow you in a hornet's nes'.

Chorus:

2. Now, shake, shake, Mattie, gonna buy that beady dress, (2)
You don't shake, shake, Mattie, throw you in a hornet's nes'.

Chorus:

3. Say, shake, shake, baby, shake if it's all night long,
Now, shake, shake, baby, shake if it's all night long,
Say, shake now, Mattie, you know you have done me wrong.

Chorus: Get you a nickel, I'll buy some wine, (2)
        If you cry 'bout a nickel, you'll die 'bout a lousy dime.

   *Smoky Babe (Robert Brown), vocal and guitar; Scotlandville,
Feb. 6, 1960.*

 167C. *Shake, Shake, Mattie Blues*

1. Shake, shake, Mattie, gonna buy you a beady dress, (2)
If you don't shake, buy you gingham like the res'.

2. Shake, shake, Mattie, gonna buy you a diamond ring, (2)
You ain't gonna shake the supple, ain't gonna buy you a doggone thing.

3. Shake, shake, mama, gonna buy you a fuzzy coa' (coat),
You don't shake, gonna buy you a billy goa' (goat).

4. Shake, shake, Mattie, gonna buy you a diamond ring,
You ain't gonna shake the supple, ain't gonna buy you a doggone thing.

   Leon Strickland, vocal and guitar; Killona, Nov. 27, 1959.

   Leon says, "That's one I learned from other peoples. I come
here an' found 'em playin' that. I picked it up from my dad

amongst, oh, one o' 'em ole guitar players." "Shake, Shake, Mattie" is fairly well-known in folk circles in Louisiana and owes its circulation primarily to direct word-of-mouth transmission.

Stanzas from "Shake, Shake, Mattie" also wander into other songs, as for example in the lines in "Tie-Tamping Chant," Lomax, *American Ballads and Folk Songs,* p. 19:

Shake, shake, Mattie, shake, a-rattle an' a-roll,
Oh, shake, shake, Mattie, Mattie want to win my gol'.

It is the final stanza in Robert Pete Williams, "Make Me a Pallet on Yo' Floor," No. 204 in this collection.

TROUBLED LOVE

168. *When the Sun Go Down*

1. In the evenin', baby, when the sun go down,
In the evenin', mama, when the sun go down,
Well, it's hard to tell, it's hard to tell, oh baby,
After the sun go down, an' the sun go down.

2. I lain down last night tryin' to take my rest,
Well, I lain down last night, baby, tryin' to take my rest,
Thinkin' 'bout the good time, sweet mama,
That I love the best, when the sun go down.

3. Sun rises in the east, goes down in the west, mama,
She gonna take in my baby where we gonna build our nest.

4. Now looka here, woman, I want to tell you before we begin,
Looka here, baby, I want to tell you before we begin,
If you stays out all night, I just swear that's gonna be the end,
When the sun go down.

5. In the evenin', baby, 'fore the sun go down,
Early in the evenin', mama, 'fore the sun go down,
Well, you love me, thinkin' 'fore the sun go down,

*Guitar (Robert) Welch, vocal and guitar; Angola, Feb. 14,
1959.*

Derived from Leroy Carr, "When the Sun Goes Down," Bb
5877, MW 5877, Chicago, Feb. 25, 1935. See also The Ink
Spots, "When the Sun Goes Down," De 1870, BrE 02606, May
19, 1938.

169. *Night Time Is the Right Time*

1. Night time is the right time to be with the one you love,
With the one you love,
I wakes in the mornin', if I feel the same,
I don't have a thing for you, darlin', I'm not to blame,

Chorus: Any time is the right time to be with the one you love,
With the one you love.

2. You gets up in the mornin' with frowns in yo' face,
I know about it, darlin', someone else takin' my place.

Chorus:

3. If you don't want me, darlin', whyn't you tell me so? (2)
I don't think I'll ever, be in love no mo',
Be in love no mo'.

4. You know I was good to you honey, when I taken you in,
I was good to you, baby, when I taken you in,
You didn't have nothin' to wear,
I thought I was yo' closest frien',
Yo' closest frien'.

5. You gave me a rotten deal, baby,
What make me so crazy about you, darlin'?
Those little dreamy eyes, those little dreamy eyes,
Yes, them dreamy eyes.

6. She got a light in her mouth, shine like the mornin' star,
Got a light in her mouth, shine like the mornin' star,
Every time I kissin' her, you don't know what it's worth,
Oh, what it's worth.

7. She gets up an' tells me a lot o' sweet names,
Then she lay down, turn out the light,
She cries out, "Sweet daddy, everythin' it is all right,
Yes, everythin' is all right for me."

Otis Webster, vocal and guitar; Angola, Nov. 19, 1960.

The same tune and stanza structure occur in Leroy Carr's "When the Sun Goes Down," Bb 5877, MW 4826, Chicago,

Feb. 25, 1935. See also Big Bill Broonzy, "Night Time is the Right Time," Vo 04149, May, 1938; Roosevelt Sykes, "Night Time is the Right Time," De 7324, 1937, Smokey Hogg, "Any time Is the Right Time," Mod 20-563 A 675-2, c. 1949.

170. *Po' Boy*

I'm the po' boy, I'm a long way from home. I'm a po'

boy and a long way from home. I'm a po' boy here and

I ain't got no-where to go.

1. I'm the po' boy, I'm a long way from home.
I'm a po' boy, and a long way from home,
I'm a po' boy here, and I ain't got nowhere to go.

2. I ain't got nowhere to lay my worried head, (2)
Rather to see you leave, I would rather see you dead.

3. When I left her house she followed me to her door, (2)
You ain't got no money, man, I would rather see you go,
Man, I'd rather see you – – –, I'd rather see you go.

4. I been talkin' on that long distance phone, (2)
Tryin' to call my little gal, but I think she been gone too long,
I think she have been gone too – – – – –.

5. Now tell me, gal, what you me to do? (2)
I tried so hard, an' I can't get along with you,
I just can't get along with– – –, get along with – – – –,
I just can't get along with – – – –.

Herman E. Johnson, vocal and guitar; Baton Rouge, May 27, 1961.

This is perhaps derived from Barbecue Bob (Robert Hicks) "Poor Boy Long Ways from Home," Co 14246-D, Atlanta, June 16, 1927, although only one stanza of Johnson's variant is close to it in text. See also "Banjo Joe" (Gus Cannon), "Poor Boy, Long Ways from Home," Para 12571, Chicago, Nov. 1927; George Rambling Thomas, "Poor Boy Blues," Para 12722,

Chicago, c. Nov. 1928; Roosevelt Sykes, "Poor Boy Blues," OK 8819, Chicago, Nov. 16, 1929.

Here Johnson accompanies himself in the archaic knife-blade style, holding the guitar flat on his lap and stopping the strings with a closed jack-knife, sliding from note to note. His instrumental style is much influenced by the records of Blind Lemon Jefferson and Blind Willie Johnson, who like many of the folk Negro performers of the twenties would omit words or portions of lines and let the guitar complete what was unsaid verbally.

171. *Cold-Hearted Mama*

1. Cold-hearted mama, I swear you's givin' me a chill, (2)
If you don't treat me nice an' kind, woman, I swear somebody
will.

2. Please, please, woman, please don't leave me here, (2)
I swear I'm a poor little boy, I can hardly see my way.

3. Yes, I love my little woman, tell the world I do,
Love my little woman, tell the world I do,
I love my little woman, tell the world I do.

4. Lord, one o' these mornin', baby, before you know,
I say one o' –,
The hearse gonna come rollin', oh Lord, before yo' do'.

5. Sometime' I wonder, swear, an' again I stand an' look,
Sometime' I wonder, then again I stand an' look,
I had my woman left me, Lord, an' I won't be back no mo'.

6. I ain't never love' but four womens in my life,
I swear I ain't never love' but four womens in my life,
That was my mother, an' my sister, sweetheart an' my wife.

*Charles Henderson, vocal and guitar; Butch (James) Cage,
fiddle; Zachary, Feb. 5, 1961.*

The first stanza resembles the last one of Blind Blake, "Cold-
Hearted Mama," Para 12710, c. June, 1928; there are no other
stanzas the two songs have in common. Probably Henderson
remembered this fragment of Blind Blake's blues and filled out
the remainder by tapping his mental reservoir of standard
verses.

172. *Backwater Blues*

1. Oh, I'm gonna leave you, mama, Lord, but I won't be back
till fall, (2)
Oh, if you don't take good care o' me, baby, Lord, I won't be
back at all.

2. I'm gonna leave you, mama, I want you to hang crepe on yo'
do',
I want you to leave, mama, I want you to hang crepe on yo' do',
Lord, if my mind don't change, little woman, Lord, I'll never
knock there no mo'.

3. I woke up this mornin', Lord, with the blues all roun' my bed,
Lord, I woke up this mornin', Lord, with the blues all roun' my
bed;
I had the blues so bad, baby, Lord, I need my baby.

4. Baby, you may be beautiful, Lord, but you swear you got to
die some day,
Yes, you may be beautiful, Lord, but I swear you got to die
some day;
Then you gonna be sorry, little woman, you ever done me
disdaway.
Spoken: Play it now, man.

Guitar (Robert) Welch, vocal and guitar; Angola, March 21, 1959.

For a recording of Welch's performance, see *Angola Prisoners' Blues*, LFS A-3, 1958.

173. *Cold, Cold Snow*

1. People, people, people, oh Lord, they do not know, (2)
I say my baby she put me down, Lord, in the cold snow.

2. I was wonderin' an' I was worried, wasn't no place to go,
Well, I was wonderin' an' I was worried, peoples, I didn't have
   nowhere to go.

3. I been wonderin' an' I been worried, wonderin' all to myself,
Mm, I been wonderin' an' I been worried, peoples, wonderin'
   all to myself,
Put me out in the cold cold snow, I didn't have nobody else.

4. People, people made her turn her back on me, (2)
The reason why I was hard to fin', baby, I was lost, lost in the
   sea.

*Smoky Babe (Robert Brown), vocal and guitar; Scotlandville,
June 14, 1961.*

For a recording of Smoky Babe's performance, see *Hottest
Brand Goin'*, PrB 1063, 1961.

174. *Crawlin' Baby Blues*

1. Well, my baby's cryin', what does his mother mean? (2)
He's cryin' for that sweet milk, she won't feed him that Jersey cream.

2. Well, he crawl from the fireplace an' he stopped in the middle of the floor,
Says, "Mama, is that my second daddy standin' right there in the door?"

3. Well, grabbed by baby an' spanked him, an' I tried to make her leave him alone,
Tried my best for to stop (her), she said, "This baby is none o' yourn."

4. But the woman rocks the cradle, I declare she rules the home,
Woman rocks the cradle, I declare she rules the home,
But a man rockin' other men's babies, an' the fool think he rockin' his own.

5. It was late last night when I got these crawlin' baby blues, (2)
My baby done put my clothes outa doors, an' I don't know what to do.

Herman E. Johnson, vocal and guitar; Baton Rouge, Nov. 3, 1960.

Probably derived from Blind Lemon Jefferson, "That Growling (*sic*) Baby Blues," Para 12880, Oct. 1929, which it closely resembles.

175A. *Shake 'em on Down*

Ah, plain words about it, we was tryin' to make love . . .
an' she was kinda hesitatin' about it a little bit, an' I say, "Do
you think we can make it? How about it?"

An' she say, "Well, all right. How long we gonna talk about
this thing?"

I say, "We can talk about it all night."
I say, "Well, must I holler, must I shake 'em on down."

It's the whole story about makin' a girl friend, an' you been
single, an' you been sleepin' by yourself . . . a man get kinda
tired sleepin' by hisself, an' he sees a girl he like an' everythin'.
She have a personality he like, he think he try to make her, an'
she talk kinda slow on it.

—*Willie B. Thomas*

1. You done, done made me love you,
Now yo' man done come,
Holler, must I shake 'em on down,
Well, I done stop hollerin',
Believe I shake 'em on down.

2. Oh, jet black woman outshine the sun,
Oh, lipstick an' powder, sho' won't help her none,
Must I holla, must I shake 'em on down,
Well, done stop hollerin', believe I shake 'em on down.

3. Oh, roll yo' belly, like you roll yo' dough,
Let me down so easy, till I want some mo';
Asked her about it, an' she said, "All right,"
Asked her how long, an' she said, "All night."

4. Repeat 3.

5. Oh, look here, woman, you done made me love you,
Now yo' man done come,
Holler, must I shake 'em on down,
Well, I done stop hollerin',
Believe I shake 'em on down.

*Willie B. Thomas, vocal and guitar; Butch (James) Cage,
vocal and fiddle; Zachary, Oct. 4, 1960.*

The opening two lines appear in many blues, the most familiar of which is "C. C. Rider." In the recording by Blind Willie McTell and Ruby Glaze, "Rollin' Mama Blues," Vic 23328, 1932, McTell sings, "I want you to roll me, baby, like a baker rolls his dough."

 175B.   *Shake 'em on Down*

1. Baby, mama, what's goin' on?
Made me love you, now your man done come.

Chorus: Lord, must I holler, oh, must I shake 'em on down,
       Baby, I done quit hollerin', mama,
       Must I shake 'em on down.

2. You took a nightcap, baby, I'd got my gown,
Just before day, baby, we gonna shake 'em on down.

Chorus:

3. One an' one is two, baby, Lordy,
Two an' two is fo', girl I used to love,
Don't love me any mo'.

Chorus:

4. Soon this mornin', mama, just before day,
I felt for my baby, Lord, done gone away.

Chorus:

5. Hey baby, I believe I shake 'em on down,
Oh Louise, Lord, I believe I shake 'em on down,
Baby, done stop hollerin', believe I shake 'em on down.

6. Looka here, sweet mama, Lord, how you done done,
Make me love you, now your man done come,
Your best man done come now.

Chorus: I believe I holler, etc.

   Guitar (Robert) Welch, vocal and guitar; Angola, Feb. 14, 1959.

   The first, second, and sixth stanzas occur in Bukka White, "Shake 'Em on Down," Vo 03711, 1937.

176. *Mean Mistreatin' Woman*

1. I got a mean mistreatin' woman, she mistreat me all the time,
(2)
I say, looka here now, good people, she don't pay poor me no min'.

2. I says, oh pretty woman, baby, now that's all right for you,
I says, all right now, pretty mama, baby, now that's all right for you,
Say, it's all right, pretty mama, any ole way you do.

3. Goin' back home, settle my fool self down,
Goin' back home, baby, settle my fool self down,
Gonna leave you here, don't need you nohow.

4. Worried, worried now as a poor boy can be,
Say now I'm worried, worried as a poor boy can be,
Says, all righty pretty boy, way you treat poor me.

5. Mm, mm, mm, I say mm, mm, uhmm,
That's all right, pretty mama, don't need me nohow,
So you a mean mistreater, mistreat me all the time, (2)
I say now goodby, pretty baby, I got other things on my min'.

Smoky Babe (Robert Brown), vocal and guitar; Scotlandville, Jan. 6, 1961.

The first stanza occurs in Leroy Carr's "Mean Mistreater Mama," Vo 02657, Cq 8741, Mlt 7-07-56, Feb. 20, 1934.

177. *You Don't Love Me, Baby*

1. Ah— — — — — —, ah— — — — — —, ah— — — — — —,
ah— — — — — — — — — — — — —,
Well, you don't love me, baby, you don't love me I know.

2. Well, you been takin', takin' all my money in my clothes, (2)
Well, an' you told all your friends that you gon' do somethin' awful.

3. Please don't leave me, please don't never, never go, (2)
Well, if you leave me, baby, I'm goin' crazy, yes I know.

Clarence Edwards, vocal and guitar; Cornelius Edwards, guitar; Butch (James) Cage, fiddle; Zachary, Oct. 27, 1960.

For Clarence Edwards' recording, see *Country Negro Jam Sessions*, FL 111, 1960.

178. Stack o' Dollars

1. You hear that rumblin', you hear that rumblin', a-deep down
in the groun', oh Lord,
Now it musta be the devil, you know, turnin' by women roun'.

2. Now stack o' dollars, stack o' dollars, just as high as I am
tall, oh Lord, (2)
Now you be my baby, mama, you can have them all.

3. She great big woman, great big woman, head right full o'
hair, (2)
Now I call her tailor-made, but her people don't want me there.

4. Now here's my han', babe, now here's my han', babe, if I
never see you any more,
Now here's my han', if I never see you any more,
Now I'm goin' t' leave you 'lone with Mr. So-and-So.

Clarence Edwards, vocal and guitar; Cornelius Edwards, gui-
tar; Butch (James) Cage, fiddle; Zachary, Oct. 27, 1959.

See Sleepy John Estes, "Stack O' Dollars," Vic 23397, May
30, 1930; Joe Williams, "Stack O' Dollars," Co 38055, c. 1946.
A variant of Edwards opening stanza occurs in William "Jazz"
Gillum, "The Devil Blues," Vic 20-3118, Chicago, Nov. 10,
1947.

For a recording of Clarence Edwards' performance of this
song, see *Country Negro Jam Sessions*, FL 111, 1960.

179. *I'm Blue as a Man Can Be*

1. I'm blue an' down as a man can be,
Oh, yassuh, I'm blue as a man can be,
I was sittin' here wonderin' where my baby — — — — —,
I wonder, do she ever think o' me?

2. I play with my baby, all night — — — —,
I play my baby, all night long,
An' I know she make a baby child.

3. I'm leavin' here, woman, just as soon as I — — —,
Yes, leavin' here, just as soon as I — — — —,
I'm goin' away, an' I ain't comin' here no mo'.

4. I got the blues so bad, can't hardly — — —,
Got the blues so — — —, I can't hardly — — —,
An' I'm worried, just as blue as a man can be.

5. I love you, babe, I love you,
Yes, I love you, I love you,
An' I always care, I always care for you.

6. Make yo' bed up, baby, turn yo' lamp way — — —,
Make yo' bed up, turn yo' lamp way — — — —,
I'm gonna change yo' min' if it takes all night long.

Robert Pete Williams, vocal and guitar; Angola, Jan. 27, 1959.

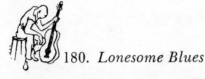

180. *Lonesome Blues*

1. You know when a man all alone, darlin', you know just how
   it feel,
When a man all alone, you know just how it feel,
Ain't got anybody to keep him company, make him feel just
   like a lost bird.

2. Well, I had you tryin' to do right, an' you just wouldn't let
   me be,
Well, I had you tryin' to do right, darlin', an' you just wouldn't
   let me be,
An' I rushed over in the corner, darlin', an' I grabbed my
   suitcase, walked out.

3. Well, I'm goin' away, an' I ain't comin' here to live no mo',
I'm goin' away to leave, darlin', I ain't a-comin' back here
   to live no mo',
The way you treatin' a man, Lord, I might sa (*sic*) well be dead
   an' gone.

4. Now, late up in the night, make me up a pallet down on yo'
   floor,
Late up in the night, baby, make me a pad down on yo' floor,
Well, I don't feel like walkin' by myself.

*Robert Pete Williams, vocal and guitar; Baton Rouge, July 31,
1961.*

181A. *44 Blues*

1. "Good mornin', Mr. Pawnshopper," as I walked in your door,
    (2)
"An' I didn't come here for no trouble, just want my 44."

2. An' I tote my 44 so long that it made my shoulder sore, (2)
Oh, I woke up this mornin' with the blues knockin' on my door.

3. Walk all night long with my 44 in my han',
Yes, I walk all night long with my 44 in my han',
I was lookin' for my woman, foun' her with another man.

4. Repeat 1.

5. My buddy got a 45, is known to kill dead a level mile, (2)
I taken a left hand 44 an' I laid him in the bar room door.

6. Well, I got a little cabin, cabin number 44, (2)
When I wake up in the mornin', blues is howlin' roun' my door.

7. Repeat 3.

8. Well, I thought I heard 44 whistle blow, (2)
Well, it blowed just like ain't gonna blow that whistle no mo'.

9. Repeat 3.

10. Repeat 5.

Butch (James) Cage, vocal and fiddle; Willie B. Thomas, vocal and guitar; Zachary, Oct. 10, 1960.

The meaning of the fifth stanza is that the singer is such a good shot that shooting even left-handed he kills a sharpshooter with a larger bore revolver.

 181B. *44 Blues*

1. I wore my 44 so long, till it made my shoulder sore, (2)
If I do what I wanta do, I won't wear my 44 no more.

2. Lord, I've worn it a prisoner so long, till it made my collar
— — —, yes;
Lord, I could hear my bossman tellin' me,
Oh, don't go down there no mo'.

3. You know I had a little woman,
She was dressed in red,
She told me, "Now looka here, man,
I'd rather see you dead."
I looked at the little girl, dead in the eye,
"I want you to be for me, honey, till the day I die;
I'm so glad, baby, I don't wear my 44 no mo',
If I find the woman I'm lookin' for,
I won't wear my 44 no mo'."
Spoken: Yeah, play it a long time, man.

Otis Webster, vocal and guitar; Angola, Nov. 19, 1960.

The Cage and Thomas variant follows closely in tune and text (except for their first and fifth stanzas which do not occur in the Sykes recording) Roosevelt Sykes, "44 Blues," OK 8702, June 14, 1929. However, their style of performance is different. Sykes, who made up words in a folk idiom for a folk tune, later accompanied on the piano James "Boodle It" Wiggins, "Forty Four Blues," Para 12860, Oct 12, 1929. Sykes also recorded the same blues on De 7586, New York City, April 13, 1939. See also Robert Johnson, "32-20 Blues," Vic 20-2028, July 5, 1945.

In "Thought I Heard That K.C. Whistle Blow," collected c. 1906 (Odum and Johnson, *The Negro and His Songs,* p. 221), two lines occur which are much like the eighth stanza sung by Cage and Thomas:

> Thought I heard whistle when it blow,
> Blow lak she ain't goin' blow no mo'.

In Webster's blues, the tune and text begin sounding much like the recordings, but he introduces a favorite theme of his, the paternalistic bossman who cautions him against getting into trouble, and also his treatment of his encounter with the woman is different. The tune changes after the second stanza.

For the Cage and Thomas performance, see *Country Negro Jam Sessions,* FL 111, 1960.

 182. *A to Z*

1. I'm gonna cut yo' doggone head four different ways,
That's long, short, deep, an' wide;
When I get through usin' this ole well-sharpen' razor,
I'm sho' you gonna take a ride.

2. I'm gonna cut out A,B,C, in the top o' yo' head,
I treat you nice an' kin', an' you ain't gonna be dead,
Gonna whop across yo' bosom with X,Y,Z,
I get through wit' you, you been clownin' wit' me.

3. A married man is a fool to think that his wife don't love
nobody but him.
Spoken: Now, come here, baby, now listen what I got to say,
I'm in love wit' you, but you don't mean me no good,
'Cause I'm in love wit' you, I'm not weak to you.

4. Repeat 1.

5. Repeat 2.

6. A married man is a fool to think that his wife don't love
nobody but him;
Cut yo' head four different ways,
That's long, short, deep an' wide;
When I get through to usin' this ole well sharpen' razor,
Sho' we gonna take a ride.

Lemon Nash, vocal and ukelele; New Orleans, Oct. 21, 1959.

More extended texts occur in Butterbeans and Susie, "A to
Z," OK 8163, New York City, Sept. 15, 1924, and Uncle Skipper,
"Cutting My ABC's," De 7353, c. 1935.

183. *Fiddle Blues*

1. Lord, I feel like jumpin' through the keyhole in yo' do', (2)
Lord, you jump this time, you sure won't jump no mo'.

2. Lord, I woke up, baby, with the blood all roun' my bed; (2)
I couldn't eat my breakfast, the blood all in my bread.

3. Lord, I love you baby, an' I'm scared to call yo' name,
Lord, I love you, baby, but I'm scare to call yo' name,
Lord, you're a married woman, I love you just the same.

Hogman (Matthew) Maxey, vocal and fiddle; Angola, April 14, 1959.

The first stanza also occurs in Blind Lemon Jefferson, "Mean Jumper Blues," Para 12631, Chicago, c. Feb. 1928; the opening line of the last stanza in Leroy Carr, "Tired of Your Lowdown Dirty Ways," Vo 1261, Supr 2255, Chicago, Feb. 1, 1929.

184. *Down by the Waterfall*

1. *Sally:* Oh, down to the waterfall, where I met you, (2)
You told me you loved me, oh yes, you know I love you, oh yes,
    I do.

2. Where in the green pastures, I an' you lay, (2)
That's where you told me that you love me.

3. *Smoky:* I say every day an' every night, every day long I
    have the blues, (2)
Baby, it's the woman I'm lovin, it's you I hate to lose.

4. I say nobody love me, an' nobody seem to care,
I say that nobody love me, an' nobody seem to care,
Well, you know I'm bad luck, boy, don't you know that I have
    had my share.

5. I'm gonna pack my suitcase, baby, I'm gonna move on down
    the line,
Yes, I'm gonna pack my suitcase, baby, I'm gonna move on down
    the line,
Where you don't see nobody laughin', an' you don't see nobody
    cryin'.

*Smoky Babe (Robert Brown), vocal and guitar; Sally Dotson,
vocal; Scotlandville, Feb. 10, 1961.*

185. *Midnight Blues*

1. Say, well, soon this mornin', when the clock was strikin' fo',
Yes, well, it was soon this mornin' when the clock was strikin' fo',
Oh, the girl I'm lovin', Lord, she don't want me no mo'.

2. You know it was late last night when the clock was strikin' fo',
Yes, it was late last night, baby, when the clock was strikin' fo',
Lord, my baby tole me, she goin' travel on.
Mm –

3. I woke up this mornin', I feelin' kinda bad,
I woke up this mornin', baby, an' feelin' kinda bad,
Yeah, the worst ole feelin' that a man most ever had.

4. I woke up this mornin' 'bout the break o' day,
You know soon this mornin', it was about the break o' day,
Yes, it was soon this mornin', about the break o' day,
Hoh, hoh, Lord, the woman I'm lovin', she didn't want me no
   mo'.
Mm –

*Guitar (Robert) Welch, vocal and guitar; Angola, March 21,
1959.*

186. *Gonna Move My Baby*

1. Woh, I'm gonna move my baby, woh gonna move her out on the 'skirts o' town,
Woh, I'm gonna move my baby, woh, gonna move on the 'skirts o' town,
Woh, the reason I'm gonna move her over there, boy, I don't want no one hangin' roun'.

2. Woh, gonna buy my groceries, baby, gonna buy 'em every day,
Woh, I don't need nobody, got to keep 'em 'way.
Boy, I got to buy my groceries, woh, Lord, an' carry 'em on out o' town,
Woh, Lord, I'm gonna stop that grocery boy, woh, from hangin' roun'.

3. Woh, I'm gonna buy me a icebox, baby, don't need no Frigidaire,
Woh, gonna buy me a icebox, woh Lord, don't need no Frigidaire,
Woh, Lord, I'm gonna break down that iceman's truck, woh, Lord, to keep him 'way.

4. *Spoken:* Play it for me, now, Hogman.
Sung: Woh, it may seem funny, baby, funny as it can be,
Woh, Lord, it may seem funny, baby, funny as it can be,
Woh, if we ever have any children, darlin', Lord, I wan' 'em to look like me.

Hogman (Matthew) Maxey, vocal and guitar; Angola, March 21, 1959.

Composed by Will Weldon and recorded by him as Casey Bill: Will Weldon, "We Gonna Move (To the Outskirts of Town)," Vo 03373, Chicago, Sept. 3, 1956. See also Big Bill (Broonzy) and his Chicago Five, "I'm Gonna Move to the Outskirts," OK 06651, Co 37196, March 6, 1942. Maxey's variant follows the recorded ones closely with the exceptions that he has confused the sense of the third stanza by reversing Frigidaire and icebox and that he has added an effective original line, "I'm gonna break that iceman's truck."

"I'm Gonna Move on the Outskirts of Town," words by Andy Razaf and William Weldon. Music by William Weldon. © Copyright MCMXLII, MCMLXIII by Music Corporation of America, 322 West 48th Street, New York, N. Y. 10036. Used by permission. All rights reserved.

187. *What Is Wrong With You?*

1. Now listen, woman, tell me what is wrong with you,
Now tell me, now tell me what is wrong with you.

2. You know I did everything you asked me to do, tryin' to keep
you pleased,
But after all you got the blues, listen woman,
Now tell me what is wrong with you,
I just can't please this woman, and it's no matter what I do.

3. You know I try double hard to get along with you,
That man that's on your mind must can do something I can't
do,
What is it woman, now tell me what is wrong with you?
I just can't please this woman, and it's no matter what I do.

4. You know I'm on my way now, must be this afternoon,
When I leave here this time, you don't see me no way soon,
Now listen woman, tell me what is wrong with you, etc.

5. Well you know I love that woman, tell this world I do,
Oh yes I love her, but she just won't be true,
But listen woman, etc.

*Herman E. Johnson, vocal and guitar; Baton Rouge, April
27, 1961.*

188. *She Was a Woman Didn't Mean*
    No One Man No Good

1. Yes, she was a woman, didn't mean no one man no good.

2. When you see me comin', baby, raise yo' window high,
When you see me comin', raise yo' window high,
When you see me leavin', hang yo' head an' cry.

3. I got a gal in town, woman sixteen years of age,
Got a gal, in town, sixteen years of age.
Yeah, she's a full-grown woman, but she just got childish ways.

4. Yeah, she's a full-grown woman, but she just got childish
ways.

*Charles Henderson, vocal and guitar; Butch (James) Cage,
fiddle; Zachary, Feb. 16, 1960.*

The second stanza has been reported by White, p. 295;
Odum and Johnson, *Negro Workaday Songs*, p. 126; Handy,
Blues: An Anthology, p. 11, and has appeared frequently in
recorded blues. The lines quoted by White were collected in
1915-1916, from a Negro block setter in a sawmill long before
they first appeared in a record.

> When you see me coming
> H'ist your window high,
> When you see me leaving
> Tuck your head and cry.

189. *Ordinary Blues* (II)

1. Eh, if you seen my baby, as I say, please won't you hurry
home,
Eeh, see my babe, please now hurry home,
You know I ain't had me no lovin', since my little girl been
gone.

2. I'm gonna write an' tell my mother, please ma'am, write an'
send for me,
Lord, I'm gonna write an' tell my mother, please, ma'am write,
send for me,
I'm in a world o' trouble an' all my trunk is free.

3. Lord, my mother tole me, my father tole me too,
Lord my mother have tole me, an' my father tole me too,
Hey, Leon, some brownskin woman gone be the death o' you.

4. Lord, I looks at my mother, swear begin to smile,
Eeh, I looks at my mother, swear begin to smile,
I say, "(If) good time kill me, Mama, please, Mama, let me die."

Leon Strickland, vocal and guitar; Killona, Nov. 27, 1959.

190. *Hesitation Blues*

1. I'm no doctor, doctor's son, but I can handle all the patient',
till the doctor come,

Chorus: Tell me how long do I have to wait?
        Do I get you when I need you?
        Don' you hesitate.

2. Oh the hesitatin' stockin' an' the hesitatin' shoe,
There's a hesitatin' woman, sing the hesitatin' blues,
Do I get you when I need you? Do I hesitate?
How long, etc.

3. Got a bran' new skillet, got a bran' new lid,
Got a bran' new woman, got a bran' new babe,
Tell me, etc.

4. Well, I ain't been to heaven, but I been tole,
The women over (there) got a sweet jelly roll,
Tell me, etc.

Butch (James) Cage, vocal and fiddle; Willie B. Thomas, vocal and guitar; Zachary, Nov. 27, 1960.

In 1915 W. C. Handy published "The Hesitating Blues," the first strain of which has essentially the same melody and the same chorus words as the variant sung by Cage and Thomas. Around the same time Smythe and Middleton of Louisville published "Hesitation Blues or Must I Hesitate." Handy built the song he copyrighted on a variant he collected from a wandering musician, who said he had it from a hymn. (Handy, *Blues: An Anthology*, p. 42.)

Blossom Seeley sang Handy's song in vaudeville in 1916. Among the early recordings were Eva Taylor and Sara Martin, "Hesitation Blues," OK 8082, New York, June 20, 1923; and Sam Collins, "Hesitation Blues," Gen 6379, Sept. 1927. See also Scarborough, pp. 276-77; White, p. 301, p. 339, p. 391.

191. Leavin' Blues (II)

1. I left my baby, sun was shinin' bright, (2)
Hey goodby gal, see you tomorrow night.

2. I'm worried an' I'm lonesome, sure I'm blue,
I ain't thinkin' 'bout nobody else but you.

3. I was standin' on the corner, baby, with my head hung down,
I was lookin' for you baby, you jus' could not be foun'.

4. Well, you left me lonesome, worried as I could be, (2)
Say, I wonder now why you wanta, little girl, mistreat pore me.

5. Now if you leavin', goodby, if you gone an' gone, (2)
That's all right, baby, I will not be here alone.

Smoky Babe (Robert Brown), vocal and guitar; Scotlandville, Nov. 3, 1960.

192A. *Baby, Please Don't Go*

1. Baby, please don't go,
Baby, please don't go,
You know I love you so.

2. Got me way down here,
You got me way down here,
An' treat me like a dog.

3. Now, mama, please don't go,
Baby, please don't leave,
An' go back to New Orleans,
I'll give anything you want,
Mama, please don't go.

4. You got me way down here,
You got me way down here,
In a rollin' fog,
An' treat me like a dog,
Now, mama, please don't go,
I give anything I got,
Mama, please don't go.

5. Baby, please don't go,
Baby, please don't go,
You know I love you so.

6. Lord, it's one man gone,
Lord, it's one man gone,
To the county farm,
He got his shackles on,
Now, mama, please don't go.

7. Baby, please don't go,
Baby, please don't go,
Back to New Orleans
To get yo' col' ice cream,
You know I love you so.

Guitar (Robert) Welch, vocal and guitar; Angola, March 31, 1959.

192B. *Baby, Please Don't Go*

1. Oh, now yo' man done gone, (3)
To the county farm,
He got his shackles on.

2. Baby, please don't go, (3)
Back to New Orleans,
You know I love you so.

3. Baby, please don't go,
Now, baby, please don't go, (2)
Back to New Orleans,
'Cause I love you so.

4. Believe yo' man done gone,
Back to the county farm,
He got his shackles on.

5. Repeat 4.

6. 'Fore I'll be yo' dog, (3)
I get you way down here,
Make you walk the log.

7. Baby, please don't go,
Now, baby, please don't go,
Now, please don't go,
Back to New Orleans,
An' get yo' col' ice cream.

8. 'Fore I'll be yo dog, (3)
I get you way down here,
I made you walk the log.

9. Repeat 2.

   *Smoky Babe (Robert Brown), vocal and guitar; Scotlandville,
Feb. 27, 1960.*

192C. *Baby, Please Don't Go*

1. Baby, please don't go, (3)
Back to New Orleans,
You know I love you so.

2. Repeat 1.

3. I believe my man is gone,
Believe my man is gone, (2)
To the county farm,
He got his shackles on.

4. Turn yo' lamp down low, (2)
I be with you all night long,
Baby, please don't go.

5. She got me way down here,
Got me way down here, (2)
Behind a rollin' fork,
You treat me like a dog,
Baby, please don't go.

6. Don't you call my name,
He got me way down here,
Got me way down here,
Behind a rollin' fork,
You treat me like a dog,
Baby, please don't go.

Charles Henderson, vocal and guitar; Butch (James) Cage, fiddle; Zachary, April 15, 1960.

"Baby, Please Don't Go" is a modern descendant of a field and prison song. Vera Hall of Livingston, Alabama, recorded an apparently related song for the Library of Congress in 1940, "Another Man Done Gone," which deals with the escape of a prisoner from the county chain gang.

The variants sung by Welch, Smoky Babe, and Henderson are directly or indirectly derived from Joe Williams, "Baby, Please Don't Go," Bb 6200, Oct. 31, 1935.

For a recording of Smoky Babe's performance, see *Hottest Brand Goin'*, PrB 1063, 1961.

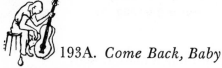

193A. *Come Back, Baby*

We's all at a saloon once, an' a boy come from up North an'
played it, an' I took it from him. He come down there for
the strawberry harvest. I seen him at a saloon, he 'roun' there
playin', him an' his wife, an' I went. But I never did see him
no mo'. 'Cause he had stopped in Hammond for the harvest,
you know, an' I was in Amite. Ridin' at night, like I out with
my guitar. I stood aroun' an' watched him play a while.

—*Leon Strickland*

1. Come back, baby, mama, please don't go,
The way'r I love you, don't nobody know,
Come back, woman, say we'll tell it over,
One more time.

2. You say goin' leave me, you goin' away,
You know'r I love you,
Whiles the blues goin' to stay.

3. Come back woman, mama, please don't go,
The way'r I love you, don't nobody know,
Come back, woman, say we'll tell it over,
One more time.

Leon Strickland, vocal and guitar; Killona, Nov. 27, 1959.

193B. *Come Back, Baby*

Chorus: Come back, honey, please don't go,
The way I love you, nobody know,
Oh, come back, baby, let's talk it over
One more time.

1. You know I love you, baby, tell the world I do,
The way I love you, honey, proud of you, so

Chorus:

2. I tell you, woman, I don't mean no harm,
I have to tell you, baby, you treat me wrong, so

Chorus:

3. She got a light in her mouth like a mornin' star,
What (you mean to me), baby, honey, you just don't know, so

Chorus:

4. Now looka here, little woman, you already know,
I don't think I'll ever be in love no mo', so

Chorus:

5. You don't want me, baby, whyn't you tell me so,
I won't be hangin' roun' your house no mo', so

Chorus:

   Otis Webster, vocal and guitar; Angola, Nov. 19, 1960.

194. *Rock Well Blues*

1. You know the reason why I sing the blues, baby,
When I get these women on my min',
I just can't be satisfie' until I catch any—oh Lord.

2. Yeah, you know what I'm talkin' about.
When I was out at night—hair like a horse's mane, oh Lord,
Well, I want to tell you, people, that black gal run me wil'.

3. Let me tell you women what I mean,
If you want me, you got to go by my rule, oh baby,
Yeah, that's what I'm talkin' about,
I might be your boy if you wear my pants.

4. If you wanta be my boss, you can take my pantses,
An' I would take yo' dress, baby,
To let you know I be a woman, run house,
An' I won't try to boss you roun'.

5. I want you to ride me, baby, the yother night, ride me till
   I say that I got enough,
Woh, ride me, babe, well I want you to ride me, baby, till I
say that I got e — — — — —.

6. Well, I got a coal black mare, you know she sure can saddle
   along,
I got a coal black mare, God knows she sure can saddle along,
She can ride me a while until I be right where (I belong).

*Robert Pete Williams, vocal and guitar; Baton Rouge, July
31, 1961.*

A metaphor for love-making like the one in the last stanza
in "Rock Well Blues" occurs in Big Bill Broonzy, "Black Mare,"
Mlt 7-01-57, April 22, 1936. See also Walter Davis, "Let Me in
Your Saddle," Bb 8282, 1938.

195. *She's A-lookin' for Me*

She a-look-in'   for,   she a-look-in'-   for me,

Yes, I know,   she a-look-in' for me.

1. She a-lookin' for, she a-lookin' for me,
Yes, I know, she a-lookin' for me.

2. I'm gonna catch me a train,
If I have to ride the top,
Because I know, she a-lookin' for me.

3. I am lookin', for my 'fiancée,
And I don't intend to stop *Spoken:* not until I finds her,
Sung: Because I know she a-lookin' for me.

4. I dreamed about her love,
And I almost cried,
Because I knew that she was lookin' for me.

5. Whenever I sees her in my dreams,
I know she's not satisfied,
That's how I knew that she was lookin' for me.
That's how I knew that she was lookin' for me.

6. Yes, she's lookin' for – – – –, she is lookin' for me,
Yes I know, she's a-lookin' for – – – – – – – – – –.

Herman E. Johnson, vocal and guitar; Baton Rouge, March 26, 1961.

196. *Ma Négresse M'a Quitté*

1. Ma Négresse m'a quitté,
Elle est partie au Texas;
Je suis bien malheureux, (2)
Ma femme m'a quitté.

2. Je suis bien malheureux, (2)
Ma Négresse m'a quitté,
Pour s'en aller bien loin de moi,
Je peux m'ennuyer. (2)

3. Depuis dimanche passé,
Depuis ma Négresse m'a quitté,
Je peux m'ennuyer, (3)
Comme un pauvre malheureux.

4. Tu es bien malheureux
Quand ta femme t'a quitté;
Y'avait pas de raison
Elle s'en va si loin de moi.

       1. My black woman has left me,
       She has gone to Texas;
       I am very unhappy, (2)
       My woman has left me.

       2. I am very unhappy, (2)
       My black woman has left me
       To go away very far from me,
       I can bore myself. (2)

       3. Since last Sunday,
       Since my black woman left me,
       I can bore myself, (3)
       Like a poor unhappy man.

       4. You are very unhappy
       When your woman has left you.
       There was no reason
       She went so far from me.

Godar Chalvin, vocal with Cajun accordion (primitive button accordion which plays in one key and has two chords, the tonic and the dominant); Abbeville, Feb. 10, 1956.

Abbeville is a town in southwest Louisiana, an area whose inhabitants are still predominantly descendants of the Acadians exiled from Acadie in French Canada in 1755 because they refused to swear loyalty forever to England and to bear arms against France. The exiles who found their way to Louisiana lived in comparative isolation from the rest of the country until well into the twentieth century with the result that even today most of the Acadians (now shortened to "Cajuns") are bilingual and there are still oldsters who speak only French, a dialect derived principally from the speech of the northern provinces of France. Chalvin sings blues in both English and Cajun French.

Traditionally in Cajun songs when a lover was rejected he departed for Texas, which to the country Frenchmen of Louisiana typified a frontier land, wild, adventurous, and remote.

197. *Anons au Bal, Calinda*

1. Anons au bal, Calinda, (3)
Dimanche matin dans le brouillard,
Ta robe est a déchirée.
Allons au bal, Calinda, (3)
Pourquoi tu ne dis pas, Calinda?

2. Dimanche matin dans le brouillard,
Ta robe est a déchirée;
Le dimanche matin dans le petit jour,
Ta robe est a déchirée.
Allons au bal Calinda, (7)
Dimanche matin dans le brouillard
Ta robe est a déchirée.

1. Let's go to the dance, Calinda;
Sunday morning in the fog,
Your dress was torn.
Let's go to the dance, Calinda, (7)
Why don't you speak, Calinda?

2. Sunday morning in the fog,
Your dress was torn;
Sunday morning at dawn,
Your dress was torn.
Let's go to the dance, Calinda.
Sunday morning in the fog,
Your dress was torn.

Godar Chalvin, vocal with Cajun accordion; Abbeville, Feb. 10, 1956.

"Anons au Bal, Calinda" is derived from a voodoo dance brought to Louisiana by Negro slaves from San Domingo and the Antilles. The state authorities considered the dance so disturbingly erotic that they banned it in 1843. The song was picked up by Cajuns and became widely known in southwest Louisiana with a text in which Calinda was the name of a girl. The incident of the girl's return early in the morning with her dress incriminatingly torn or disordered also occurs in variants of "Alberta" or "Corinne, Corinna," which was a best selling rock-and-roll hit as recorded by Fats Domino. For Godar Chalvin's performance, see *A Sampler of Louisiana Folksongs*, LFS A-1, 1957.

198A. *Alberta*

1. Ole Alberta, ole Alberta, Lord, don't you hear me callin' you,
Well, you three times seven, an' you know what you want to
– – – –.

2. Repeat

3. Well, I pawn my pistol, an' I pawn my watch an' chain,
I pawn poor Alberta, but she wouldn't even sign her name.

4. Alberta, Alberta, don't you hear pore Bob callin' on – – – –,
You three times seven, an' you soon will be twentyone.

5. Well, I love you Alberta, an' I tell the world I do,
An' the day that you quit me, Alberta, that day you die.

6. Well, I'm down an' I'm worried, but I won't be worried
always,
Say you flyin' high now, but you comin' down to my size.

7. Tell me, tell me, Alberta, Alberta, baby, why don't you
change yo' lowdown ways,
You better not leave home, or I'll haunt you all yo' days.

8. I say, tell me, Berta, Berta, when you comin' back home to
– – – – –,
Don't you know that I'm lonesome without yo' love?

Robert Pete Williams, vocal and guitar; Denham Springs, Feb.
21, 1960.

 198B. *Corinna*

1. Corinna, Corinna, where you been so long, (2)
Been long since I had some lovin',
Since you been gone.

2. First you build yo' playhouse,
Now ya actin' the fool,
Well it's a lowdown shame,
Ya broke yo' daddy's rule.

3. I know you been to Hammond, how in the world you know
(2)
I can feel it by yo' apron, an' the dress you wore before.

4. Corinne, Corinne, what's yo' head doin' red? (2)
The Devil stole my derby, sun done burned my head.

5. Corinne, Corinne, you ain't treatin' me right, (2)
It's a lowdown shame, you broke yo' daddy's rule.

Charles Henderson, vocal and guitar; Butch Cage, fiddle; Zachary, Oct. 10, 1960.

198C. *Tomorrow Gonna Be My Tryin' Day*

1. Oh tomorrow, oh tomorrow, gonna be my tryin' day,
Oh I'm goin' down yonder, see what that mean ole judge gonna say.

2. That mean Alberta, where you stay last (night),
Your hair all wild, an' you know you ain't talkin' right.

3. An' I met, I met Alberta, 'way cross the sea,
She wouldn't write me no letter, she wouldn't (care for me).

4. Alberta, Alberta, what you gonna do?
I done everything for to try an' get along with you.

5. Oh tomorrow, oh tomorrow, gonna be my tryin' day,
Oh I'm goin' down yonder, see what that mean ole judge gonna
— — — —.

6. Well I met, I met Alberta, 'way 'cross the sea,
Well, she wouldn't write me no letter, an' she don't care for me.

Butch (James) Cage, vocal and fiddle; Willia B. Thomas, vocal and guitar; Zachary, Dec. 5, 1960.

198D. *C. C. Rider*

1. Well now, C. C. Rider, gal will you see what you have done?
You know you made me love you, and now your man has come.

2. It was a great long engine and a little small engineer,
It took my woman away along and it left me standin' here.
But if I just had listened unto my second min',
I don't believe, I'd-a been here, wringin' my hands an' cryin'.

3. But there is no mo' potatoes, you see the frost have killed
the vine,
And the blues ain't nothin' but a good gal on your min'.

4. I been tellin' you little woman and I told your partner too,
That you're three times seven, and you know what you wants
to do.

5. Now, if you see Corinna, will you tell her to hurry home,
but I ain't had no true love, since Corinna been gone.

*Herman E. Johnson, vocal and guitar; Baton Rouge, March
26, 1961.*

"Alberta," or "Corinna" as it is alternatively called, is at
least half a century old, widely familiar in folk circles and frequently recorded. The same tune is also well-known in the
many variants of "The Midnight Special," a favorite prison
song in the South, localized to fit various prisons. See John
and Alan Lomax, *American Ballads and Folksongs,* pp. 71-75.

An early reference to Alberta occurs in a song collected by
Odum around 1906, "I'm on My Last Go-Round":

God knows Albirdie won't write to me,

(*The Negro and His Songs,* p. 181) a precursor of the lines in
the Cage and Thomas song, "Tomorrow Gonna Be My Tryin'
Day":

Well, I met Alberta 'way 'cross the sea,
Well, she wouldn't write me no letter, an' she don't care for me.

Another early appearance of a stanza is given by Anna Franz
Odum, "Some Negro Folksongs from Tennessee," JAF, XVII,
1914, p. 265:

> Where did you stay last night?
> Where did you stay last night?
> Your hair all rumpled up,
> Your clothes ain't on you right.

Herman Johnson's "C. C. Rider," which has the standard tune usually associated with that title, comes from Blind Lemon Jefferson, "Corinna Blues," Para 12367, Chicago, c. May 1926. Except for Herman's omission of the repetitions of the last line of each stanza and minor variations in phrases, the texts are essentially identical.

The line in the Robert Pete Williams "Alberta"—

> An' the day you quit me, Alberta, that day you die

also appears in Tommy McClennan, "Black Minnie,"

> But the day you quit me, Black Minnie, I swear that's the day
> you die.

The Cage and Thomas variant is a combination of a prison song, which is represented by the opening stanza, and standard Alberta-Corinna verses such as appear in Tampa Red and Georgia Tom, "Corinne Corinna," Vo 1450, Chicago, Dec., 1929.

In Henderson's variant the fourth stanza is descended from a nineteenth century Negro song about a woodpecker, one form of which runs:

> Way the woodpecker's head is red,
> Bill Billix say to dat woodpecker bird:
> W'at makes yo' topknow red?
> Says he: "I'se picked in de red-hot sun,
> Till it's done burned my head,"

(Talley, p. 207)

The same basic idea found its way from the song of the woodpecker to "De Ballit of de Boll Weevil." (Lomax, *Amercian Ballads and Folk Songs,* p. 113.)

See also Huddie Ledbetter, "Alberta," Bb B8559, Stin SLP 48, New York City, June 15, 1940; Jesse James, "Corinna's Boogy," SIW 569, c. 1950; Cat Iron, "Don't Your House Look Lonesome," Fkwy, FA 2389, c. 1957, and Fats Domino, "Corinne Corinna," Im, c. 1956, Rock-and-Roll hit.

199. *Fast Life Woman*

1. Woh, fast life woman, well your life won't last you long,
Woh, fast life woman, your life won't last you long,
Well, you done run around so long, baby, you gon' lose your happy home.

2. Oh, the moon risin', darlin', oh the sun shinin' in the west,
Oh Lord, the moon risin', baby, oh Lord, the sun shinin' in the west,
Oh Lord, I had to leave you, baby, I know that for the best.
Spoken: Play it for me a little while, Hogman.

3. *Sung:* Woh, operator, operator, what time your next train leave goin' east, (2)
Woh, you know I got to leave here, darlin', don't I never have no peace.

4. Woh, Katy May, Katy May, where you stay last night,
Oh, Katy May, wonder where you stay last night,
Oh you know your hair all tore down, darlin', your clothes don't fit you right.

Hogman (Matthew) Maxey, vocal and guitar; Angola, March 27, 1959.

The last stanza is a variant on lines in "Alberta" and "Corinna."

200. *The Deceitful Brownskin*

1. I got a brown cross town, an' she's tall as a sycamore tree, (2)
That's the gal that walks through the rain an' snow, just to ease
    that pain for me.

2. Brownskin gal is deceitful, till gets you all worn down, (2)
When she get all your pocket change, then she drive you from
    her town.

3. I went home last night an' found a note in my brownskin'
    do', (2)
"Daddy, stay away, has got yo' room an' you can't live here no
    mo'."

4. I been walkin' an' walkin', walk till my feet got soakin' wet,
I commence to walkin', walk till my feet got soakin' wet,
Tryin' to find some good old mama, but I ain't found her yet.

5. But the sun is gonna shine in my back do' some day, (2)
I'll have one more drink, gonna drive these blues away.

6. She's a heavy hipted woman, an' the meat shakes on her bone',
She's a heavy hip-fasted woman, an' the meat shakes on her
    bone',
Every time it shake, some poor boy leavin' home.

Herman E. Johnson, vocal and guitar; Baton Rouge, May 10,
1961.

Follows closely Blind Lemon Jefferson, "Deceitful Brown
Skin Blues," Para 12551, 1927.

201. *Sundown Blues (II)*

1. Oh it's been a long time, since I carried your books to school,
(2)
Well we used to laugh and have fun, ride home on grandpa's
mule.

2. Woh, can't tell my baby, when I'm comin' back home,
Mm, mm, can't tell my baby when I'm comin' back home,
Lord, I miss her so bad, I'm rollin' in my room.

3. Woke, woke up this mornin', looked out my door,
Oh, somebody else done told me, "You can't live here no mo',
No use to cryin', baby, you can't live here no mo',
Lord, that key you got baby, won't fit my lock no mo'."

4. Woh, left walkin', my head hangin' down an' cryin', (2)
Know my baby done quit me, it really stand on my min',

5. Don't let it worry you, she'll be back home one day,
Woh, don't let it worry you, baby, she'll be back home one day,
Oh, she must have had to leave me, she wouldn't-a never went
away.

6. Oh I know you gonna miss me, oh Lord, 'fore the sun go
down,
Mm, mm, know you gonna miss me, baby, woh 'fore the sun
go down,
Oh to be your dog, baby, but I just can't let you dog me aroun'.

*Hogman (Matthew) Maxey, vocal and guitar; Angola, March
27, 1959.*

202A. *Careless Love*

1. Well it's love, oh love, oh careless love, (2)
Love done made, she done made me weep and moan,
Love have made me lose my happy home.

2. Well don't you see what careless love have done,
Don't you see what careless love have done,
It have made me weep, love made me weep and moan,
It have made me lose my happy home.

3. Love made me wish that I was dead,
Love have made me wish that I was dead,
Love have made me lose my happy home.

4. Well it's love, oh love, oh careless love,
Let me show you what careless love will do,
It will make you weep, then it will make you moan,
It have made you leave your happy home.

   Guitar (Robert) Welch, vocal and guitar (bottle-neck style); Angola, Feb. 14, 1959.

202B. *Careless Love*

1. You see what careless love will do, (2)
You leave my home, you can't stay long, (2)
You left me baby, standin' lone.

2. You left me once, you left me twice, (2)
You left me, baby, standin' cryin',
You say, you see what careless love will do,
You see what careless love,
Oh cause me to leave my home to follow you.

3. You cause me to weep, you cause me to moan,
You cause me to leave my happy home,

I love you, baby, woh, and your sister too,
You say, you say what careless love will do.

Hogman (Matthew) Maxey, vocal and guitar; Angola, March 21, 1959.

W. C. Handy had heard and played the tune as early as 1892 in Bessemer, Alabama. (Handy, *Father of the Blues,* p. 147.) A variant collected around 1906 appears in Odum and Johnson, *The Negro and His Songs,* p. 194 as "Kelly's Love." (Since *Kelly's* and *careless* sound essentially identical in Negro folk speech, I suspect someone, either the informant or the collector, confused the two words.) See also Handy's copyrighted variant, "Careless Love," *Blues: An Anthology,* pp. 55-57, which includes several folk stanzas (he published a "Loveless Love," in which only the tune of the chorus is folk, pp. 75-78), Richardson, p. 50; Sandburg, p. 21; White, pp. 326-327; Lunsford, pp. 40-41; Randolph, pp. 306-308.

Among numerous recordings are Lulu Jackson, Vo 1193, Per 195, Supt S2227, Ban 32387, 1928; Lonnie Johnson, OK 8635, 1928; Ruth Johnson, Para 13060, 1930; Bessie Smith, Mlt 8-02-66, Vo 03456, 1937.

203. *Bastard Child*

1. I'm, yeah, a-worried, yeah, a-worried by myself,
Yes, I'm a-worried, Lord, I'm a-worried by myself,
I was thinkin' 'bout you, darlin', God know I know you with
   someone else.

2. Yeah, I'm leavin' you this evenin', yes, I'ma leave you all
   alone,
I'm gonna leave you this evenin', an' I leave you all alone,
I'm gonna tell you all that happen, 'cause God knows that you
   done me wrong. Yeah!

3. Yeah, now my mother ain't worrie', Lord, my father laid
   down an' died,
Yeah, my mother, poor lone gal, an' my father laid down an'
   died,
I'm gonna tell you about it, Lord knows you know the reason
   why.

4. Now you know my mother, poor thing, ain't married, God
   knows I have to be a bastard child,
Spoken: Now you know that.
Sung: Now my mother, poor thing, ain't married, Lord, I have
   to be bastard,
Ain't no need o' me askin' you no question now, sir, God knows
   she ought to know what's the reason why.

*Roy Lee Jenkins, vocal and guitar; Scotlandville, May 19,
1960.*

204. *Make Me a Pallet on Your Floor*

1. I woke up this mornin', baby, blues all round my bed, (2)
Oh, looked in my breakfast, blues all in my — — — — — — —.

2. "Won't you run here, woman, sit down on my knee,"
I said, "Run here, woman, sit down on my — — — — — — —,
I got somethin' to tell ya, baby, make the hair rise on yo'
— — — — — —."

3. "Make me down a pallet, make it down on yo' floo',
Make me down a pallet, make it down on yo' — — — —,
Make it any way, darlin', that the yother man won't know.

4. "Shake, shake, woman, I'm gonna buy you a diamond ring,
Shake, shake, baby, I'm gonna buy you a diamond ring,
If you don't shake, darlin', I ain't gonna buy you a doggone
thing."

*Robert Pete Williams, vocal and guitar; Angola, Oct. 21,
1959.*

For a recording of Williams' performance, see *Those Prison
Blues,* FL 109, 1959.

205. *I Won't Be Yo' Lowdown Dog No Mo'*

1. I sent for you yesterday, here you come today,
Yeah, I sent for you yesterday, here you come today,
Lord, with your mouth wide open, and I wonder what you have
to say.

2. I so long for wrong, baby, been your dog,
I so long for wrong, baby, I been your dog,
'Fore I do it again, baby, I sleep in a hollow log.

3. Heh, sent for you yesterday, here you come today,
Yeah, sent for you yesterday, here you come today,
Lord, your mouth wide open, and you ain't got a word to say.

4. Ain't gonna be your lowdown dog no mo',
Ain't gonna be your lowdown dog no mo',
'Fore I'll go do (it) now, woman, gonna pack my clothes and go.

5. Yeah, fare you well, fare you well, good-by,
I'm gonna see you, baby, when your trouble get like mine.
Spoken: Goin' out here, boy! That's what I'm about. Yeah,
heh! Quit your foolishness.

Lucius Bridges: Yeah, stop it now. Just like they did. Cut
up like I don't know who. Where you been?

Percy Strickland: Church.

Lucius: You been to church? And come back doing all that
boogy-woogyin' like that? Huh? Let me see what you did.
That boy boogyin' up a wow. Good gracious alive!

*Leon Strickland, vocal and guitar; Lucius Bridges, thimbles
and washboard; Leslie Anders, banging the back of a guitar;
Killona, Nov. 27, 1959.*

When I was having an all-day recording session at Leon's
country shack on a Sunday his wife, mother, and several of his
children (he said he had " 'bout eleven") went off to church.
After they had returned, Percy Strickland, then seven years old,
started to tap dance exuberantly to his father's swingy guitar
playing. Lucius Bridges, a visitor from New Orleans reproved
him with mock indignation.

206. *Steppin' in the Valley*

1. Oh mama, talk to your daughter, (2)
Talk to your daughter, she sure look good to me.

2. Talk to your daughter, where she stay last night?
Oh talk to your daughter, where she stay last night,
Her hair tore down, and her clothes don't fit her right.

3. She rock an' roll, she rock, baby, all night long, (2)
Love to rock, but she just won't stay at home.

4. She start that rockin', she wasn't but nine years old, (2)
She got to rock to satisfy her soul.

5. Oh I like your lovin', I'm crazy about the way you do, (2)
Say I love you, baby, you oughta love me too.

Hogman (Matthew) Maxey, vocal and guitar; Angola, Feb. 27, 1959.

The second stanza, here somewhat changed to fit the context, is usually associated with "Alberta" and "Corinna," but is also one of the most common wandering stanzas since it fits so aptly into any blues about an unfaithful woman.

207A. *Louise*

Chorus: Louise is the sweetest gal I know, (2)
          She made me walk from Chicago to the Gulf o' Mexico.

1. Now looka here, little Louisa, who been fishin' in my pon',
He catchin' all my perchie, an' grindin' up the bone,

Chorus: Louise, that will never do,
          Here you made me walk from Chicago to the Gulf o'
          Mexico.

2. Now the big boat is up the river, she's on a bank o' san',
If she don't strike the water, I don't believe she'll never lan',

Chorus: Louise, sweetest gal I know,
          She made me walk from Chicago to the Gulf o' Mexico.

3. Now looka here, little Louisa, what you want me to do,
Be yo' mother an' yo' father, an' yo' doctor too?

Chorus:

Charles Henderson, vocal and guitar; Butch (James) Cage, fiddle; Willie B. Thomas, guitar; Zachary, May 15, 1962.

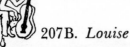

207B. *Louise*

1. Louise, you's the sweetest gal I know, (2)
She made me walk from Chicago, right t'the Gulf o' Mexico.

2. Tell me, Louise, what you tryin' to do,
Give the yother man my lovin' an' me too?
You know, Louise, Louise, that won't do,
Tryin' to love me, baby, an' love some yother man too.

3. Big boat's up the river out on a bank o' san',
If she never get the water, I swear she never lan',
You know, Louise, baby, why don't you hurry home?
I ain't had no lovin' since Louise been gone.

4. Somebody been fishin' in my pon',
Catchin' all my perchie,
Grindin' up my bone,
Louise, baby, what is you tryin' to do,
Give some yother man my lovin' an' try to love me too?

5. Louise is the sweetest gal I know,
She made me walk from Chicago to the Gulf o' Mexico.

6. Some like a rattlesnake piled, when it's in its coil,
When it get to lovin', gets all out its coil,
Louise, baby, what is you tryin' to do,
Give some yother man my lovin', an' try to love me too?

Robert Pete Williams, vocal and guitar; Angola, Sept. 22, 1959.

The above two blues are folk variants of "Louise, Louise Blues," words and music by Johnny Temple and J. Mayo Williams, © copyright MCMXXXIV, MCMLXIII by Music Corporation of America, 322 West 48th Street, New York, N. Y. 10036, used by permission, all rights reserved.

Some of the recordings which may have influenced Henderson and Williams are Big Bill Broonzy, "Louise, Louise," Mlt 7-08-65, Vo 03075, June 9, 1937; Bob Crosby and his orchestra, "Louise, Louise, Blues," De 2032, DeE F6930, March 1938.

208. *Trouble in Mind*

1. Trouble in mind, I'm blue,
But I won't be blue always,
For the sun gone shine,
In my back door some day.

2. Trouble in mind, I do,
Never had no trouble,
Trouble in my life,
My life before.

3. My good gal has quit me,
An' it sho' do grieve my min',
Some time I feel like laughin',
Some time I feel like dyin'.

4. Goin' to the river, gonna take me a rockin' chair,
If the blues overtake me,
Gonna rock away from here.

5. Trouble in mind, I do,
Never had no trouble,
In my life, before.

Roosevelt Charles, vocal, Otis Webster, guitar; Angola, Nov. 19, 1960.

Composed by Richard M. Jones in 1926, first recorded by Thelma La Vizzo (with Jones at the piano), "Trouble in Mind Blues," Para 12206, Chicago, 1924. "Trouble in Mind," words and music by Richard M. Jones, © copyright MCMXXVI, MCMXXXVII by MCA Music a division of MCA Inc., New York N. Y. © Copyright renewed MCMLIII and assigned to MCA Music, a division of MCA Inc., New York, N. Y. Used by permission, all rights reserved.

209. *Moon Is Risin'*

1. You know the moon is risin', baby, an' the sun is sinkin' low,
You know the moon is risin', baby, Lord, an' the sun is sinkin'
  low,
Oh, I was just wonderin', why me and my baby have to go away.

2. Lord I been standin' by, waitin' for my phone to ring,
Lord, I call up Central, I can't even hear my phone ring,
Lord, moon is risin', yes an' the sun is sinkin' low,
Trouble in my mind, wonderin' where my time.

3. Thinkin' 'bout my baby, she might call today,
I don't know why do my trouble come thisaway,
Spoken: Now I just wanta call my baby,
Just one more time in life.
Sung: Baby, hey, woh, baby way, why don't you please call me
  today,
Because tomorrow is too far away.
I wanta know why my baby won't call me today,
Because I love that woman, Lord, an' I tell the world I do,
If she don't call today, she might call me tomorrow night.

   *Roosevelt Charles, vocal; Otis Webster, guitar; Angola, Nov.
5, 1960.*

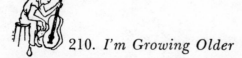

210. *I'm Growing Older*

1. I'm growing older, I'm growing older,
But I just can't help myself, I just can't help myself,
After she got all of my little pocket change, she run off with
   someone else.

2. I can't tell hardly, I can't tell hardly,
That's Monday from Tuesday, and Tuesday from Wednesday
   noon,
But either Thursday, Friday, or Saturday, but Sunday I'll be
   there soon.

3. Now don't deny me, woman, don't deny me,
That all that I, that's all that I can do,
But I want you to remember that some day you'll be old too.

4. Now, don't mistreat me, now don't mistreat me,
Because I am growing, because I am growing old,
Now you can have your another boy friend without you bein'
   so bold.

5. You treats me mean gal, you treats me mean, gal,
An' you treats me dirty, filthy an' dirty too,
An' there is no tellin', what a gal like you won't do.

6. I'm gonna leave here walkin', gonna leave here walkin',
But I don't know where I will go,
Because the woman I been lovin', she drove me from her door.

7. I got a gal, man, I got a gal, man,
An' she's tall as a cypress, she's tall as a cypress tree,
An' she walk through the rain, cold weather, just to be with me.

8. But she's deceitful, man, she's deceitful,
An' she's tryin' to get me all worn down,
After she get all o' my little pocket change,
She gonna drive me from her town.

*Herman E. Johnson, vocal and guitar; Baton Rouge, May 12,
1961.*

The tune resembles that in Memphis Minnie, "Me and My
Chauffeur Blues," OK 6288, May 1941, Chicago.

211. *Teasin' Blues*

1. Now, looka here, woman, what you call yourself tryin' to do,
Now looka here, baby, what you call yourself tryin' to do pore
  Bob,
Try to walk out on me, baby, do you think pore Bob was lyin'
  here asleep?

2. Now don't cheat me, woman, I don't stand no cheatin' roun',
Now, looka here, baby, I don't stand no cheatin' aroun',
I want you to know, baby, you know me better'n that.

3. Well, you don't want me, woman, just because I done growed
  old,
You don't want me, baby, just because I done growed old,
Well, that's all right, woman, you gonna want me one day.

4. You find a young man, you like better than you do me,
You find a young man, darlin', one you like better'n you do me.

*Robert Pete Williams, vocal and guitar; Baton Rouge, July
31, 1961.*

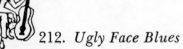

212. *Ugly Face Blues*

1. I got up this mornin', now I put on my shoes,
I string my shoes, then I wash my face,
I walk to the mirror, for to comb my hair,
I made a move, didn't know what to do,
I stepped forward, start to break an' run,

Chorus: Oh baby, oh baby, baby this ain't me,
       I done got so ugly, I don' even know myself.

2. I'm goin' to town, have some pictures made,
I'm gonna bring 'em back, put 'em side by side,
I'm gonna take a good look,
See if they's the same as me.

Chorus: Oh no, oh no, baby, oh this ain't me,
       I done got so ugly, I don't even know myself.

3. Mama said, when I was a baby,
Pretties' thing she had,
Now look what remain of the thing in the past,

Chorus: Baby, baby, this ain't me,
       I done got so ugly, I don't – – – – – – – – – – – – – –.

4. I was standin' on the porch, lookin' down the street,
I looked like somethin' hadn't seen in a week,
Baby, this ain't me, oh baby, this ain't me.
I got so ugly, I don't even know myself.

Robert Pete Williams, vocal and guitar; Baton Rouge, Oct. 20, 1960.

An original song. For Williams' performance, see *Free Again,* PrB 1026, 1960.

213. *You Don't Know My Min'*

1. You don't know, you don't know, you don't know, doggone you,
You don't know, you don't know, my min',

Chorus: But when you sees me laughin', that's just to keep from cryin'.

2. I served my little woman sweet jelly roll, took the shoes off my feet, an' put me out in the col',
Man, you don't know, you don't know my min',

Chorus:

3. I asked my little woman, could she stand to see me cry,
Told me, "Why heck yes, I can stand to see you die,"
You don't know, now can you know my min',

Chorus:

4. Got a handful o' nickels, pocketful o' dimes,
Houseful o' children, neither one of them is mine,
How can you know, man, you don't know my min',

Chorus:

5. You don't know, you don't know, you don't know, doggone you,
Spoken: Woman, you don't know, I say.

Chorus:

Herman E. Johnson, vocal and guitar; Baton Rouge, May 12, 1961.

First recorded by Virginia Liston, "You Don't Know My Mind," OK 81344, New York City, Nov. 15, 1923. Among numerous other recordings are Clara Smith, "You Don't Know My Mind Blues," Co 14013-D, New York, Jan. 29, 1924; Barbecue Bob (Robert Hicks), "Honey, You Don't Know My Mind," Co 14246-D, Atlanta, June 15, 1927; Tampa Red, "She Don't Know My Mind," Bb 6498, Chicago, April 1, 1936. Odum and Johnson, *Negro Workaday Songs*, p. 210, reports that it was sung by Left Wing Gordon, who (like Butch Cage and Willie B. Thomas) would use the chorus as a wandering stanza, and readily fit it into many different songs. Odum and Johnson also state, p. 210, "numerous vulgar versions of the same title were current among Negroes long before the formal song was published."

Herman Johnson's performance is a folk variant of "You Don't Know My Mind," words and music by Virginia Liston, Samuel Gray, and Clarence Williams, © Copyright MCMXX-III, MCMXXIV by MCA Music, a division of MCA Inc., New York, N. Y. © Copyright renewed MCML, MCMLI and assigned to MCA Music, a division of MCA Inc., New York, N. Y. Used by permission, all rights reserved.

214. *Worried Blues* (I)

1. You can carry me to the river, you sure can't make me swim, (2)
Woh, baby, I know you love me, woh, I know you in love with him.

2. Woh, you can tell when your baby, woh, if she's got another man, (2)
Oh, she don't wanna do nothin' you tell her, woh, she's so hard to understan'.

3. Oh decided this mornin', oh gonna let her go,
Mm, mm, decided this mornin', woh Lord, I let her go,
Woh, she had spent all my money, she don't want me no mo'.

4. Woh, woh, woke up this mornin', blood all round my bed,
Woke up this mornin', blood all round my bed,
Woh, know she was goin', woh, I heard what she said.

Hogman (Matthew) Maxey, vocal and guitar; Angola, March 27, 1959.

215. *I Just Keeps on Wantin' You*

Had a little female difficulty, cause me to compose this little thing, but after all, we won't discuss that, that's the cause o' me composin' it, a little female difficulty. Another guy gettin' between me an' my little female, cause me to want a little bit; I'm gonna pull the trigger if you won't do better.
—Herman E. Johnson

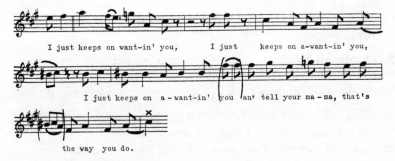

I just keeps on want-in' you, I just keeps on a-want-in' you,

I just keeps on a-want-in' you an' tell your ma-ma, that's

the way you do.

Chorus: I just keeps on wantin' you,
I just keeps on a-wantin' you,
I just keeps on a-wantin' — — —
An' tell your mama, that's the way you do.

1. An' tell your mama, that's the way you do,
You don't cook, you don't wash my clothes, (3)
But every time I look, you is in the road.

Chorus: Now, I just keeps on wantin' — — — —,
I just keeps on wantin' — — — —,
I just keeps on wantin' — — — —,
An' tell your mama, that's the way you do.

2. Can you remember last Friday night? (3)
I put my arm around your sister, an' she wanted to fight.

Chorus: But I just keeps on wantin' you,
I just keeps on wantin' — — — — —,
I just keeps on wantin' — — — — —,
Mama, that's not the way to do.

3. Seem like you just gotta have your way, (3)
But you keeps me broken hearted both night an' day

Chorus: I just keeps on wantin' you,
   I just keeps on wantin' – – –,
   An' tell your mama – – – – – – – –.

Herman E. Johnson, vocal and guitar; Baton Rouge, May 10, 1961.

The text is original, the tune is derived from a folksong which has been widely recorded, e.g., James "Boodle It" Wiggins, "Keeps A-Knockin' An' You Can't Get In," Para 12662, Bwy 5086, Chicago, c. Feb. 1928.

Odum and Johnson quote a text of an early variant, collected c. 1906, "I Couldn't Git In," the complaint of the lover of a prostitute who is busy with an all-night customer:

> Lawd, I went to my woman's do',
> Jus' lak I bin goin' befo';
> "I got my all-night trick, baby,
> An' you can't git in."

> "Come back 'bout half pas' fo',
> If I'm done, I'll open de do'.
> Got my all-night trick, baby,
> An' you can't git in."

(*The Negro and His Songs*, p. 189)

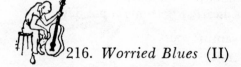

216. *Worried Blues* (II)

1. You know I'm worried baby, Lord, but I won't be worried long,
You know I'm worried, mama, Lord, but I won't be worried long,
Companion I'm lovin', Lord, she done been here an' gone.

2. You know my suitcase packed, Lord, an' my trunk's already gone,
My suitcase packed, baby, Lord, an' my trunk's already gone,
You know 'bout that my little woman, Lord, is somethin' goin' on wrong.

3. I believe, I believe, Lord I believe, baby, I believe I make a change,
I believe, little woman, Lord, I'll make a change,
I'm gonna find me another little woman,
Go back to your other man.
Spoken: Play it a while, man.

Spoken: Play it a while, man.

4. *Sung:* May be the last time you can hear your baby say, (2)
Well it's your time, baby, but it's gonna be mine some day.

Guitar (Robert) Welch, vocal and guitar; Angola, March 27, 1959.

217. *Out in West Texas*

1. I say the blues left Texas, lopin' like a mule, (2)
Takes a high brown woman, I swear she's hard to fool.

2. You can fall from the mountain, mama, down in the deep blue sea,
You can fall from the mountain, mama, down in the deep blue sea,
You ain't done no fallin', baby, till you fall in love with me.

3. Lord, I can't see why old Guitar can't get no mail,
Well, I can't see why old Guitar can't get no mail,
Lord I dreamed last night that a black cat done crossed my trail.

4. I'm gonna get me a rocker, I'm gonna rock on away from here, (2)
'Cause the woman I'm lovin', she sure don't feel my care.

5. Lord, excuse me, baby, knockin' on your door,
Lord, excuse me, mama, for knockin' on your door,
Lord, if my mind don't change, mama, I never knock there no more.

6. I see my baby comin' way on down the road,
Lord, I see my baby comin' way on down the road,
Lord, there's nobody here, I swear I can't do my roll.

7. Put me in your rocker, mama, rock me away from here,
Put me in your rocker, baby, an' rock me away from here,
Lord, there's no one here seems to feel my care.

Guitar (Robert) Welch, vocal and guitar; Angola, March 27, 1959.

The first stanza occurs in Blind Lemon Jefferson, "Got the Blues," Para 12354, Feb., 1926.

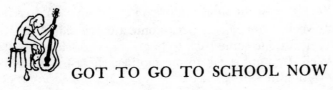

GOT TO GO TO SCHOOL NOW

218. *Broke My Mother's Rule*

1. You know I'm all down an' worried, because I broke my
   mother's rule,
   You know that I'm all down an' worried, you know I broke my
   mother's rule,
   Been out on the solid highway, keep from goin' to school.

2. Well, I done come back home ain't to school at all,
   Well, I done come back to home, ain't to school at all,
   Well, I go an' speak to me mother, she ask me, "How you get
   along in school today?"

3. "Well, I got along all right, mother,"
   She wanta know I been workin' har',
   "Well, I was a good boy today, mother,"
   I didn't catch no beatin' at all.

4. Well, when my mother foun' out, she sho' laid the hard wood
   on me,
   When she foun' out that I wasn't goin' to school,
   My mother beat me with a rawhide whip.

5. Woh, in this town, the people all call me a fool,
   In this town, in this town, peoples all call me a fool,
   The peoples all call me a fool, darlin', because I didn't go to
   school at all.

6. Well, I'm leavin' Louisiana, I just don't like here no mo',
   Well, I'm leavin' Louisiana, darlin', Lord knows I don't like
   here no mo'.
   Well the peoples here seem to be so aggravatin', they don't
   know how to treat no man.

*Robert Pete Williams, vocal and guitar; Baton Rouge, June
1, 1960.*

This song is largely original, but it is in a well-established
tradition in which the singer tells how he broke his mother's
rule, for example, Mississippi Moaner (Isaiah Nettles), "So
Cold in China," Vo 03166, Jacksonville, Oct. 1935:

> I was a li'l boy, on ma way to school,
> Was a little boy—ooh—on ma way to school,
> An' a high-brown woman, an' she broke my mammy's rule.

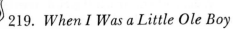

219. *When I Was a Little Ole Boy*

1. When I was a li'l ole boy,
I was not but ten years old,
An' many man an' wife was pickin' cotton, too,
They work' so hard, I was sittin' on a tree.
When I growed up, he said, "Son, you know things are hard."
An' I said, "What, Daddy?" He told me,
"Son, you know one thing?" I say, "What?"
"I work so hard in my days to raise you."
I say, "Yessuh." "Have to go outside, pickin' cotton,
Pullin' corn." I say, "Yessuh."
An' he told me that I want you to do, do do the same thing.

2. Then I told my daddy, "Looka here, Daddy."
He say, "What?" "You know one thing?"
I say, "The day way back there is over with."
He say, "Yeah?" I say, "Everybody got to go to school now these
    days."
He say, "Well, son, you right about that."
An' he didn't tell me nothin' else then.

3. Ever since then he sent me to school
To learn what I can in school,

4. Well, I stayed in school round about
Till I got round about twelfth grade,

Then I came outa school an' I got me a little job,
An' I start to teachin' them children.

5. An' he told me, "What did you teach the children?"
An' I told him, "I teach the children science."
An' he told me, "Lord, you know one thing, You so good to my
   children."

Clyde Causey, vocal and harmonica; Baton Rouge, June 10,
1961.

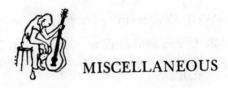

MISCELLANEOUS

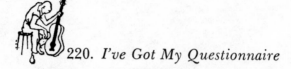

220. *I've Got My Questionnaire*

1. Well, now I've got my questionnaire, an' it lead me to the war,
Well, now I've got my questionnaire, an' they lead me to the war,
Well, I'm leavin', pretty baby, can't do anythin' at all.

2. Uncle Sam ain't no woman, but he sho' can take yo' man, (2)
Boy, they got 'em in the service, doin' somethin' I can't understan'.

3. Uncle Sam ain't no woman, but he sho' can take yo' man, (2)
Boy, they got 'em doin' somethin' that I just can't understan'.

4. Well, now I've got my questionnaire, an' they lead me to the war,
Well, now I've got my questionnaire, an' it lead me to the war,
Boy, they doin' somethin', an' I'm goin' over there an' have a shot.

Snooks Eaglin, vocal and guitar; New Orleans, Nov. 10, 1958.

A line like the first also occurs in Arthur "Big Boy" Crudup, Bb 9019, 1941-42. The opening line of the second stanza is duplicated in Brownie McGhee, "Million Lonesome Women," OK 06329, May 23, 1941.

For a recording of Eaglin's performance, see *Snooks Eaglin: New Orleans Street Singer*, Fkwy, FA 2476, 1958.

221. *Hottes' Bran' Goin'*

1. *Spoken:* Well, I say I work in the Conoco Station on 1668 Plank Road,
I work for Mr. Domaine, I say now, Conoco, oil station, happy motor, super service,
You know they got the hottes' bran' goin'.

2. You want super service, come to the Conoco Station on Plank Road,
You want super service, baby, come to the Conoco Station on Plank Road,
I say, come to Mr. Ed Domaine service station, he got the bes' goin', be all over,

3. *Sung:* You want yo' car to be served,
You want it served jus' right,
Get some of that Royal gasolene in there,
Roll all night or day.

4. 1668 Plank Road, that's where Robert Brown work,
You might need a tune-up job,
Your brakes might be out o' fix,
You might need tires, everythin's all right.

5. Come to 1668, 1668 Plank Road, I say down by that Conoco Station, I know,
Spoken: People know what I'm talkin' about,
I'm talkin' about the hottes' bran' goin',
Get that Royal feelin' with that royal gasolene.

6. *Sung:* Come down on 1668, 1668 Plank Road,
Say, you want super service, right at Mr. Ed Domaine,

Spoken: I'm talkin' about my boss now, that's my boss where I work at,
1668 Plank Road, you want super service, come right there.

7. Buy that Royal Gasolene, get that royal feelin', that royal ride,
An' I'm tellin' you, it's the hottes' bran' goin'.'

This was put out by Robert Brown, an' he know me, an that's
   my boss;
Come out on 1668 Plank Road, an' buy the hottes' bran' goin'.
Now, you want yo' car super-service,
Just go to super right there.
Spoken: Talkin' 'bout the Conoco station.

*Smoky Babe (Robert Brown), vocal and guitar; Scotlandville,
April 18, 1961.*

Here Smoky expresses unqualified enthusiasm for his job as
grease monkey and mechanic at a Conoco filling station in
Scotlandville, for his boss, for the service, and for Conoco
products. The supercharged energy and exuberance of his
performance communicate his message admirably well.

For a recording of Smoky Babe's performance, see *Hottes'
Brand Goin'*, PrB 1063, 1961.

DISCOGRAPHY OF PERFORMANCES
IN THIS COLLECTION

BROWN, ROBERT [SMOKY BABE]

COUNTRY NEGRO JAM SESSIONS, Folk-Lyric Records, FL 111, 1960: *Goin' Downtown Boogie.*

HOTTEST BRAND GOING, Prestige Bluesville 1063, 1961: *Baby, Please Don't Go* (issued as *Now Your Man Done Gone*); *Cold, Cold Snow; Hottes' Bran' Goin'; I'm Goin' Back to Mississippi; Insect Blues; Long Way from Home.*

BROWN, ROBERT, AND DOTSON, SALLY

COUNTRY NEGRO JAM SESSIONS, Folk-Lyric Records, FL 111, 1960: *Your Dice Won't Pass.*

CAGE, JAMES [BUTCH] AND THOMAS, WILLIE B.

COUNTRY NEGRO JAM SESSIONS, Folk-Lyric Records, FL 111, 1960: *Brownskin Woman; 44 Blues; Jelly Roll.*

CHALVIN, GODAR

A SAMPLER OF LOUISIANA FOLKSONGS, Louisiana Folklore Society (reissued by Folk-Lyric Records), LFS A-1, 1957: *Anons au Bal, Calinda.*

CHARLES, ROOSEVELT

BLUES, PRAYER, WORK AND TROUBLE SONGS, Vanguard Recording Society, VRS 9136, 1964: *Boll Weevil an' the Bale Weevil; Cane Choppin' Song; Freight Train Blues; Greenback Dollar Blues; I'm a Gamblin' Man; Mean Trouble Blues; Mule Blues; Pick 'em Up Higher; Wasn't I Lucky When I Got My Time?*

DUTSON, TOM

ANGOLA PRISON SPIRITUALS, Louisiana Folklore Society (reissued by Folk-Lyric Records), LFS A-6, 1959; *Dig My Grave with a Silver Spade.*

EAGLIN, SNOOKS

SNOOKS EAGLIN: NEW ORLEANS STREET SINGER, Folkways Records, FA 2476, 1958: *I Got My Questionnaire.*

EDWARDS, CLARENCE

COUNTRY NEGRO JAM SESSIONS, Folk-Lyric Records, FL 111, 1960: *Smokes Like Lightnin'; You Don't Love Me, Baby.*

MAXEY, MATTHEW [HOGMAN]
ANGOLA PRISONERS' BLUES, Louisiana Folklore Society (reissued by Folk-Lyric Records), LSF A-3, 1958: *Black Night Blues.*

SOUTHERN PRISON BLUES, Storyville (I. S. Dansk Grammofonplade-forlag), SLP 125, 1962: *Rock Me, Mama.*

WELCH, ROBERT [GUITAR]
ANGOLA PRISONERS' BLUES, Louisiana Folklore Society (reissued by Folk-Lyric Records), LFS A-3, 1958: *Backwater Blues; Electric Chair Blues.*

SOUTHERN PRISON BLUES, Storyville (I. S. Dansk Grammofonplade-forlag), SLP 125, 1962: *Boll Weevil Blues.*

WEBSTER, OTIS
SOUTHERN PRISON BLUES, Storyville (I. S. Dansk Grammofonplade-forlag), SLP 125, 1962: *Standin' at the Greyhound Station.*

WILLIAMS, ROBERT PETE
ANGOLA PRISONERS' BLUES, Louisiana Folklore Society (reissued by Folk-Lyric Records) LFS A-3, 1958: *Motherless Children Have a Hard Time; I'm Lonesome Blues; Levee Camp Blues; Prisoners' Talking Blues; Some Got Six Months.*

THOSE PRISON BLUES, Folk-Lyric Records, FL 109, 1959: *Army Blues; Pardon Renied Again; Make Me a Pallet on Your Floor.*

FREE AGAIN, Prestige Bluesville, 1026, 1960: *Almost Dead Blues; Death Blues; Free Again; Hay Cuttin' Song; Hobo Worried Blues; I've Grown So Ugly; Rollin' Stone; Thousand Miles from Nowhere; Thumbin' a Ride.*

All the above albums are Long-Playing, 33⅓ RPM recordings. Except for SNOOKS EAGLIN: NEW ORLEANS STREET SINGER, which was collected by Harry Oster, edited by Kenneth S. Goldstein, all the material was collected *and* edited by Harry Oster.

BIBLIOGRAPHY

Abrahams, Roger D. "Playing the Dozens," *Journal of American Folklore,* LXV (1962), 209-220.

————*Deep Down in the Jungle,* Hatboro, 1965.

Allen, William F., C. P. Ware and L. M. Garrison. *Slave Songs of the United States,* New York, 1867.

Ames, Russell. "Implications of Negro Folk Song," *Science & Society,* XV (1951), 163-173.

————"Protest and Irony in Negro Folksong," *Science & Society,* XIV (1950), 193-213.

————*The Story of American Folk Song,* New York, 1955.

Backus, E. M. "Negro Song from Georgia," *Journal of American Folklore,* X (1897), 216.

Berendt, Joachim E. *Blues,* Munich, 1957.

Blesh, Rudy. *Shining Trumpets,* New York, 1946.

Botkin, B. A. (ed.). *Lay My Burden Down: A Folk History of Slavery,* Chicago, 1945.

Broonzy, William and Yannick Bruynoghe. *Big Bill Blues,* London, 1955.

Brown, Sterling A. "Blues, Ballads, and Social Songs," *75 Years of Freedom,* Washington, D. C., 1943.

Burlin, Natalie (Curtis). *Hampton Series Negro Folksongs,* New York, 1918-1919, 4 v.

Butcher, Margaret Just. *The Negro in American Culture,* New York, 1956.

Carey, Dave and Albert J. McCarthy. *The Directory of Recorded Jazz and Swing Music (Including Gospel and Blues Records).* London, 1949-1957, 6 v.

Chase, Gilbert. *America's Music,* New York, 1955.

Charters, Samuel B. *The Country Blues,* New York, 1959.

————*The Poetry of the Blues,* New York, 1963.

Cunard, Nancy. *Negro Anthology,* London, 1934.

Dixon, Robert M. W. and John Goodrich. *Blues & Gospel Records 1902-1942,* Kenton, England; 1963.

Dollard, John. "The Dozens: The Dialect of Insult," *American Imago,* I (1939), 3-24.

Douglass, Frederick. *My Bondage and My Freedom,* New York and Auburn, 1855.

Embree, E. R. *Brown Americans: The Story of a Tenth of a Nation,* New York, 1944.

Fenner, Thomas P., Fred. G. Rathburn, and Bessie Cleveland. *Cabin and Plantation Songs as Sung by the Hampton Students* (3rd edition), New York and London, 1901.

Fenner, Thomas P. *Religious Folk Songs of the Negro as sung on the Plantations,* Hampton, Va., 1909.

Fisher, Miles M. *Negro Slave Songs in the United States,* Ithaca, 1953.

Handy, William C. (ed.). *Blues: An Anthology,* with an introduction by Abbe Niles, New York, 1925.

———*Father of the Blues: An Autobiography of W. C. Handy,* ed., Arna Bontemps, foreword by Abbe Niles, New York, 1955.

Haywood, Charles. *A Bibliography of North American Folklore and Folksong,* New York, 1961, 2 v.

Herskovits, Melville J. *The Myth of the Negro Past,* New York, 1941.

Hughes, Langston and Arna Bontemps. *The Book of Negro Folklore,* New York, 1958.

Johnson, Charles S. *Shadow of the Plantation,* Chicago, 1934.

Jones, LeRoi. *Blues People, Negro Music in White America,* New York, 1963.

Kemble, Frances. *Journal of a Residence on a Georgia Plantation in 1838-1839,* New York, 1863.

Krehbiel, Henry E. *Afro-American Folksongs,* New York, 1914.

Lang, Iain, *Jazz in Perspective: The Background of the Blues,* London, 1947.

Lee, George. *Beale Street, Where the Blues Began,* Foreward by W. C. Handy, New York, 1934.

Locke, Alain Le Roy. *The Negro and His Music,* Washington, D.C., 1936.

Lomax, Alan. The Folk Songs of North America, Garden City, 1960.

———*Mister Jelly Roll,* New York, 1950.

Lomax, John A. and Alan. *American Ballads & Folk Songs,* New York, 1934.

———*Folk Song: U.S.A.,* New York, 1947.

———*Negro Folk Songs as Sung by Leadbelly,* New York, 1936.

———*Our Singing Country,* Ruth Crawford Seeger, music ed., New York, 1941.

Lomax, John A. *The Adventures of a Ballad Hunter,* New York, 1946.

Louisiana Writers' Project. *Louisiana: A Guide to the State,* New York, 1941.

Lunsford, Bascom Lamar and Lamar Stringfield. *30 and 1 Folk Songs (from the Southern Mountains.),* New York, 1919.

McCormick, Mack. "Mance Lipscomb, Texas Sharecropper and Songster," booklet of notes for LP, Arhoolie F1001.

Metfessel, Milton. *Phonophotography in Folk Music,* Chapel Hill, 1928.

Mezzrow, Milton and Bernard Wolfe. *Really the Blues,* New York, 1946.

Myrdal, Gunnar. *An American Dilemma,* New York, 1944.

Niles, Abbe. "Blues Notes," *New Republic,* XLV (1926), 292-293.

Odum, Anna Kranz. "Some Negro Folksongs from Tennessee," *Journal of American Folklore,* XXVII (1914), 255-265.

Odum, Howard W. "Folksong and Folk-Poetry of the Southern Negro," *Journal of American Folklore,* XXIV (1911), 255-294, 351-296.

Odum, Howard W. and Guy B. Johnson. *Negro Workaday Songs,* Chapel Hill, 1926.

————*The Negro and His Songs: A Study of Typical Negro Songs in the South,* Chapel Hill, 1925.

Oliver, Paul. *Blues Fell This Morning,* London, 1960.

————*Conversation with the Blues,* New York, 1965.

Peabody, Charles. "Notes on Negro Music," *Journal of American Folklore,* XVI (1903), 148-152.

Perrow, E. C. "Songs and Rhymes from the South," *Journal of American Folklore,* XXV (1912), 137-155, XXVI (1913), 123-173, XXVIII (1915), 129-190.

Pucket, Newbell N. *Folk Beliefs of the Southern Negro,* Chapel Hill, 1926.

Ramsey, Frederic Jr. *Been Here and Gone,* New Brunswick, 1960.

Richardson, Ethel Park. *American Mountain Songs,* New York, 1927.

Ruspoli, Mario (ed. and translator). *Blues; poesie de l'Amerique noire.* Paris, 1947.

Stearns, Marshall. *The Story of Jazz,* New York, 1958.

Sandburg, Carl. *The American Songbag,* New York, 1927.

Scarborough, Dorothy. "The Blues as Folksongs," *Texas Folklore Society Publication,* II (1917), 52-66.

————*On the Trail of Negro Folk-Songs,* Cambridge, Mass., 1925.

————"The Blues as Folksongs," *Texas Folklore Society Publication,* II (1917), 52-66.

Shirley, Kay and Frank Driggs. *The Book of the Blues,* New York, 1963.

Tallant, Robert. *Voodoo in New Orleans,* New York, 1946.

Talley, Thomas W. *Negro Folk Rhymes,* New York, 1922.

Van Vechten, Carl. "The Blues," *Vanity Fair* (Aug.) 1925; (March) 1926.

White, Newman L. *American Negro Folk Songs.* Cambridge, Mass., 1928.

Wilgus, D. K. *Anglo-American Folksong Scholarship Since 1898,* New Brunswick, 1959.

Wilson, David, ed. *Twelve Years a Slave—Narrative of Solomon Northrup,* New York, 1853.

Work, John Wesley. *American Negro Songs,* New York, 1940.

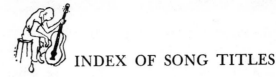

INDEX OF SONG TITLES

THE TITLE OF EACH SONG is followed by a number in parenthesis that indicates the number of the song in the book, followed by the number of the page on which it appears. An asterisk (*) immediately after the number of the song indicates music is supplied with the text.